Policy Research Project Participants

Project Director

Leigh B. Boske, Ph.D.
Professor of Economics and Public Affairs

Students

Mustafa Akcay, B.S. (Civil Engineering), Middle East Technical University, Ankara, Turkey

Angelica Cervantes, B.A. (Government/English), The University of Texas at Austin

John Cuttino, MPAff, MA, University of Texas at Austin

Cara Dougherty, B.A. (Latin American Studies), Columbia University

Celestino Gallegos, B.A. (International Studies), University of Washington at Seattle

Ricardo García Babún, B.A. (Latin American Studies & Spanish/Spanish American Literature), Vanderbilt University

Matthew Gever, B.A. (History), University of California at Los Angeles

Bryan P. Hykes, B.A. (Government and MAS), The University of Texas at Austin

Anna Okola, B.S. (Civil Engineering), Northeastern University

Sarah Fox Özkan, B.S. (Natural Resources and the Environment), University of Michigan at Ann Arbor

Michael L. Pratt, B.A. (History/Spanish), Texas Tech University

Richard J. Rodarte, B.A. (Business Administration), Colorado State University

Cindy E. Rosales Bush, B.A. (Political Science), B.A. (History), Southern University, Baton Rouge, Louisiana

Daniel Stein, B.A. (Spanish, International Relations), University of Rochester

Ravi Subramanian, B.S. (Mechanical Engineering), The University of Texas at Austin

David Wortman, P.E., B.S. (General Engineering), University of Illinois at Urbana/Champaign

Table of Contents

List of Tables

List of Figures

Foreword

The Lyndon B. Johnson School of Public Affairs has established interdisciplinary research on policy problems as the core of its educational program. A major part of this program is the nine-month policy research project, in the course of which two or more faculty members from different disciplines direct the research of ten to twenty graduate students of diverse backgrounds on a policy issue of concern to a government or nonprofit agency. This "client orientation" brings students face-to-face with administrators, legislators, and other officials active in the policy process and demonstrates that research in a policy environment demands special talents. It also illuminates the occasional difficulties of relating research findings to the world of political realities.

This report is the product of a policy research project conducted in the 2000-2001 academic year with funding from the U.S.-CIDI Specific Fund of the Organization of American States (OAS) and the William and Flora Hewlett Foundation through the Center for Inter-American Policy Studies at The University of Texas at Austin. Also participating was the United Nations Economic Commission for Latin America and the Caribbean (ECLAC). The purpose of the study is to examine the role of maritime transportation and seaports in fostering international trade, economic integration, and sustainable development throughout Latin America and the Caribbean.

The curriculum of the LBJ School is intended not only to develop effective public servants but also to produce research that will enlighten and inform those already engaged in the policy process. The project that resulted in this report has helped to accomplish the first task; it is our hope that the report itself will contribute to the second.

Finally, it should be noted that neither the LBJ School, The University of Texas at Austin, the OAS, nor ECLAC necessarily endorses the views or findings of this report.

Edwin Dorn
Dean

Acknowledgments

This policy research project could not have been completed without the generous donation of time and information by hundreds of individuals, most especially Dr. Jan Hoffmann, Maritime Economist, International Trade, Financing and Transport Division, United Nations Economic Commission for Latin America and the Caribbean, Santiago, Chile, and the project's primary editors Mr. Matthew S. Miller II and Ms. Irene Aldrich. The following individuals also deserve special recognition for assisting members of our research team on various aspects of the study.

Lic. Arturo Cruz Aguilera, Director of Trainmar in Mexico, Veracruz, Mexico;

Mr. Marcelo de Andrade Almeida, Manager, Wilport Port Operations S.A., Santos, Brazil;

Mr. Rômulo Otoni Andrade, General Cargo and Containers Associate, Commercial Division, Navegação Vale do Rio Doce S.A. (Docenave), Rio de Janeiro, Brazil;

Mr. Karel Jan O. Aster, Managing Director, Curaçao Port Services Inc., Curaçao, Netherlands Antilles;

Sr. John Ballestero, General Director, H. L. Boulton and Company/Terminal Port Services, Puerto Cabello, Venezuela;

Mr. Nicholas Baylis, Security/Safety Manager, Kingston Terminal Operators, Kingston, Jamaica;

Mr. André Freire Bittencourt, Marketing Division Manager, Hamburg Süd, São Paulo, Brazil;

Mr. Alberto C. Borquez , General Manager, San Antonio Terminal Internacional, San Antonio, Chile;

Sr. Uwe Breitling, Port, Transport and Training Consultant, TRAINMAR, San Jose, Costa Rica;

Mr. Odair Busoli Filho, Director, Net Marinha, São Paulo, Brazil;

Mr. Paulo Augusto Camello, Manager, Cabotage Operations Center, Aliança Navigation and Logistics Ltd., Rio de Janeiro, Brazil;

Ms. Pedrita V. Castiglioni, Technical Adviser, Mideast Region, Operational Consortium of the Mideast Transportation Corridor, Mercosul Atlantic Corridor Consortium, Vitória, Brazil;

Ms. Kim Bergmann Christiansen, Vice President, Barwil Agencies, S.A. Panama, Panama City, Panama;

Sr. Luis Blanco, General Director, P&O Nedlloyd Maritime of Venezuela, Puerto Cabello, Venezuela;

Ing. Libardo Bru, Surveyor and Marine Consultant, Marpol Engineers and Consultants, Balboa, Panama;

Captain Marvin D. Castillo B., Surveyor and Marine Consultant, Marpol Engineers and Consultants, Balboa, Panama;

Mrs. Marguerite Cooke, Public Relations and Community Manager, Port Authority of Jamaica, Kingston, Jamaica;

Mr. Caio Morel Corrêa, Director, Transroll Navegação S.A., Rio de Janeiro, Brazil;

Mr. Fernando Mário Santana Correia, Executive Secretary, National Union of Maritime Shipping Companies (Syndarma), Rio de Janeiro, Brazil;

Ing. Ricardo H. Del Valle, Interventor, General Port Administration S.E., Puerto Buenos Aires;

Ms. Vanessa Deeke, Marketing Division Associate, Hamburg Süd, São Paulo, Brazil;

Ing. Wenceslao Tejeda Delagado, Director of Operations, Terminales de Cargas Especializadas (TCE), Veracruz, Mexico;

Mr. Agustin M. Diaz, Director, Curaçao Port Authority, Curaçao, Netherlands Antilles;

Mr. Pablo Duarte, Manager of Operations, Exolgan S.A., Container Terminal, Buenos Aires, Argentina;

Mr. Ralph Edwards, Attorney at Law, Office of International Affairs, U.S. Maritime Administration, Washington, D.C.;

Msc. Gilberto Brown Fairclough, Coordinator of the Regional Plan of Development, JAPDEVA, Puerto Limón-Moín, Limón, Costa Rica;

Arq. Jorge Pedro Falcon, Manager, Institutional Relations and Training, Administracion General de Puertos S.E., Puerto Buenos Aires, Buenos Aires, Argentina;

Prof. Anilton Salles Garcia, Department of Information Technology, Federal University of Espírito Santo, Vitória, Brazil;

Mrs. Mireya Babún García, Vice President and Equipment Control Manager, Antillean Marine Shipping Company, Miami, Florida;

Mr. Rodolfo García, Executive Vice President, Camara Maritima de Chile, Valparaiso, Chile;

Mr. Gonzalo García Babun, Sales Executive, Farovi Shipping Corporation, Miami, Florida;

Mr. Gonzalo García Herrera, President, Overseas Forwarding Corporation, Miami, Florida;

Eng° Fernando Gazal, TRAINMAR Brasil, Santos, Brazil;

Prof. Andrés Gómez-Lobo, University of Chile, Santiago, Chile;

Sr. Oswaldo Guerreiro Silva, General Director, Planning and Marketing, Puerto Cabello Port Authority (IPAPC), Puerto Cabello, Venezuela;

Prof. Hercules E. Haralambides, Editor, *International Journal of Maritime Economics*, Rotterdam, The Netherlands;

Mr. Kevin Harrington, Adviser to the Minister of Canal Issues of the Ministry of the Presidency, Panama City, Panama;

Mr. Alvin C. Henry, F.C.A., General Manager, Shipping Association of Jamaica, Kingston, Jamaica;

Mr. Roger Hindes, Chief Executive Officer, Transocean Shipping Limited, Kingston, Jamaica;

Mr. Dalton Seiji Honda, Marketing Division Associate, Hamburg Süd, São Paulo, Brazil;

Mr. Thomas H. Kenna, Marketing Director, Panama Canal Railway Company, Balboa, Panama;

Mr. Robert Kinlocke, Managing Director, Kingston Terminal Operators, Kingston Jamaica;

Mr. Chris Koch, Director, World Shipping Council, Washington, D.C.;

Mr. Byron G. Lewis, Senior Vice President, Special Projects, Port Authority of Jamaica, Kingston, Jamaica;

Sr. John de Lima, Operations Coordinator, P&O Nedlloyd Maritime of Venezuela, Puerto Cabello, Venezuela;

Mr. Marco Antonio Lopes, Customer Service, Terminal 37, Santos, Brazil;

Mr. Joseph Lowe, Managing Director, Hamburg Süd/Columbus, Kingston, Jamaica;

Ing. Carlos Lucas Amador, Port Director, JAPDEVA, Puerto Limón-Moín, Limón, Costa Rica;

Mr. Gilberto Marchena, President, Christian Port Workers Union of Willemstad, Curaçao, Netherlands Antilles;

Mr. Jose Luis Mardones Santander, Former Director, Emporchi Privatization Committee, Santiago, Chile;

Sr. Gerardo Martinez, Director of Port Operations, Crowley Liner Services, Limón, Costa Rica;

Mr. Peter McGivern, Chief Operating Officer, San Antonio Terminal Internacional, San Antonio, Chile;

Sr. Karl B. McQueen Williams, Port Superintendent, JAPDEVA, Puerto Limón-Moín, Limón, Costa Rica;

Mr. Jacques Michaux, Deputy Head of Unit, European Commission, Directorate General for Energy and Transport, Maritime Policy, Brussels, Belgium;

Gustaaf de Monie, Consultant, Policy Research Corporation, Antwerp, Belgium;

Lic. Tomás R. Montero, Sub-Director of Operations, Dominican Port Authority, Santo Domingo, Dominican Republic;

Mr. Enrique Morales, Manager of Development and Concessions, Empresa Portuaria Valparaiso, Valparaiso, Chile;

Cap. Aldo O. Moroz, Superintendent, Buenos Aires Container Terminal Services S.A., Buenos Aires, Argentina;

Sr. Carlo Muir, Manager, Department of Steamers, Cor Mar, Limón, Costa Rica;

Mr. Joe Naranjo, Operations Manager, Antillean Marine Shipping Company, Miami, Florida;

Ms. Eyra Mercedes Ng Schouwe, Marketing Manager, Siclamar, S.A., Balboa, Panama;

Mr. Roberto N. Nogueira, President, Belo Horizonte Integration Roundtable, Mercosul Atlantic Corridor, Belo Horizonte, Brazil;

Mr. Fabio Ferraro Oliari, Administrator, Porto de Santos, Santos, Brazil;

Mr. Miguel Oses Lorca, Coordinator, I.T.F.—Chile, Valparaiso, Chile;

Sr. Tomas Palacios, Operations Supervisor, H. L. Boulton and Company/Terminal Port Services, Puerto Cabello, Venezuela;

Mr. Marcelo Patricio, Engineer, Terminal 37, Santos, Brazil;

Mr. Juan Bautista Perez Rocha, Shippers Association of the Dominican Republic, Santo Domingo, Dominican Republic;

Lic. Alberto Ramirez, General Manager, Camara de Puertos Privados Comerciales, Buenos Aires, Argentina;

Mr. José Carlos da Rocha Ramos, General Cargo and Containers Manager, Navegação Vale do Rio Doce S.A. (Docenave), Rio de Janeiro, Brazil;

Mr. Ruben Reyna, President, International Mar Consult, Panama City, Panama;

Mr. Sidney Rezende, International Trade, Transport and Financing Division, United Nations Economic Commission for Latin America and the Caribbean, Santiago, Chile;

Ms. Rosa Amélia Ribeiro, Manager of Research and Analysis, Research Division, Merchant Marine Department, Rio de Janeiro, Brazil;

Mr. Henry James Robinson, Technical Director, Terminal 37, Santos, Brazil;

Lic. Freddy Rodríguez Soldevila, Executive Sub-Director, Dominican Port Authority, Santo Domingo, Dominican Republic;

Sr. Jose Sabatino Pizzolante, Sabatino Pizzolante Maritime and Commercial Attorneys, Puerto Cabello, Venezuela;

Mr. Onesimo V. Sanchez, Manager, Competitive Intelligence Unit, Corporate Planning and Marketing Department, Panama Canal Authority, Panama City, Panama;

Mr. Federico F. Schad, Managing Vice President, F. Schad Shipping Agents, Santo Domingo, Dominican Republic;

Mr. Danny Scorpecci, Maritime Unit, Organization for Economic Co-operation and Development, Paris, France;

Mr. L. E. Jorge Sempe, Assistant Director of Marketing, Internacional de Contenedores Asociados de Veracruz S.A. de C.V. (ICAVE), Veracruz, Mexico;

Mr. Edward Sheppard, Attorney at Law, Thompson Coburn LLP, Washington, D.C.;

Lic. Marlon Clarke Spencer, Port Consultant, JAPDEVA, Puerto Limón-Moín, Limón, Costa Rica;

Mr. Justin Stares, Latin America Correspondent, *Lloyd's List*, São Paulo, Brazil;

Engª Sandra Maria Ferraz Stehling, Director of Operations, Mercosul Atlantic Corridor Consortium, Vitória, Brazil;

Mr. Alain Stekke, Principal Administrator, European Commission, Directorate-General Information Society, Brussels, Belgium;

Mr. Condell G. Stephenson, BSc. (Hons), General Manager—Operations, Kingston Terminal Operators, Kingston, Jamaica;

Mr. Grantley Stephenson, President, Shipping Association of Jamaica, Kingston, Jamaica;

Sr. Carlos Thomas, Director of Port Operations, Chiquita Brands, Limón, Costa Rica;

Ing. Rommel Troetsch G., Manager, Customer Service and Public Relations, Panama Ports Company, Panama City, Panama;

Mr. Carlos M. Urriola Tam, Vice President of Marketing, Manzanillo International Terminal, Colon, Panama;

Mr. Silvio Ureña Mendoza, Secretary General, Dominican Federation of Port Workers, Santo Domingo, Dominican Republic;

Mr. Ubiratan Vargas Xavier, Supervisor of Operations, OGMO, Santos, Brazil;

C.P. Gustavo Jimenez Vazquez, Director of Marketing, Corporacion Integral de Comercio Exterior, S.A. de C.V. (CISE), Veracruz, Mexico;

Ing. Serafin Vazquez, Director of Planning and Development, Administracion Portuaria Integral de Veracruz, S.A. de C.V. (APIS), Veracruz, Mexico;

Mr. José Luis Vidal, President, São Paulo Integration Roundtable, Mercosul Atlantic Corridor Consortium, São Paulo, Brazil;

Sr. German I. Vierma L., President, EMESCA Stevedoring Terminal Operators, Puerto Cabello, Venezuela;

Eng° Paulo Augusto Vivacqua, President, Mercosul Atlantic Corridor Consortium, Vitória, Brazil;

Lic. Gilberto E. Wilson Wilson, Director of Planning, JAPDEVA, Puerto Limón-Moín, Limón, Costa Rica;

Mr. Antonio J. Zuidwijk, Director, Murchison S.A. Estibajes y Cargas I. y C., Buenos Aires, Argentina;

Mr. Guillermo Zuidwijk, Operations Manager, Mediterranean Shipping Company S.A., Buenos Aires, Argentina.

Executive Summary

This research report provides a comprehensive examination of the role played by maritime transportation and ports in fostering international trade and economic development in Latin America and the Caribbean (LAC). The report is composed of six chapters, which address various aspects of maritime commerce: trade liberalization and formation of regional trade blocs, liner shipping services, ports and port reform, existing and emerging transshipment hub ports, the Mercosur Atlantic Corridor Consortium, and cabotage law in the Americas.

Chapter 1: Latin American and Caribbean International Trade

This first chapter examines global trade liberalization, formation of regional trade blocs, and both intra- and interregional international trade flows. Five Western Hemispheric regional trade blocs—the Southern Common Market (Mercado Común del Sur, or MERCOSUR), the North American Free Trade Agreement (NAFTA), the Andean Community, Caribbean Common Market (CARICOM), and the Central American Common Market (CACM)—are discussed in terms of their histories, key provisions, trends in trade, exports of leading products, and tariff structures. Also discussed in detail are intraregional international trade flows (exports and imports) between the MERCOSUR, NAFTA, Andean Community, CARICOM, and CACM trade blocs and interregional international trade flows between these five trade blocs and Europe, Africa, the Middle East, Asia, and Oceania.

Continued increases in international trade within the Western Hemisphere and between the Western Hemisphere and the rest of the world raise hopes for achieving higher standards of living and the prospect of further hemispheric economic integration such as the proposed Free Trade Area of the Americas (FTAA).

Chapter 2: Liner Shipping Services

Chapter 2 provides an overview of the logistics of maritime trade and of trends in the maritime service industry, looking at Latin American and Caribbean (LAC) countries within a global context. Emphasis is given to containerized services. The chapter begins by discussing trends and critical issues in the industry and then proceeds to describe the effects of globalization. An analysis of fluctuations in freight rates is used to explore how these trends and issues interact to affect services provided. An overview of the fleets of the largest shipping lines follows.

Finally, two major features offer the reader the opportunity to understand the issues from the perspective of industry insiders. The first is the inclusion of four case studies (Hamburg Süd, Antillean Marine Shipping, Aliança, and Docenave) researched through personal contacts with officials within the industry. The case studies are examples of liner operations on different types of routes, including transoceanic, regional, and cabotage. The second feature is found throughout the chapter. It is a mix of tables and figures of maritime industry data from the year 2000, consolidated by researchers participating in the research project, primarily using statistics provided by *Containerisation International*. These statistics provide a useful picture of general trends in the LAC maritime industry.

Globally, principal attitudes of the liner industry include preferences for stability over expansion in the short run, balance in volume of trade on all round-trip routes, and port efficiency. In addition, increasing globalization has caused concentration in multiple aspects of the industry: movement toward mergers, alliances and vessel sharing agreements, increases in vessel size, rising fixed costs and concurrent decreasing variable costs, and growing use of transshipment. In the face of this concentration, the report recommends that national governments ensure the maintenance of healthy competition through enactment and enforcement of antimonopoly laws and some prohibitions against mergers. However, warning is also given to governments that excessive regulation can cause dramatic decreases in efficiency of the entire industry, consequently affecting local economies. The dissolution of conferences already has meant that companies must distinguish themselves through intense competition in pricing. As a result, many companies are now faced with a problem of overcapacity. Dismally low freight rates in Latin America today underscore the effect of these global trends on Latin American shipping lines.

Three methods of measuring shipping activity are employed: vessel deployment, vessel carrying capacity, and number of services provided. These measurements are analyzed within each LAC country, within the region, and between the region and the rest of the world. Within LAC countries, vessels deployed account for approximately 10 percent of the world container fleet and 15 percent of the total capacity. Panama emerges as the leader among the LAC countries in terms of capacity and vessel size–with an average vessel size 50 percent greater than that of the rest of the region. However, in terms of total number of vessels, it is only the third largest. The West Coast of Mexico is served by vessels significantly above average, although many of these are on routes that also serve Panama.

An intraregional service, as defined in the chapter, is a carrier that has port calls within the LAC region, whether or not the service extends to port calls in other parts of the world. However, services that operate only within LAC account for just 10 percent of LAC deployment. Nearly one-quarter of all containerized maritime trade in LAC occurs with LAC countries, implying that a majority of intraregional trade is carried by vessels continuing on to other parts of the globe.

Of the intraregional routes considered, Panama also has the largest deployment, with connections to the West Coast of Mexico and the West Coast of South America occupying the top two spots. The service between the North Coast of South America and the Caribbean has the greatest number of vessels, but the average vessel size in this trade lane is relatively small, making it only the third largest in terms of twenty-foot equivalent units (TEUs) deployed. Also, within the region, some of the most active routes in LAC are the trade lanes of the North Coast of South America, with top destinations being the

East Coast of South America, the Caribbean, and eastern Mexico. This activity occurs despite the fact that this region has only a moderate level of total deployment.

In discussing services between LAC and the rest of the world, it is noted that, of the 9.6 million TEUs traded by LAC in 2000 (imports and exports combined), approximately 60 percent is evenly split between North America and Europe, and 15 percent is with Asia/Pacific. Using numbers of vessels as a measurement, service between the North Coast of South America and the Caribbean emerges as the top route. Overall, the trends between LAC and the rest of the world are consistent with the logic that the benefits of economies of scale are greatest on the longest routes.

Panama's connections to the world dominate LAC in terms of total deployment and carrying capacity. However, when the number of services in operation is considered, Panama ranks fairly low. The implication is that trade lanes with smaller trade flows are not necessarily served by fewer services. On the contrary, these lanes have some of the greatest liner activity but are served by primarily small vessels.

Finally, the world fleet, measured in deadweight tonnage, has increased 20 percent since 1990 and that of LAC (excluding flags of convenience) has increased 35 percent. The greatest increase, both globally and within LAC, however, has occurred in the container industry. The world container fleet has more than doubled in each of the last two decades, and the LAC container fleet has seen a sixfold increase in the last decade. The top three ranking international shipping companies with large presence in the region demonstrate the strength of the LAC market, as they each maintain approximately one-quarter of their fleets in LAC.

Chapter 3: Ports and Port Reform

Seaports are complex organizations that provide essential services to a nation. While seaports have historically been labor intensive, recent technological advances in the transportation industry, such as containerization of cargo, have shifted the industry toward capital-intensive production. For this reason, many ports have been forced to devise plans to increase investment in order to maintain a competitive position. One of the ways that a port can attract investment is by privatization.

The history of Latin America during the 20th century was characterized by models of centralized governance and heavy state intervention in the economy. Latin American governments often focused on development of national industries and domestic markets as a development strategy. But as the world moved toward global integration, it became clear that this economic model was inhibiting domestic economic growth rather than stimulating development. Many Latin American countries have decided to undertake an economic transformation in order to adapt to the new global economy. One of the key policy tools used in an economic aperture is privatization of state-run industries. Privatization promises national governments both revenue from the tender of its assets and funds saved from the devolution of responsibility for operation and maintenance as well as increased investment from the private-sector operators. At the same time, however, privatization also implies that some sectors of the economy and certain political interests will lose privileges enjoyed under the previous scheme.

In chapter 3, we examine the recent trend of port reform in Latin America. We begin with an overview of the levels of privatization that have occurred in this sector, especially those types that are common to Latin America. We then take a closer look at how Latin American ports have either undertaken or plan to undertake a reform process, on a case-by-case basis. Analysis of the following 11 ports is presented: Buenos Aires, Argentina; Curaçao, Netherlands Antilles; Kingston, Jamaica; Puerto Cabello, Venezuela; Limón/Moín, Costa Rica; Rio Haina, Dominican Republic; San Antonio, Chile; Santos, Brazil; Veracruz, Mexico; and the ports of Panama. The case of Panama, which also includes the Panama Canal, is treated separately because of its unique position in the world market. The case studies were selected from a spectrum of port administrative models, levels of production, types of markets served, and levels of development. Each case study discusses port infrastructure, operations, management and labor issues, strategic plans, economic impact, reform process, and lessons learned from the reform process.

Port organization has been classified into three types: the "service" port, where the state owns both the infrastructure and the port equipment and is the provider of port services; the "tool" port, where the state owns the infrastructure and port equipment but allows private operators to provide port services; and the "landlord" port, where the state owns the infrastructure but allows private operators to invest in port equipment as well as provide port services. While all three types of ports are present in Latin America, the recent trend has been a shift toward adopting the "landlord" model because it offers the most potential for capital investment needed to accommodate containerized cargo.

The effects of port reforms have varied. While privatization processes have resulted in increased efficiency and lower port costs, they have also resulted in a displacement of laborers (whose functions in the modern port have become obsolete), which has a detrimental effect on the local economy. The gains to port users and consumers become the subject of greater public scrutiny in light of the fact that most of the private-sector operators are multinational corporations. The key issues in analyzing port privatization in each case have been to weigh the overall gains and losses to national economies, as well as to identify individual winners and losers.

It is important to analyze how each country has faced the political and economic challenges presented by the port-reform process. For each case study, the lessons learned from the process are instructive for evaluating the successes and shortcomings of the respective approaches to port reform implemented in LAC countries.

Chapter 4: Hub Ports

Transshipment is the transfer of cargo from one ship to another in a hub-and-spoke style of operation between ports, similar to air service provided by commercial airlines.

The aim of chapter 4 is to analyze transshipment in Latin America and the Caribbean, identifying existing and emerging transshipment hub ports, ranging from the larger global transshipment centers to the smaller regional transshipment ports in the region. The chapter also evaluates hub ports in the region based on a set of criteria characterizing successful transshipment ports in an attempt to predict which port(s) have the potential to become transshipment centers.

Experts generally consider the region's global transshipment hub ports to be Kingston, Jamaica; Colón, Panama; and Freeport, Bahamas. Of these, only Freeport was originally designated as a hub port. Kingston and Colón grew into their roles as global hubs, though certainly not by accident. Both satisfy the minimum criteria as outlined by experts, particularly their potential locations near major shipping lanes. Location is a particularly important criterion: the presence of the Panama Canal is a major factor contributing to Colón's development into a global hub, as is Kingston's location along shipping lanes from the canal to North and South America and Europe.

Experts tend to agree that a successful hub port should (a) be well located in relation to feeder ports and shipping lanes, (b) have adequate draft to handle large ships, (c) possess adequate facilities to handle containerized cargo, (d) maintain high efficiency and low costs, and (e) sustain an environment free from the threat of labor unrest. It must be noted, however, that these criteria represent a minimum standard; satisfying these criteria by no means guarantees that a port will become a hub. Investment is a key issue, as is a willingness to adapt to and successfully implement a new system of port operations.

This chapter also investigates existing and emerging transshipment hub ports through the use of statistical regression analyses and other prediction techniques. The investigation begins with a descriptive, principal component model as a means to compare the region's three global transshipment centers (Kingston, Colón, and Freeport) with other ports in the region. The model shows that the four terminals comprising these three transshipment centers group together (cluster) apart from other ports in the regions. The analysis reveals that these four terminals require less infrastructure for handling their TEU movements than do other ports.

The second model is a linear regression of TEU transshipment traffic in the Caribbean. An analysis of this prescriptive model suggests that in the case of global hub ports, deviation distance from the Panama-North American trade lane is a statistically significant factor; in other words, a port's distance from this lane is a key factor in predicting future hub ports. However, a similar model suggests that a port's deviation distance from the Panama-South American trade lane is NOT statistically significant.

For the ports found on South America's northern and eastern coasts, the importance of location must be evaluated in a different manner. Because these ports will most likely be acting as concentration points for regional trade, a location loading factor (LLF) is considered. The LLF assigns diminishing values to containerized trade taking place at greater distances from a port. Container movements occurring at the port itself are weighted with a factor of 1, while movements at a distance of 100 miles are weighted as 50 percent as important. The weighted values for all trade taking place around the port are then summed together to create the LLF, designed to gauge the amount of containerized trade that takes place in a port's surrounding area. The factor measures the degree to which a port's location influences its ability to act as a concentration point for regional transshipment, that is, as a regional port that acts as one end of a spoke that connects to a global hub port. The LLF is included in a criteria matrix for the ports located on the East Coast of South America to identify any and all ports likely to excel in transshipment as containerization increases in the region.

The chapter closes with an analysis of ports on the East Coast of South America. Santos, which operates most of the transshipment in the region, is discussed, as are Buenos Aires, Suape, and Sepetiba. Transshipment services and physical attributes of these four ports are examined. The LLF is also a key component in forecasting the future of transshipment in the region. Although Buenos Aires handles approximately 50 percent more TEU movements per year than does Santos, Buenos Aires' low draft does not allow the accommodation of ships large enough to carry more than 1,500 TEUs. Santos, however, boasts a draft that can already accommodate ships carrying up to 3,000 TEUs. While Suape and Sepetiba both possess depths that allow them to receive ships carrying 7,000 TEUs, their low level of containerized trade renders them less competitive than Santos in the transshipment market. Our conclusion is that Santos will continue to lead South America's East Coast region in transshipment for years to come, provided that labor disruptions are addressed.

Chapter 5: The Mercosur Atlantic Corridor Consortium

During the August 31, 2000, South American Summit, transportation and trade issues formed a major part of a collective continental development agenda. Specifically in the area of transportation infrastructure, efforts addressed facilitating trade through multimodal transportation corridors, making clear the importance of effective transportation networks in light of upcoming trade negotiations involving MERCOSUR, the Andean Community, and the United States. Notwithstanding South America's recent coalescence around transport and trade, a rapidly changing Latin America bears witness to the limited capacity of governments to invest in transportation and arbitrate disputes in a timely fashion. Chapter 5 focuses on the emergence of the Mercosur Atlantic Corridor Consortium as a nonprofit organization attempting to generate economic development, facilitate trade, ameliorate transportation bottlenecks, promote a rationalization of freight carriage, and resolve trade- and transportation-related problems.

Building the context for the analysis of the Mercosur Atlantic Corridor Consortium, the chapter makes a careful delineation illustrating the differences between transportation corridors and trade corridors. Put simply, trade cannot exist without a transportation corridor, but there are many transport corridors where no meaningful trade takes place. Moreover, a trade corridor comprises many important value-added services, including logistics services within transportation corridors. The Mercosur Atlantic Corridor Consortium incorporates these concepts into its day-to-day activities, hinging on the operation of integration roundtables that assemble various actors involved in transport and trade.

After a brief synopsis of its genesis, the chapter presents the organizational structure of the consortium and its evolution into a multifaceted organization. The consortium can now provide door-to-door multimodal transport service for its members in addition to resolving disputes via its roundtables. The key component of the consortium is its regularly scheduled integration roundtable meetings in dozens of exporting and port cities in Brazil, Argentina, Peru, and Chile. This Latin American initiative closely resembles the development of port networks in Europe that seek to leverage development through synergies of integrated intermodal terminals, ports, railways, and productive industry. Though the South American roundtables are predominantly led by the funnel port, which receives or exports cargo, the issues addressed venture far into a port's hinterland.

Since they moved to the nonprofit sector in 1994, the Mideast Corridor Consortium and Mercosur Atlantic Corridor Consortium have accomplished many transportation improvements. Some of the most compelling improvements are enumerated. With much underway and in development, the Mercosur Atlantic Corridor Consortium is also at risk of hypertrophy. Several criticisms address its rapid growth. One possible explanation for the rapid growth is the high demand to improve transportation and expand trade. The Mercosur Consortium's most ambitious project is the creation of a backbone transportation network separate from trunk highways. It is an attempt to pool the strength of shippers, transportation providers, and government to shift cargo away from highways to more economic and environmentally sound modes of freight carriage (barge, inland waterway, cabotage, rail, intermodal). To accomplish this task, the Dorsal Fin Project is one instrument that consortium members can use to attract new cargo and increase frequency of coastal shipping. The project is also occurring at a time when MERCOSUR cabotage has been consistently growing. The recent passage (1998) and implementation (2001) of Brazil's Multimodal Transportation Operator Law now increase the possibility of more door-to-door logistics services and, hence, a shift away from costly highway travel.

The intriguing aspect of the Mercosur Atlantic Corridor Consortium lies in its ability to bring diverse interests together on a variety of transportation and trade issues. The trademark integration roundtables resolve disputes and fix problems. As a vehicle for fomenting integration, the roundtables are an easily exportable model outside the realm of the state and national frontiers.

Through an analysis of its integration roundtables, an attempt is made to identify the most pressing problems that inhibit Latin American trade. First and foremost is the lack of fully regulated legislation concerning port labor regimes and multimodal transportation operators. Second, the arbitrariness of customs officers in liberating cargo at ports and recently constituted inland dry ports illustrates that however well designed a system is, it is only as strong as its weakest link. Third, there is considerable angst over the high cost of terminal-handling charges and add-on fees (dredging funds à la Santos) of Brazilian ports. Fourth, the tax regime is also punitive to exporters, with multimodal movements suffering double charges on the value-added state tax in Brazil. Finally, the absence of more frequent cabotage service is a deterrent for those wishing to use less costly means of transport.

As the chapter pertains to maritime transportation in the Americas, it shows the increasing growth of efforts for more access to cabotage trade. Moreover, it illustrates how a nonprofit organization is addressing the issues that have plagued Latin America, such as an unintegrated transport infrastructure directed by vertically integrated industries in mining, steel, and agriculture and a hegemonic legacy of development by road and automobile.

Chapter 6: Cabotage Law in the Americas

Chapter 6 begins with an overview and brief history of the types of regulatory restrictions that nations place on maritime shipping companies seeking to operate within their domestic markets. A survey of selected countries in the Western Hemisphere is offered to establish the nature of restrictions placed on cabotage operators and the reasons for doing so. Unique national restrictions and policies that favor nationally registered vessels are also discussed in a nation-by-nation analysis. Attention is given to the debate that currently exists in the maritime community over the possible reform of these laws. Arguments are presented for both sides of this debate. The case of the European Union (EU) is discussed as a notable example of a region that has recently undergone cabotage reform.

The great majority of nations sampled in this report maintain some form of restriction on shipping companies seeking to operate within their domestic markets. Nations that restrict domestic trade typically do so with some combination of registration requirements, crewing requirements, domestic ownership requirements, or domestic shipbuilding requirements. Thirteen of the fourteen nations discussed in this chapter limit domestic waterborne trade to vessels registered in that nation and employing at least some number of their citizens. Twelve nations also require that vessels used in domestic trade be owned at least in part by citizens of that nation. Notably lacking among these nations is Panama, which maintains an open-coast policy for shipping between its own ports. Only three nations in the survey—Brazil, the United States, and Peru—require that vessels used for cabotage be constructed domestically.

Shippers of low-cost bulk commodities have spearheaded the public debate to reform cabotage laws in the United States as they believe that opening domestic waterborne trade to vessels from all nations will significantly lower the overall cost of transporting their products. Cabotage opponents have found support for their economic argument against cabotage laws in a series of biannual reports of the U.S. International Trade Commission. These reports concede that shipyards may well lose revenue as a result of any liberalization of cabotage law but conclude that projected cost savings to shippers and consumers would more than likely offset such losses.

A number of groups have rallied behind existing cabotage laws, claiming that the continued existence of these policies protects domestic employment and ensures the availability of a well-trained merchant marine fleet in times of war. Supporters of the continued existence of cabotage restrictions also point out that projected declines in shipping costs resulting from cabotage reform assume that freight rates would drop if cabotage markets were opened to foreign vessels. Groups such as the Maritime Cabotage

Task Force contend that a number of factors might keep freight rates from dropping to levels predicted by the U.S. International Trade Commission.

One possible template for cabotage reform is that of the EU, which, under Council Regulation 3577/92, opened waterborne trade within the EU to vessels from any of its member states. Cabotage liberalization proceeded faster among the northern European members of the EU than the southern member states. The difference in the pace of reform between these two regions can be explained by the fact that a much stronger market in passenger service exists in southern Europe than in northern Europe. One EU study indicates that the opening of cabotage in the EU has had only a marginal effect on maritime employment.

The chapter concludes by outlining the type of research that must be conducted to resolve the supporting and opposing arguments for eliminating cabotage restrictions in the United States and for determining whether the EU model is cost effective and whether it would be applicable to the proposed FTAA. Differences in geography, comparative market size, and the availability of alternative modes of transportation are factors (among others) that could contribute to the eventual success or failure of a regional cabotage system for the Americas.

Note: Unless otherwise specified, all references to currencies are in U.S. dollars.

Chapter 1. Latin American and Caribbean International Trade

Introduction

Over the past two decades, the Western Hemisphere has experienced trade liberalization, formation of regional trade blocs, governmental deregulation of key sectors of national economies, and privatization of former government-owned and -operated industries. The rationale for the formation of regional trade blocs is fairly straightforward: there are undeniable benefits resulting from market expansion, as well as the increasing gains from trade. Economic integration facilitates the creation of larger competitive markets, which permit greater specialization, greater allocative efficiency of factors of production, and the realization of economies of scale. Economic integration is particularly attractive to smaller nations, where domestic demand for manufactured goods is simply insufficient to absorb the output necessary to establish a cost-effective industrial base or to attract the necessary private foreign direct investment in cases in which inadequate savings mean inadequate capital formation.

If external barriers are removed and the market base is extended, industrial manufacturing can be established at a level conducive to the realization of economies of scale, resulting in a lower cost per unit of output and greater productivity per worker or unit of capital input. Thus, not only will a more rational pattern of production be achieved, but also trade within the region will increase. Secondary benefits include greater specialization through comparative advantage as well as more favorable terms of trade in a highly competitive global economy. Nations enter into regional arrangements because they believe the outcome will be higher levels of welfare and improved standards of living. In effect, many of the same arguments used to advocate global free trade are used to justify regional integration. However, while regional integration serves to improve welfare within a region, does it increase global welfare? At the heart of the debate is the issue of trade creation versus trade diversion.

Article XXIV of the General Agreement on Tariffs and Trade (GATT) permits such arrangements, provided that all trade between member countries is liberalized and that external tariffs imposed by these countries are not higher, on average, than those prevailing before the formation of the regional arrangement or bloc.

It is important to note that regional trade liberalization does constitute an exception to the GATT system in that member countries are treated more favorably than nonmember countries. There is a considerable debate among economists whether regional trade blocs represent a complement to the multilateral system or a substitute for global trade liberalization because of their discriminatory nature. Nevertheless, between 1947 and 1990, more than 80 regional arrangements were registered with GATT as specified under Article XXIV. While many of these blocs have failed, generally for political reasons, at the establishment of the World Trade Organization (WTO) nearly two dozen regional trade blocs at varying levels of integration were in existence—with more being planned.

Responsibility for ensuring that these regional trade blocs play a complementary role to global trade liberalization will fall to the WTO as a forum for trade negotiations and in its role of monitoring national trade policies. Trade barriers between regional blocs must be lowered, as well as barriers within blocs, in order to maximize the potential benefits from trade.

Forms of Regional Trade Blocs

Regional trade blocs at differing stages of integration have different institutional frameworks, posing different challenges to policymakers concerned with reducing barriers to trade. Three types of integration are free-trade areas, customs unions, and common markets.

Free-Trade Areas

A free-trade area is established when a group of nations agrees to abolish restrictions on mutual trade between countries, while each country maintains its own external tariff system on trade with nonmember countries. The North American Free Trade Agreement (NAFTA) represents such a system. In a free-trade area, tariffs are eliminated on the trade in goods and services. However, there is no common external tariff (CET), and there continue to be restrictions on the movement of labor and capital. Furthermore, there is no harmonization of economic policies among member countries, and there are no supranational institutions.[1] As barriers to trade are lowered, facilitating greater trade between member nations, disputes that do arise have few established institutional arrangements to provide a dispute-settlement mechanism. The governments of member nations must try to resolve the disputes as best they can, subject to considerable domestic pressures. In the case of NAFTA, there are disputes over labor and wage policy as well as environmental issues. Interest groups, such as labor unions and environmental advocacy organizations, have no means of redress except to apply pressure on domestic lawmakers. Thus, a certain level of continual uncertainty exists because the gains from free trade may be obscured in acrimonious partisan debate.

Customs Unions

A customs union is created when a group of nations agree not only to remove restrictions on mutual trade but also to establish a CET system with respect to nonmember countries. Again, restrictions remain in place on the movement of labor and capital, member nations do not harmonize their economic policies, and there are no supranational institutions.[2] It is at this level of integration where the trade-diversion problem begins to manifest itself. It is the CET that provides the incentive for trade to shift from low-cost nonmember countries to high-cost member countries. The Southern Common Market (Mercado Común del Sur, or MERCOSUR) represents an example of a customs union. Related to the customs union issue is the dilemma of Chile, which in general maintains a lower tariff rate than does the MERCOSUR customs union. Both NAFTA and MERCOSUR would like to bring Chile into their own trade blocs.[3] There are both political and economic ramifications either way Chile decides to go. If the proposed Free Trade Area of the Americas (FTAA) is ultimately established, then of course the issue is resolved. Latin American governments are very sensitive to the possibility that the United States might disrupt their current arrangements, where, in effect, Latin American economies would become part of the domestic U.S. market. For its part, the United States has some reservations over negotiations between MERCOSUR and the European Union (EU). The newly liberalized Latin American markets offer huge future trade potentials, which both the United States and EU recognize.

Common Markets

A common market is created with the removal of all restrictions on the movement of factors of production, such as labor, capital, and natural resources. This free flow of production factors represents the most efficient allocation of resources and production possibilities, allowing the greatest gains from trade to be realized. Common markets can then move toward full economic union, with the establishment of supranational authorities responsible for economic policymaking. Of course this arrangement may require considerable sacrifice of national sovereignty. When full economic union has been reached, virtually all restrictions on trade have been removed. The EU is currently in a transitional phase from common market to full economic union. European integration has required a difficult 40-year process. An economic union involves creation of a single monetary system, a central bank, a unified fiscal system, and a common foreign economic agenda. The next step will involve political union or the creation of some type of federal system—for which the EU has already created an institutional framework, including a European Parliament, Court of Justice, the European Council, and the Council of Ministers.[4]

Regional Trade Blocs in the Americas

Two very significant inter-American trade agreements stand out in the region and will be closely examined: NAFTA and MERCOSUR. NAFTA alone covers a combined market with a gross domestic product (GDP) exceeding $10 trillion, 406 million people, and an area of 21 million square kilometers encompassing three countries. MERCOSUR consists of four South American countries, including the region's largest, Brazil.

Three other free-trade agreements worth noting in this chapter are the Caribbean Community (CARICOM), the Andean Community, and the Central American Common Market (CACM).

Latin American and Caribbean (LAC) countries have sought to widen their integration schemes in a variety of ways. First, they have established closer ties within their own region, expanding existing regional groups or negotiating new trade agreements with their LAC neighbors. Second, they have launched negotiations to create a FTAA. Last, LAC countries have also pursued closer commercial links with Europe and Asia. The result has been a proliferation of trade agreements among LAC countries and between their extraregional partners. Such efforts are in line with one of the basic premises of

3

"open regionalism," namely to facilitate LAC integration into the global economy through progressive market opening.

One recent trend regarding trade agreements in the Americas is the collaboration of individual countries with regional trade blocs. Out of the thirteen trade agreements between 1994 and 1999, six trade agreements have involved single-member countries with multinational trade blocs. Brazil, for example, signed a free-trade agreement with the Andean Community in 1999 that came into effect in 2000. Additionally, some countries that have a limited role in regional trade blocs have signed their own agreements with either individual countries or regional trade blocs. Chile, for example, is not a formal member of any trade bloc but has signed a total of eight trade agreements; seven being bilateral trade pacts with other individual countries. Finally, extraregional organizations, most notably the EU and South Korea, have established trade agreements with LAC countries or trade blocs.

MERCOSUR

Overview

As of January 1995, MERCOSUR integrated a large regional market uniting Brazil, Argentina, Paraguay, and Uruguay. The four countries signed the Treaty of Asunción on March 26, 1991, establishing an imperfect customs union to accomplish the following goals:

- elimination of tariff and nontariff barriers;

- adoption of a CET and a CET policy;

- coordination of macroeconomic and sectoral policies; and

- member-country commitment to the free movement of services, labor, and capital.

MERCOSUR functions within the greater frameworks of the Latin American Integration Association (Asociación Latinoamerica de Integration, or ALADI) and GATT, which permit members to provide preferential treatment within customs unions, while prohibiting additional tariffs to be levied on outside countries. In targeting the end of duty requirements and nontariff restrictions, the trade-opening program eliminated customs rights on foreign trade and prohibited the member countries from unilaterally impeding mutual trade.

MERCOSUR's Atlantic coast stretches 3,500 miles along eastern South America, and the combined geographic area of 4,583,629 square miles is considerably larger than that of the United States. It is the fourth-largest integrated market in the world after NAFTA, the EU, and Japan.

The current CET covers 85 percent of all traded goods, with the normal average external tariff being 11.3 percent. In December 1997, the maximum external tariff was temporarily raised to 23 percent. All goods entering any of the MERCOSUR countries are subject to a uniform tariff. Since MERCOSUR's implementation on January 1, 1995, the members adopted a CET ranging between 0 and 20 percent that applies to approximately 9,000 items. Not all items are included in this list; some of them are subject to specific negotiations, such as sugar and automobiles. In addition, foreign enterprises are increasing investment in the region, and there are attractive opportunities for new investment in the infrastructure sector, particularly in areas that will require huge building projects, such as energy, telecommunications, transportation, and tourism.

The Treaty of Asunción provides for the possibility of other nations joining MERCOSUR. Its members can examine applications for any such nations if the interested parties are not already a part of any subregional integration or extraregional associations. MERCOSUR has brought in associate members in the hopes of building a South American coalition. Chile signed a free-trade agreement with MERCOSUR that went into effect in October 1996, and Bolivia signed on in March 1997. These new agreements point to the creation of a customs union in a maximum of 18 years and establish the framework for integration, commercial safeguards, and dispute settlement.

MERCOSUR had its foundations when Latin America started to take steps toward regional integration. The treaty that created the Latin American Free Trade Association (Asociación Latinoamericana de Libre Comércio, or ALALC), signed in 1960, provided for the creation of a free-trade zone by means of periodic and selective negotiations between its member states. The negotiations, at the discretion of the member states, rather than automatic reduction of import duties, made the ALALC trade-opening program develop reasonably well in its first years, lose impetus from 1965, and almost come to a complete standstill in the 1970s.[5]

ALADI was created in 1989 to replace ALALC. ALADI used means other than those previously adopted to attempt greater member-state integration. In place of the free-trade zone established by ALALC, an economic preference zone was established, creating conditions favorable to the growth of bilateral initiatives as a prelude to the initiation of multilateral relationships in Latin America. ALADI thus made possible agreements and joint actions between countries in the region, which previously had only limited ties. The establishment of a common market, however, was still far off in the horizon.[6]

Under the ALADI system, Brazil and Argentina signed 12 commercial protocols in 1986. They were the first concrete steps toward bringing the two countries closer together. In order to improve on their former agreements, Brazil and Argentina signed a "Treaty for Integration, Cooperation and Development" in 1988, which set the stage for a common market between the two countries within ten years. It contemplated the gradual elimination of all tariff barriers and the harmonization of the macroeconomic policies of both nations. After the addition of Paraguay and Uruguay, all four countries signed a new treaty on March 26, 1991, in Asunción, Paraguay, providing for the creation of a common market among the participants, to be known as the Southern Common Market (MERCOSUR).[7]

Since the four-member structure was cemented, MERCOSUR has been actively pursuing expansion. With Chile and Bolivia already associate members, talks with other prospective members are under way. Peru made a formal application for membership. Mexico and Venezuela also have been considered.[8] Since 1996, representatives of the Andean Community have held various rounds of talks with MERCOSUR officials to prepare for a biregional free-trade accord. The most-recent discussions took place in March 1998, at which a target of October 1 was set for the first phase of a free-trade pact between the two groups. However, differences regarding tariff reductions and export exclusions made this deadline difficult to meet.[9] Last, the final goal of negotiations with other South American countries is to create a type of South American Free Trade Agreement (SAFTA), an entity first proposed by Brazil in 1992. This type of agreement is considered an important step in the eventual creation of a hemispheric free-trade area.

Trade Trends

The MERCOSUR trade bloc has experienced a consistent increase in trade since 1990. Total exports from the region almost doubled from $46.4 billion in 1990 to $81.4 billion in 1998, illustrating an increase of more than 75 percent during this period, with an average annual growth rate of more than 6 percent per year. In addition, imports grew at a faster rate, from $27.4 billion to $95.6 billion for an increase of nearly 250 percent in the same period and an average annual growth rate of nearly 15 percent.

Argentina and Brazil are responsible for most of the trade bloc's exports. In 1990, 94.3 percent of total exports originated in these countries; by 1998, they accounted for 95.2 percent of exports. Brazil and Argentina also accounted for most of the total imports: they imported 89.9 percent of imported goods in 1990, climbing up to 93.1 percent in 1998. Argentina led an increase in both exports and imports during the period, with an average annual growth rate of 8.8 percent in exports and 25.5 percent in imports. Brazil followed at more modest rates of 5.6 percent and 12.1 percent for exports and imports, respectively.

Exports from the region's most important partner, Brazil, grew 62.7 percent during the period, while Argentina's exports doubled (growing 114 percent). Uruguay had a similar performance as Brazil, with a trade increase of 62.2 percent. Paraguay, on the other hand, witnessed a slow growth in its exports, growing only 15.8 percent during this period. Brazil's imports rose more than its imports, rising 180.2 percent, while Argentina's imports grew dramatically, at a 25.5 percent annual rate, the highest in the region.

Brazil is the prime exporter of the region. In 1998, its exports accounted for almost two-thirds (62.8 percent) of the bloc's total; Argentina's exports accounted for 32.5 percent; Paraguay and Uruguay represented 4.8 percent. During the 1990-98 period, a reconfiguration in the relative importance of the member countries in the region's total exports took place. In 1990, Brazil had 67.7 percent, while Argentina accounted for 26.6 percent. Paraguay and Uruguay accounted for only 5.8 percent of the bloc's exports. Brazil's share of total imports fell from 75 percent to 60.2 percent over the nine-year period, while Argentina's more than doubled, from 14.9 percent in 1990 to 32.9 percent in 1998. Meanwhile, Paraguay and Uruguay's combined import share fell from 10.0 percent to 6.9 percent.

As the commercial ties between the four countries increased during the 1990s, intraregional trade powered the export and import growth of the trade bloc. While MERCOSUR's total exports grew at a 6.4 percent average annual rate, its intraregional exports grew three times as fast, at a 22.2 percent rate, while exports to the rest of the world grew at a 4.7 percent rate during this period.

Brazil's main destination is still the EU, which purchased 29.1 percent of its exports in 1998; the United States comes in second with 18.4 percent. Argentina accounted for 13.2 percent of Brazil's exports, growing from a meager 2.1 percent in 1990 for an average growth rate of 34.1 percent. The main destinations for Paraguay are Brazil and Argentina, accounting for roughly 30 percent for each country. The most dynamic market within the trade bloc for Paraguay was Argentina, with a 24.3 percent average annual growth rate during 1990-98. For Uruguay, Brazil has been the primary export destination, taking 29.6 percent of its exports in 1990 and around one-third (33.8 percent) in 1998. During this decade, the EU bought between 20 and 25 percent of Uruguay's exports; but the EU lost its second-place ranking to Argentina, which accounted for 18.6 percent of Uruguay's exports in 1998. Uruguay's exports to Argentina grew at a rate of 25.8 percent over the 1990-98 period.

Exports of Leading Products

Between 1980 and 1998, MERCOSUR exhibited an unexpectedly small degree of change in its leading exports of the regional trade bloc. Table 1.1 illustrates the leading exported products of the MERCOSUR region since 1980. While the product vegetable oil residues decreased 35 percent of its share of all exports, it still remains the leading exported product of the region since 1980, years before MERCOSUR came into effect. Trade liberalization, import-substitution initiatives, and industrialization throughout the region allowed for a number of products to become leading exported products. Other motor vehicle parts and passenger motor vehicles, both absent in the ten leading products category of the region in 1990, became leading exported products by 1998. On the other hand, a number of products fell sharply in their share of exports. Bovine fresh meat, raw beet and cane sugar, and petroleum products are all exported goods that experienced a sharp decreasing share of total exported products from MERCOSUR.

Andean Community

Overview

The Andean Community is a regional organization composed of Colombia, Ecuador, Peru, Bolivia, and Venezuela with various institutions and "organs" that work toward the common goal of regional "Andean" integration.[10] This integration process recently celebrated its 30th anniversary in 1999, after establishing the Andean Community (formerly known as the Andean Group) in 1969. Located primarily in the northwestern portion of South America, the five member countries constitute a population of more than 110 million. There are four principal objectives of the Andean Community:

1. promote and foster stable economic development,

2. accelerate growth by means of integration and economic and social cooperation,

3. encourage participation in the process of regional integration toward a gradual formation of a common market, and

4. increase the quality of life of the total population of the Andean Community. [11]

Table 1.1
Exports of Leading Products: MERCOSUR
(as % share each year)

Product	1980	1990	1998
Vegetable oil residues	6.2%	6.1%	4.6%
Soybeans, excluding flour	3.5%	4.0%	4.1%
Iron ore, excluding pyrites	5.3%	5.2%	4.1%
Passenger motor vehicles, excluding buses	2.0%	0.0%	4.0%
Coffee, green, roasted, etc.	8.4%	2.4%	2.9%
Other motor vehicle parts	0.0%	0.0%	1.8%
Soybean oil	0.0%	0.0%	1.8%
Maize, unmilled	1.7%	0.0%	1.7%
Fruit or vegetable juice	0.0%	3.2%	1.6%
Wheat, etc., unmilled	2.8%	1.9%	1.6%
Bovine meat, fresh, frozen	2.3%	0.0%	0.0%
Raw beet and cane sugar	4.1%	0.0%	0.0%
Petroleum products	3.0%	3.2%	0.0%
Aluminum, alloys, unwrought	0.0%	2.1%	0.0%
Piston engines, nonair	0.0%	1.9%	0.0%
Footwear, leather	0.0%	2.3%	0.0%
Average share of leading products (%) exported to the world market	**39.3%**	**32.3%**	**28.2%**
Millions of U.S. dollars	**$29,467.70**	**$46,429.90**	**$80,224.50**

Source: Data from United Nations Economic Commission for Latin American and Caribbean (ECLAC), *Statistical Yearbook for Latin America and the Caribbean* (Santiago, Chile, 1999), p.16.

The decision by the presidents of the member countries of Bolivia, Colombia, Ecuador, Peru, and Venezuela in establishing broad guidelines for transforming the Andean Community into a common market by the year 2005 was a fundamental step in the long integration process of the community. Although the Andean Community has been in existence since 1969, free-trade was not exercised until the early 1990s. On November 11, 1990, the presidents from the five member countries implemented plans to accelerate the establishment of a free-trade zone. On December 5, 1991, the Andean Community approved the adoption of the Barahona Act, in which it sought to gradually phase out the CET by 1994.[12] The first two Andean countries to achieve free-trade status were Colombia and Venezuela in January 1992, when they finalized their tariff-elimination program (Arancel Externo Comun). By October of the same year, Bolivia joined in and was followed by Ecuador in January 1993. By January 31, 1993, the "free-trade zone" was in full effect for Bolivia, Colombia, Ecuador, and Venezuela.

Peru, on the other hand, has been slow to liberalize its tariff lines. On August 8, 1992, Peru was temporarily suspended from its member obligations in respect to the Andean Community's trade liberalization program. In 1998, however, Peru, marred with border disputes for many years, signed a peace agreement with Ecuador that led to their bilateral free-trade agreement in 1999. This action not only gave Peru credibility within the Andean Community but also solidified its plan to gradually eliminate its tariffs with 85 percent completion by 2000 and full liberalization by 2005.[13]

Trade Trends

The Andean Community has undertaken a serious effort in liberalizing its markets both intraregionally and through "third" countries. These efforts have apparently paid off because trade nearly doubled during the 1990s, from $49 billion in 1990 to $96 billion in 1997. While total imports grew by an average of 15 percent between 1991 and 1997, total exports grew at a much slower pace of 7 percent during the same period principally because of the Asian financial crisis. In fact, during the height of the crisis and Peru's close relationship with Japan, total exports declined by 11 percent. In addition, intra-Andean trade is mostly in manufactured exports, accounting for more than 90 percent of total trade.[14]

Colombia and Venezuela are the largest, most productive members of the Andean Community, accounting for 35 percent and 40 percent of intragroup exports, respectively. Trade between these two countries account for the bulk of trade within the region. Conversely, Bolivia is the smallest market in inter-Andean exports at 3 percent, exhibiting very little change in proportion toward the rest of the region between 1990 and 1998. The same story applies to intraregional imports, where Bolivia has only accounted for 5 percent within the region during the same period.

The overall region destinations of Andean Community exports have also relatively remained unchanged during the 1990s. The U.S./Canada region, the largest recipient, accounting for 45 percent of Andean exports in 1990, fell to 40 percent in 1998. Other important destinations of exports include the EU (15 percent in 1998), other LAC countries (17 percent), and countries within the Andean region (12 percent).[15]

The Andean region has witnessed some significant changes from its own subregion during the 1990s. The level of imports proportional to the rest of the world has nearly doubled. In 1990, the Andean Community imported only 6 percent while the U.S./Canada region was a robust 37 percent. By 1998, however, the Andean subregion swelled to 11 percent while the U.S./Canada region dropped slightly to 34 percent. Finally, EU imports also decreased in relation to the rest of the world from 22 percent in 1990 to 18 percent in 1998.[16]

The liberalization of merchandize trade and the CET have been instrumental in moving toward the eventual formation of a common market.[17] But expanding the Andean Community's influence outside the region has been equally as important as reaching important integration goals. The community has focused in deepening its intraregional links in recent years, such as the Andean-MERCOSUR initiative, for example. Free-trade agreements with Mexico and Chile and current negotiations with Panama have also illustrated the community's flexibility in engaging in agreements with individual countries.

Exports of Leading Products

Even though the Andean Community has kept crude petroleum as its leading exported product since 1980, its share of the total exported products from the Andean Community has progressively shrank. In 1980, crude petroleum owned a little more than a 47 percent share of the total products exported by the community, but by 1998 that figure had shrank to 27.7 percent (see Table 1.2). Moreover, petroleum products were the second-leading exported product and hence made petroleum and its by-products the most dominant goods exported, owning almost a 70 percent share of the total products exported in 1980. By 1998, however, the exports share of two product categories had fallen to less than 40 percent, more than a 70 percent decrease from its 1980 level. Other natural resource products that became leading exported products by 1998 included gold, coal, and cut flowers (categorized among the ten leading exported products by 1998). A number of products that experienced a decrease in their exports as a percentage share of exports from the community included a number of minerals, such as lead, zinc, copper, and aluminum.

CACM

Overview

The Central American region also possesses a common market. But unlike the other inter-American trade agreements, the CACM is a relatively new model, displacing the region's 1960 founding treaty.[18] The CACM seeks to unify the economies of Central American countries and jointly to promote the development of Central America in order to improve the living conditions of their people.[19]

Table 1.2
Exports of Leading Products: Andean Community
(as % share each year)

Product	1980	1990	1998
Crude petroleum	47.1%	33.8%	27.7%
Petroleum products	20.3%	17.6%	11.5%
Coffee, green, roasted, etc.	8.8%	5.3%	5.8%
Bananas, plantains, fresh	1.0%	3.9%	4.0%
Gold, or dust, noncurrent	0.0%	0.0%	3.4%
Coal, excluding briquettes	0.0%	2.5%	2.7%
Shellfish, fresh, frozen	0.0%	1.7%	2.2%
Cut flowers	0.0%	0.0%	1.8%
Copper, refined	1.4%	1.6%	1.6%
Aluminum, alloys, unwrought	1.1%	2.0%	1.3%
Meat or fish meal fodder	0.0%	1.5%	0.0%
Iron ores, concentrates	1.2%	0.0%	0.0%
Lead ores, concentrates	0.9%	0.0%	0.0%
Zinc ores, concentrates	0.0%	1.2%	0.0%
Gas, natural	1.4%	0.0%	0.0%
Copper, unrefined	0.9%	0.0%	0.0%
Average share of leading products (%) exported to the world market	**84.1%**	**71.1%**	**62.0%**
Millions of U.S. dollars	**$30,126.00**	**$30,831.80**	**$80,224.50**

Source: Data from United Nations Economic Commission for Latin American and Caribbean (ECLAC), *Statistical Yearbook for Latin America and the Caribbean* (Santiago, Chile, 1999), p. 26.

Intra-CACM trade liberalization has indeed advanced significantly in the 1990s, particularly because of the reestablishing of the CET. The new CET structure was to range from a minimum of 5 percent to a maximum of 20 percent. In 1995, the governments of CACM-member states agreed to accelerate tariff reduction, with the goal of reaching a CET level of 0-15 percent in the year 2000. CACM-member states also agreed to sign the Uniform Central American Customs Code (CAUCA) in 1993 to iron out the details in regards to customs procedures.[20]

Customs procedures within the CACM are critical to trade and investment protocol. These customs procedures are roughly divided into two relevant articles. The first article emphasizes the procedure of goods followed by the customs offices of exit and of entry in the member states. The second article focuses on the inspection by the central customs office of exit in the importing country.

Trade Trends

In 1998, total CACM exports and imports reached $15.6 and $19.4 billion, respectively, causing a trade deficit of $3.8 billion (about 8 percent of the region's GDP). The Central American region's total exports grew during 1995-98 at an average annual rate of 22 percent compared to 13 percent during the previous four years. Imports, on the other hand, maintained their average annual rate of growth of around 15 percent throughout the 1990s.

The aggressive growth in trade has been very evident for the Central American region during the last decade. In 1990, for example, global exports rose past $4 billion. By 1998, global exports for the CACM topped $15.6 billion, almost four times the amount in 1990. The same story applies to imports, where global imports in 1990 accounted for more than $6.5 billion. Eight years later, these same imports grew past $19 billion, also about three times as much as in global exports.

The CACM is actively pursuing agreements with other trade organizations, particularly within the Western Hemisphere. The CACM has initiated free-trade talks with Panama, where, for historical reasons, Panama has never been a member of a subregional integration scheme. In April 1998, the presidents of the Central America countries and Chile met to negotiate a comprehensive free-trade agreement for their countries. Finally, countries within the CACM subregion have also initiated their independent free-trade agreements with other countries outside the Central American community. In addition, El Salvador, Guatemala, and Honduras, otherwise known as the "Northern Triangle," have been negotiating a free-trade agreement with Mexico.[21]

Exports of Leading Products

Central America's leading exported commodity throughout the years consistently has been coffee (see Table 1.3). In 1980, coffee products made up more than 30 percent of the share of all exported products; however, by 1998 that figure had shrank to less than 18 percent, experiencing a 72 percent drop. Its second-leading exported product, bananas, is also an agricultural product, which owned more than a 9 percent share of total products exported in 1998 but was significantly less than the 15 percent share it owned in 1990. Moreover, a number of exported products increased their shares and became leading exports by 1998. Some of these products include medicaments, men's outerwear, transistors, and office machine parts. At the other end of the spectrum, some products fell sharply and are no longer leading exported goods in the region. These commodities include raw cotton, bovine fresh meat, fresh/frozen fish, and some types of minerals such as nickel.

Table 1.3
Exports of Leading Products: CACM
(as % share each year)

Product	1980	1990	1998
Coffee, green, roasted, etc.	30.7%	25.5%	17.9%
Bananas, plantains, fresh	8.0%	14.8%	9.3%
Office machine parts	0.0%	0.0%	5.1%
Transistors, valvex, etc.	0.0%	0.0%	4.2%
Raw beet and cane sugar	4.0%	5.4%	4.0%
Women's outerwear, nonknit	0.0%	0.0%	1.8%
Men's outerwear, nonknit	0.0%	0.0%	1.4%
Shellfish, fresh, frozen	1.5%	1.3%	1.4%
Medicaments	2.0%	2.4%	1.3%
Tropical fruit, fresh	0.0%	1.0%	1.2%
Bovine meat, fresh, frozen	4.9%	4.2%	0.0%
Fish, fresh, chilled, frozen	0.0%	1.0%	0.0%
Other fresh fruit	3.5%	0.0%	0.0%
Oil seeds, nuts, etc.	0.0%	1.2%	0.0%
Raw cotton, excluding linters	6.4%	1.7%	0.0%
Vegetables used in pharmaceuticals	1.1%	0.0%	0.0%
Nickel alloys, unwrought	1.4%	0.0%	0.0%
Average share of leading products (%) exported to the world market	**63.5%**	**58.5%**	**47.6%**
Millions of U.S. dollars	**$4,412.50**	**$4,019.00**	**$10,720.70**

Source: Data from United Nations Economic Commission for Latin American and Caribbean (ECLAC), *Statistical Yearbook for Latin America and the Caribbean* (Santiago, Chile, 1999), p. 38.

NAFTA

Overview

NAFTA, which took effect on January 1, 1994, is a detailed, broad-based pact governing trade between the United States, Mexico, and Canada. The objectives of the agreement are to eliminate barriers to trade, promote conditions of fair competition, increase investment opportunities, provide adequate protection of intellectual rights, and establish effective procedures for implementation of the agreement and for resolution of disputes.

NAFTA's 22 chapters are consistent with GATT and incorporate most of the provisions of the 1989 U.S.-Canada Free Trade Agreement.[22] Each nation affirmed its rights and obligations under GATT (now superseded by the WTO) and other international agreements. For purposes of interpretation, NAFTA establishes that it takes precedence over other international agreements to the extent that conflict arises but provides exception to this general rule. As an example, the provisions of certain environmental agreements take precedence, subject to a requirement to minimize inconsistencies with NAFTA.

NAFTA shares with GATT the aim of reducing tariff and nontariff barriers but, unlike GATT, focuses on the North American region—Canada, Mexico, and the United States. However, NAFTA goes beyond GATT in some significant respects. NAFTA grants national treatment not only for imported goods (as under GATT) but also for investments and services as diverse as banking, brokerage, insurance, law, and transportation.[23] In 1996, U.S. exports to Mexico set a record of $57 billion. Even during the severe downturn in the Mexican economy in 1995, NAFTA served to prevent Mexico from closing its market, as it did during the last Mexican financial crisis in 1982.

By 1999, trade between the three countries had grown by about 75 percent since NAFTA came into force. From less than $289 billion in 1993, trilateral trade has now reached $507 billion. Investment between the three economies has also significantly increased, with more than $189 billion invested in each other's economies in 1997. Moreover, total foreign direct investment into the NAFTA countries has meanwhile reached $864 billion, and job creation has surged in all three NAFTA countries, with employment levels now at record highs. Since NAFTA was implemented, employment has grown by 10.1 percent (1.3 million jobs) in Canada, by 22 percent (2.2 million jobs) in Mexico, and by more than 7 percent (12.8 million jobs) in the United States.[24]

Trade Trends

The United States, Mexico, and Canada have experienced significant increases in trade with the rest of the world. Between 1994 and 1999, the United States alone experienced a rate of growth of 36 percent in exports and 54 percent in imports. Correspondingly, Mexico's exports grew 125 percent and its imports 79 percent, while Canada's exports grew 58 percent and its imports 57 percent.

The amount of intraregional trade within the United States, Mexico, and Canada has increased exponentially since NAFTA took effect January 1, 1994. In 1993, trilateral trade was $289 billion; but, by 1999, the combined amount surpassed $500 billion. Thus, trade between the three nations has increased by more than 76 percent since 1994. In addition, investments in all three nations have increased; since 1997, an estimated $189 billion has been invested trilaterally.

The United States has a long-standing trading relationship with Canada. The two nations enacted the U.S.-Canada Free Trade Agreement in 1989. U.S. exports to Canada in 1999 increased 3.1 percent over 1998. In 1999, U.S. exports to Canada amounted to $166.2 billion, while imports from Canada totaled $198.3 billion. Imports from Canada have increased about 31 percent since 1994, while U.S. exports to Canada have increased 35 percent since 1994.

The U.S. monetary value of exports and imports with Canada is larger than with Mexico. However, since NAFTA took effect, there has been a larger increase in the percentage of trade between the United States and Mexico than between the United States and Canada. Overall, U.S.-Mexico trade has increased by a total of 120 percent during NAFTA's first five years.[25] In 1993, the total trade between the two nations was $85.2 billion. But just in the first six months of 1999 alone, U.S.-Mexico trade surpassed the $107 billion threshold.

Exports of Leading Products

The NAFTA-member countries witnessed a consistent increase in exports from all top commodity products. The single biggest commodity exported by the NAFTA countries has been parts and accessories of motor vehicles (see Table 1.4), which has experienced an increase of more than 31 percent, from $17.3 billion in 1995 to $22.8 billion in 1999. Though this exported product had a significant increase, other commodities experienced a much more aggressive growth in value exported. Telecommunications equipment, for instance, nearly doubled its exports in only five years, growing more than 87 percent from $3.7 billion in 1995 to nearly $7 billion by 1999. In addition, the product electrical apparatus for switching increased nearly 67 percent, growing from $4.3 billion in 1995 to $7.2 billion in 1999.

Table 1.4
Exports of Leading Products: NAFTA
(millions of U.S. dollars)

Product	1995	1999	% change
Parts and accessories of motor vehicles	$17,388	$22,815	31.21
All motor vehicles	$7,883	$11,684	48.22
Thermionic, cold cathode, and photocathode valve	$8,165	$12,125	48.50
Internal combustion piston engines	$5,737	$8,896	55.06
Automatic data processing machines	$5,296	$7,432	40.33
Telecommunications equipment	$3,700	$6,921	87.05
Electrical apparatus for switching or protecting	$4,319	$7,211	66.96
Electrical machinery and apparatus	$3,777	$5,746	52.13
Special purpose motor vehicles	$3,035	$4,329	42.64
Estimated low value shipments	$3,675	$4,651	26.56

Source: Data from United Nations Economic Commission for Latin American and Caribbean (ECLAC), *Statistical Yearbook for Latin America and the Caribbean* (Santiago, Chile, 1999), p. 49.

CARICOM

Overveiw

Established more than 25 years ago, CARICOM is one of the oldest integration organizations in the hemisphere. The largest trade bloc in terms of membership, CARICOM is also the smallest in economic and geographic size. After experiencing relative stagnation in its integration process during the 1980s, CARICOM-member countries have actively sought to revitalize their regional links, leading to a more outward-development, export-led growth process in the 1990s. Today, CARICOM is a multilingual, multiethnic organization of 15 member countries experiencing the challenges of transforming its free-trade area and customs union into a single market economy.[26]

The foundation of CARICOM is based on its three objectives:

- economic cooperation through the Caribbean single market economy;

- coordination of foreign policy among the independent member countries; and

- common services and cooperation in functional matters, such as health, education and culture, communications, and industrial relations.[27]

Touching on a wide array of issues from key elements in CARICOM's single market economy, from industrial policy to rules of competition, CARICOM is a very interdependent regional organization bound by common natural ties.

CARICOM has undertaken steps to improve its free-trade area in goods. Most tariffs to intraregional trade and a significant number of nontariff measures (NTMs) have now been eliminated. Member countries are also working to establish regional product standards to facilitate cross-border transactions in the community. Furthermore, CARICOM has made considerable progress with respect to lowering external protection and simplifying the structure of its CET. In fact, member countries approved a new CET structure in 1992, in which it implemented a gradual tariff reduction process to be completed in four phases over a five-year period. By mid-1999, several countries had completed Phase IV of the new CET program.[28] The final tariff rates of the CET range from 0 to 20 percent, with exceptions for some products, mostly agricultural. The CET process has, therefore, represented a significant market-opening effort for CARICOM. When the process is complete, the unweighted average tariff rate will be around 10 percent, down from 20 percent in 1991.[29] However, rapid global trade liberalization and the forming of new trade alliances worldwide have eroded some of the important trade preferences long enjoyed by CARICOM and its traditional export markets.

Trade Trends

The growing challenges faced by CARICOM in international markets are reflected by the group's modest export performance in recent years. Between 1990 and 1998, CARICOM's total merchandise exports expanded from $5.8 to $7.5 billion for an average annual growth of 3 percent. In 1990, the U.S./Canada region, easily the Caribbean region's largest export market, accounted for 44 percent of CARICOM's exports in proportion to other regions in the world, whereas in 1998 the same North American region accounted for 40 percent for a slight decrease of 4 percent. Other major export markets for CARICOM in 1990 were the EU (25 percent), and within its own

Caribbean region (8 percent). Though there were some minor changes by 1998, the 1990 figures have remained relatively consistent.

In terms of importing to CARICOM during the last decade, the U.S./Canada region also has been the largest importer. In 1990, the U.S./Canada region accounted for 46 percent of CARICOM's imports. In 1998, the same region imported a proportional lower amount (42 percent) in respect to the rest of the world. Other major markets that import into CARICOM include the EU (20 percent in 1998, a 4 percentage point increase from 1990), and Japan (8 percent in 1998, down from 11 percent in 1990). One of the group's main trade initiatives was concluded in August 1998, when CARICOM signed a comprehensive free-trade agreement with the Dominican Republic based on the NAFTA model.[30]

Exports of Leading Products

The 15 member countries in the Caribbean region have witnessed a sharp increase in the export of manufactured goods (see Table 1.5). In 1980, manufactured material goods made up less than 2 percent of all exports. By 1990, however, this type of goods swelled to nearly 31 percent (and 32.6 percent by 1996) of all exported products in the free-trade community. On the other hand, the export of crude materials has fallen since 1980, decreasing from 44.5 percent in 1980 to only 2.2 percent by 1996 as the share of total exports from the community. Other trends in CARICOM include the increase in the export of chemicals, food and animals, and machinery and transport equipment. Finally, aside from crude materials, exported goods also fell for miscellaneous manufactured articles and animal and vegetable oils.

Table 1.5
Exports of Leading Products: CARICOM
(as % share each year)

Product	1980	1990	1996
Manufactured goods (material)	1.8%	30.9%	32.6%
Mineral fuels, lubricants, and related materials	32.3%	3.9%	20.0%
Chemicals and related products	3.1%	16.4%	19.9%
Food and animals	5.1%	12.3%	11.5%
Machinery and transport equipment	3.0%	7.8%	7.8%
Beverages and tobacco	0.9%	2.2%	3.9%
Crude materials, inedible, except fuel	44.5%	24.1%	2.2%
Misc. manufactured articles	8.4%	1.7%	2.2%
Animal and vegetable oils, fats	0.3%	0.0%	0.0%
Commodities and transactions	0.5%	0.6%	0.0%

Source: Data from United Nations Economic Commission for Latin American and Caribbean (ECLAC), *Statistical Yearbook for Latin America and the Caribbean* (Santiago, Chile, 1999), p. 54.

Interregional Trade Flows

Interregional trade means trade conducted between different "trade" regions. There are two types of interregional trade that will be examined in this section: "hemispheric" interregional trade within the major trade blocs in the Americas (i.e., MERCOSUR–NAFTA) and "global" interregional trade between trade regions in the Americas and major geographic regions in the world (i.e., MERCOSUR–Africa).

Western Hemispheric Trade Flows

Interregional trade flows within the Western Hemisphere are examined in terms of the five major regional trade blocs that were previously discussed in this chapter. Hemispheric interregional trade easily accounts for the better part of total hemispheric trade.

MERCOSUR

MERCOSUR's interregional exports with the hemisphere's other major trade blocs are largely consumed by NAFTA. In fact, as Figure 1.1 shows, MERCOSUR's 1999 exports to NAFTA exceeded $14 billion. On the other hand, the CARICOM trade bloc received the least amount of exports from the MERCOSUR trade region, importing only $169 million in 1999, about 1 percent of all MERCOSUR exports made in the Americas. MERCOSUR intraregional trade (trade within its own bloc) makes up more than 40 percent of its total exports in the hemisphere. Exports to the NAFTA region and within its own region make up more than 83 percent of all its hemispheric exports. Finally, MERCOSUR's exports to the Andean Community region and the Central American region, which collectively make up only more than 8 percent of its total hemispheric trade, were about $2.8 million.

Andean Community

Just like the MERCOSUR region, the main importing hemispheric region for the Andean Community's goods is the NAFTA trade bloc. As Figure 1.2 illustrates, NAFTA countries imported about $19.5 billion from the Andean Community in 1999, more than two-thirds of all the Andean Community's exports in the hemisphere. Its own intraregional exports were second, receiving approximately $3.5 billion, more than 12 percent of all its hemispheric exports. Other trade blocs in the hemisphere making up nearly 13 percent of all its hemispheric exports include the MERCOSUR region ($1.2 billion), the Central American region ($1.1 billion), and the Caribbean region ($1.5 billion).

CACM

Hemispheric interregional exports of the CACM are also mostly destined to NAFTA-member countries. While the Central American regional trade bloc exported a total of more than $8.2 billion to the Western Hemisphere, NAFTA-member countries received more than $5.8 billion (or 70 percent) of its exports. Intraregional exports to the members of its own trade bloc was the second-leading region to receive CACM's exports with a total of $2.2 billion, nearly 27 percent of all its hemispheric exports in 1999 (see Figure 1.3).

NAFTA

The NAFTA trade bloc is the leading exporting region in the Americas, exporting a total of more than $603 billion to the rest of the hemisphere in 1999. However, more than 90 percent of this amount consists of intraregional trade, made within its own member countries. The leading hemispheric regional recipient of NAFTA exports is MERCOSUR, with nearly $20 billion (see Figure 1.4).

CARICOM

The majority of CARICOM's trade is conducted with NAFTA, more than 40 percent of CARICOM's exports and 42 percent of its imports. The Andean Community, largely led by Colombia and Venezuela, also actively engages in trade with the Caribbean region, exporting more than $1.5 billion and importing nearly $400 million. However, MERCOSUR, the largest trade bloc in Latin America, only exported nearly $170 million to CARICOM countries and only imported nearly $200 million from the Caribbean countries (see Figure 1.5).

Figure 1.1
MERCOSUR Trade with Western Hemisphere Trade Blocs, 1999
($ millions)

Note: Figures are preliminary estimates for 1999.

Source: Adapted from Inter-American Development Bank (IADB), *Integration and Trade in the Americas* (Washington, D.C.: IADB Publications, October 1999), p. 60. Map created by Mustafa Ackay using GIS software.

Figure 1.2
Andean Community Trade with Western Hemisphere Trade Blocs, 1999
($ millions)

Note: Figures are preliminary estimates for 1999.

Source: Adapted from Inter-American Development Bank (IADB), *Integration and Trade in the Americas* (Washington, D.C.: IADB Publications, October 1999), p. 60. Map created by Mustafa Ackay using GIS software.

Figure 1.3
CACM Trade with Western Hemisphere Trade Blocs, 1999
($ millions)

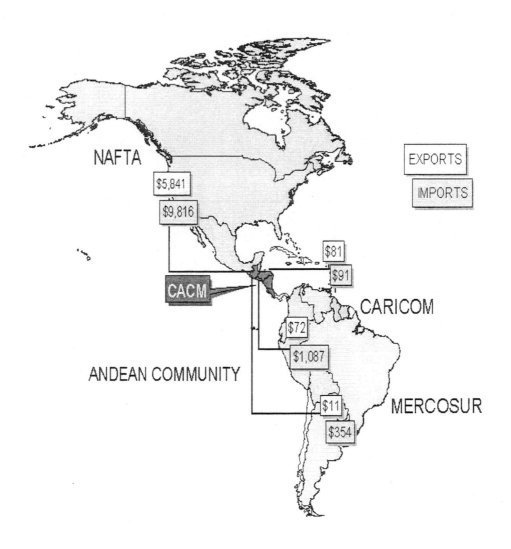

Note: Figures are preliminary estimates for 1999.

Source: Adapted from Inter-American Development Bank (IADB), *Integration and Trade in the Americas* (Washington, D.C.: IADB Publications, October 1999), p. 60. Map created by Mustafa Ackay using GIS software.

Figure 1.4
NAFTA Trade with Western Hemisphere Trade Blocs, 1999
($ millions)

Note: Figures are preliminary estimates for 1999.

Source: Adapted from Inter-American Development Bank (IADB), *Integration and Trade in the Americas* (Washington, D.C.: IADB Publications, October 1999), p. 60. Map created by Mustafa Ackay using GIS software.

Figure 1.5
CARICOM Trade with Western Hemisphere Trade Blocs, 1999
($ millions)

Note: Figures are preliminary estimates for 1999.

Source: Adapted from Inter-American Development Bank (IADB), *Integration and Trade in the Americas* (Washington, D.C.: IADB Publications, October 1999), p. 60. Map created by Mustafa Ackay using GIS software.

Global Trade Flows

The five major regional trade blocs located in the Western Hemisphere exhibited major increases in both global exports and imports during the 1990s. In fact, the entire LAC region exhibited positive growth rates every year during the period between 1990 and 1998, averaging an annual growth rate of 11.4 percent in total global exports. On the other hand, this growth is not as aggressive when the entire Western Hemisphere is analyzed (including Canada and the United States). The aggregate average annual hemispheric growth rate in global exports during this period was only 7.9 percent.

MERCOSUR

Global exports from the MERCOSUR region exhibited an annual rate of growth of 6.1 percent during the 1990s, expanding from $46 billion in global exports in 1990 to more than $81 billion by 1998. Primarily led by Brazil and Argentina, the MERCOSUR region suffered a slight decline in exports in 1998, when the region experienced an overall slowdown in its trade activity primarily because of the Asian financial crisis.

As illustrated in Figure 1.6, MERCOSUR's biggest recipient of its exports in the world outside the Western Hemisphere is the EU, which imported more than $22 billion from MERCOSUR in 1998. The rest of the world combined for only $14.5 billion, primarily led by the Asian region, which imported nearly $9 billion in goods from MERCOSUR. On the other hand, Oceania, principally Australia, was the smallest recipient of MERCOSUR exports, importing only $277 million.

Andean Community

The Asian financial crisis heavily affected the export industry in the Andean region as well. While global exports from the Andean Community witnessed an average annual growth rate in its exports of 7 percent between 1990 and 1997, it only experienced a 4.6 percent growth if 1998 is included. In fact, the amount of exports actually decreased by more than 10 percent in a single year, from $50.7 billion in 1997 to $45.4 billion in 1998. However, the Andean Community did experience an overall growth of more than 30 percent in its exports during the 1990s.

Outside the Western Hemisphere, the Andean Community, like most trade blocs in Latin America, heavily engages in trade with the EU. In 1998 alone, the Andean region imported more than $6 billion and exported more than $5.8 billion just to the EU. By contrast, the Andean region exported only $264 million and imported $490 million from the regions of Africa, the Middle East, and Oceania combined. Finally, Asia, led primarily by Japan, imported $1.4 billion from the Andean region but exported more than $4.2 billion (see Figure 1.7).

CACM

While most of CACM's exports remain in the hemisphere (82 percent in 1998), most of its exports outside the Western Hemisphere are also consumed by the EU. In 1998, the

CACM exported a total of more than $2 billion and imported more than $1.8 billion from the EU, considerably more than the rest of the world. The Asian region, the second-leading recipient of CACM's exports, imported more than $1.7 billion but exported only $533 million to the Central American region.

This region displayed the most aggressive growth in exported goods in the entire Western Hemisphere. Moreover, the five countries of the CACM did not experience similar financial setbacks from the Asian financial crisis that affected other Latin American trade blocs such as MERCOSUR and the Andean Community. The CACM saw its exports grow from $4.4 billion in 1990 to $15.7 billion by 1998 for an average annual growth of 17.3 percent during this period (see Figure 1.8).

NAFTA

Member countries of NAFTA exhibited steady growth in exports throughout the 1990s, experiencing little effect from the Asian financial crisis in 1998. The NAFTA region experienced an average annual growth rate in its exports of 8 percent, nearly doubling from $547 billion exported in 1990 to more than $1 trillion by 1998. However, exports from the NAFTA region typically remain inside the region, where over half (56 percent) of its total exports remain within NAFTA-member countries. The other two biggest recipients of NAFTA exports are the EU (18 percent) and Asia (12 percent).

The NAFTA trade bloc is the largest and most active exporting trade bloc in the Western Hemisphere to the rest of the world. Like most trade blocs in Latin America, the EU is the largest recipient of NAFTA's exports outside the Western Hemisphere, importing more than $185 billion in 1998 alone. The Asian region also imports a similar amount from NAFTA, importing more than $178 billion in 1998. Other regions importing from NAFTA include Africa ($11.6 billion), the Middle East ($24.1 billion), and Oceania ($15.4 billion) (see Figure 1.9).

CARICOM

Exports from CARICOM exhibited a less-pronounced growth rate than did other hemispheric trade regions. CARICOM's exports grew form $5.8 billion in 1990 to $7.5 billion by 1998, illustrating an average annual growth rate of 3.7 percent. While it is evident that the Caribbean region was affected by the Asian financial crisis in 1998, this region still exhibited positive, though limited, growth of exports between 1997 and 1998. In addition, CARICOM's global exports are concentrated in the U.S./Canada region (40 percent) and the EU (24 percent).

The CARICOM region is active in exporting to all regions of the world, but, like the other Latin American trade blocs, it is heavily dependent on the EU. In 1998, the Caribbean region exported nearly $1 billion, while it also imported almost $1.2 billion from the EU. The Asian region is also heavily active in trade with CARICOM, exporting more than $815 million and importing more than $30 million from the Caribbean region (see Figure 1.10).

Figure 1.6 Global Exports and Imports of MERCOSUR, 1998

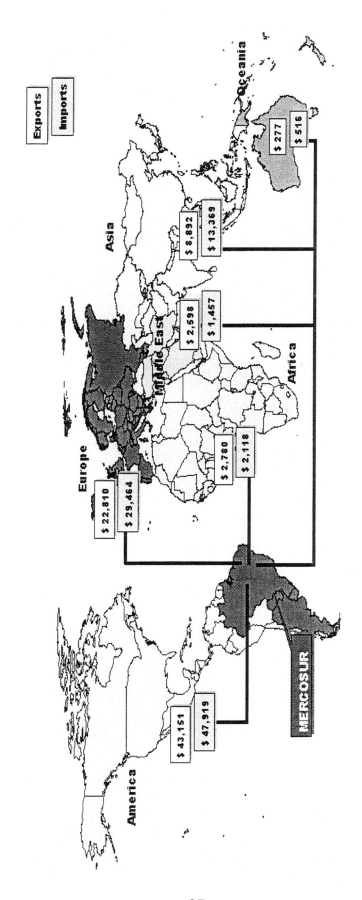

Sources: Adapted from Inter-American Development Bank (IADB), *Integration and Trade in the Americas* (Washington, D.C.: IADB Publications, October 1999), pp. 58-59; and United Nations Commission for Latin America and the Caribbean, *Maritime Profiles*. Online. Available: http://www.eclac.cl/espanol/ investigation/trenasporte/perfil. Accessed: February 4, 2001. Map created by Mustafa Ackay using GIS software.

Figure 1.7 Global Exports and Imports of Andean Community, 1998

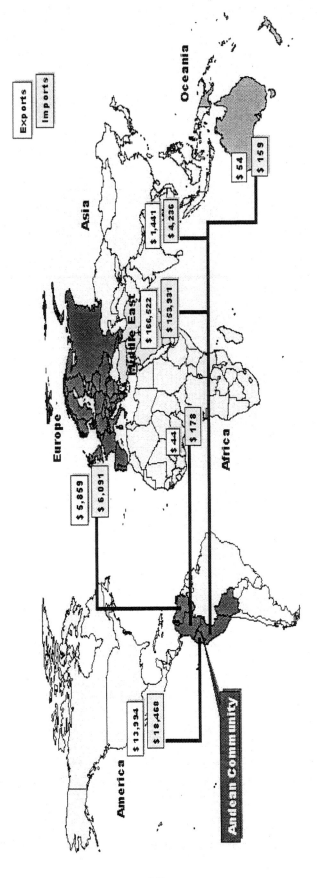

Exports
Imports

Asia
$ 1,441
$ 4,236

Oceania
$ 54
$ 159

Europe
$ 5,859
$ 6,091

Middle East
$ 166,522
$ 153,931

Africa
$ 44
$ 178

America
$ 13,994
$ 18,468

Andean Community

Sources: Adapted from Inter-American Development Bank (IADB), *Integration and Trade in the Americas* (Washington, D.C.: IADB Publications, October 1999), pp. 58-59; and United Nations Commission for Latin America and the Caribbean, *Maritime Profiles*. Online. Available: http://www.eclac.cl/espanol/ investigation/trenasporte/perfil. Accessed: February 4, 2001. Map created by Mustafa Ackay using GIS software.

Figure 1.8 Global Exports and Imports of CACM, 1998

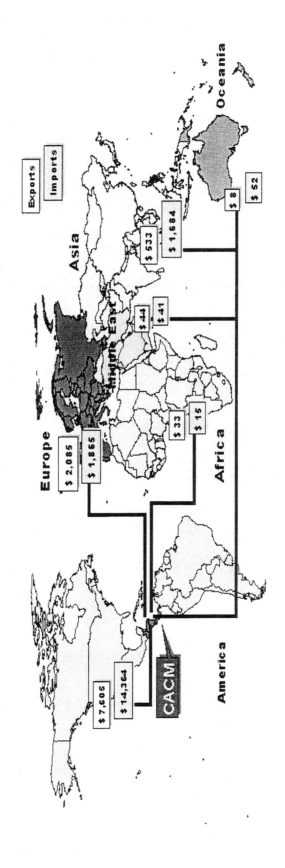

Sources: Adapted from Inter-American Development Bank (IADB), *Integration and Trade in the Americas* (Washington, D.C.: IADB Publications, October 1999), pp. 58-59; and United Nations Commission for Latin America and the Caribbean, *Maritime Profiles*. Online. Available: http://www.eclac.cl/espanol/ investigation/trenasporte/perfil. Accessed: February 4, 2001. Map created by Mustafa Ackay using GIS software.

Figure 1.9 Global Exports and Imports of NAFTA, 1998

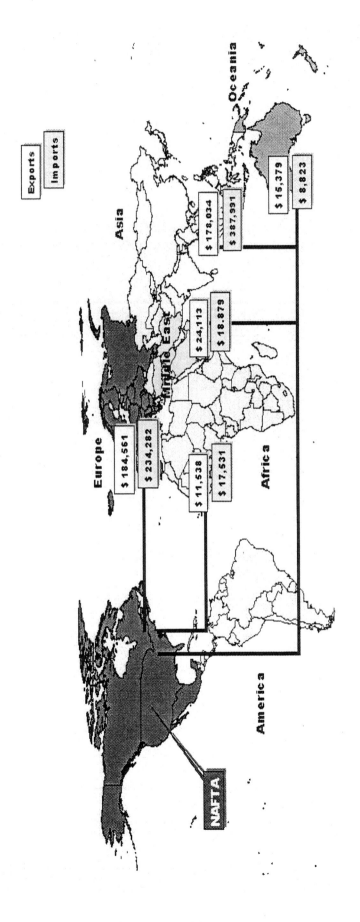

Sources: Adapted from Inter-American Development Bank (IADB), *Integration and Trade in the Americas* (Washington, D.C.: IADB Publications, October 1999), pp. 58-59; and United Nations Commission for Latin America and the Caribbean, *Maritime Profiles.* Online. Available: http://www.eclac.cl/espanol/ investigation/trenasporte/perfil. Accessed: February 4, 2001. Map created by Mustafa Ackay using GIS software.

Figure 1.10 Global Exports and Imports of CARICOM, 1998

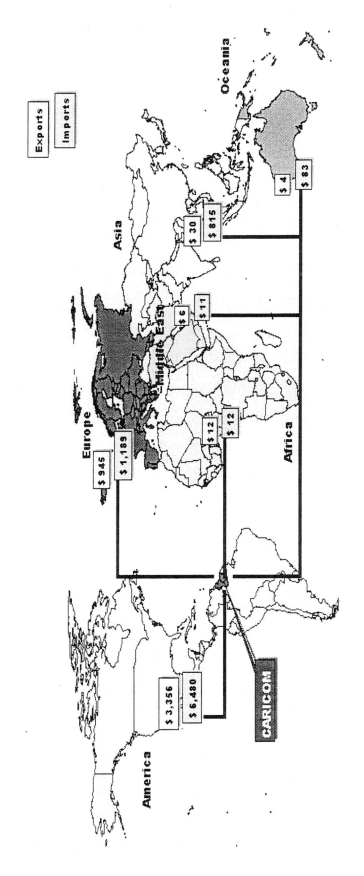

Sources: Adapted from Inter-American Development Bank (IADB), *Integration and Trade in the Americas* (Washington, D.C.: IADB Publications, October 1999), pp. 58-59; and United Nations Commission for Latin America and the Caribbean, *Maritime Profiles*. Online. Available: http://www.eclac.cl/espanol/ investigation/trenasporte/perfil. Accessed: February 4, 2001. Map created by Mustafa Ackay using GIS software.

Notes

[1] Franklin R. Root, *International Trade and Investment* (Cincinnati: South-Wales Publishing, 1994), p. 253.

[2] Ibid.

[3] Maria Beatriz Nofal, "The Economic Integration of Argentine and Brazil, MERCOSUR, and the Regionalization of the Southern Cone Market," in *NAFTA and Trade Liberalization in the Americas*, ed. Elsie Echeverri-Carroll (Austin, Tex.: Bureau of Business Research and IC2 Institute, The University of Texas at Austin, 1995), p. 217.

[4] Root, *International Trade*, p. 254.

[5] U.S. Department of Commerce, International Trade Administration. *Overview*. Online. Available: http://www.mac.doc.gov/ola/mercosur/mgi/overview.htm. Accessed: November 16, 1999.

[6] Americas Net. *MERCOSUR, Historical Background*. Online. Available: http://www.americasnet.com/mauritz/mercosur/english/page02.html. Accessed: November 17, 1999.

[7] U.S. Department of Commerce, International Trade Administration, *Country Information Overview*. Online. Available: http://www.mac.doc.gov/ola/mercosur/mgi/overview.htm. Accessed: November 16, 1999.

[8] Universidad del Salvador, Departamento de Desarrollo Regional y Medio Ambiente—OEA, "Las Negociaciones en el MERCOSUR" (Situación Actual y Perspectiva Seminar, Buenos Aires, Argentina, 1995).

[9] Economist Intelligence Unit, *Business Guide to MERCOSUR*, research report (New York, 1998).

[10] Comunidad Andina (Andean Community), *Quienes Somos*. Online. Available: http://www.comunidadandina.org/quienes.htm. Accessed: March 30, 2000.

[11] Inter-American Development Bank (IADB), *Integration and Trade in the Americas* (Washington, D.C., IADB Publications, October 1999), pp. 50-60.

[12] Ibid.

[13] Departamento de Integración y Programas Regionales, *Comunidad Andina*. Online. Available: http://www.iadb.org/intal. Accessed: February 13, 2000.

[14] Ibid.

[15] Ibid.

[16] Ibid.

[17] Departamento de Integración y Programas Regionales, *Comunidad Andina* (online).

[18] Departamento de Integración y Programas Regionales, *Secretaría de Integración Economica Centroamericana*. Online. Available: http://www.iadb.org/intal/. Accessed: February 13, 2000.

[19] Foreign Trade Information System (SICE), *General Treaty on Central American Economic Integration*. Online. Available: http://www.oas.org. Accessed: March 30, 2000.

[20] Ibid.

[21] Ibid.

[22] Gary Hufbauer and Jeffrey Schott, *NAFTA Assessment* (Washington, D.C.: Institute for International Economics, 1993), p. 2.

[23] National Law Center for Inter-American Trade, *NAFTA in the Grand and Small Scheme of Things*. Online. Available: http://www.natlaw.com/pubs. Accessed: April 19, 2000.

[24] NAFTA Commission: Joint Statement of Ministers, *Five Years of Achievement*. Online. Available: http://www.mac.doc.gov/nafta/joint.htm. Accessed: April 20, 2000.

[25] Mexican Secretariat of Commerce and Industrial Economic Development (SECOFI), "Nogales Sets Industry Standard for Border Crossing Facilities," *NAFTAWORKS*, vol. 4, no. 7 (July 1999), pp.1-2.

[26] IADB, *Integration and Trade in the Americas*.

[27] Caribbean Community, *Structure of the Community*. Online. Available: http://www.caricom.org/expframes2.htm. Accessed: March 29, 2000.

[28] IADB, *Integration and Trade in the Americas*.

[29] Ibid.

[30] Ibid.

Chapter 2. Liner Shipping Services

Introduction

Liner shipping services involve vessels operating on fixed itineraries or regular schedules and established rates available to all shippers. Martin Stopford notes:

> Providing liner services that cover the globe is a daunting task. In the "Maritime Transport Study" the United Nations identified thirty-two maritime coastal regions. There are 1,024 potential liner routes between these areas. Some of the coastal regions cover thousands of miles of coastline and all have many ports. The task of the liner market is to sort out a route network that cost-effectively meets the changing needs of these coastal regions.

> The industry generally divides the trade routes into three groups. The East-West trades, which account for 44 percent of the cargo, circle the globe in the Northern Hemisphere, linking the major industrial centers of North America, Western Europe and Asia. The North-South trades which operate mainly between the three major industrial areas and the economies in the Southern Hemisphere account for another 22 percent, while the remaining 34 percent of the trade is intraregional cargo, which is shorter-haul and uses smaller ships. This global network is constantly evolving to meet the changing needs of the world economy. Because liner services straddle the world in a complex network of arterial routes, spurs and feeder services that often overlap, it is not possible to describe the routes in a precise way.[1]

After an overview of the global trade trends in maritime transport, this chapter examines liner shipping in Latin America and the Caribbean (LAC) in terms of scheduled services, freight rates, number and types of vessels, aggregate carrying capacity, and trade lanes. Case studies of particular routes provide illustrative examples of how four shipping companies operating in LAC are dealing with global and hemispheric issues. The case studies include a transoceanic route, an intraregional route, and a coastal route.

Global Trends in Maritime Transport

Types of Ships

In the maritime trade industry, different types of ships have been designed to transport different types of cargo. Tankers transport crude oil, processed petroleum products, and various other liquids. Bulk carriers transport coal, ores, and bulk foodstuffs (grain, rice, etc.) General-cargo ships carry goods such as iron, steel, and breakbulk (bulk goods packaged in bags or boxes); and container vessels carry standard-sized containers loaded with manufactured goods or breakbulk commodities. The world fleet size of these types of ships, measured in deadweight tons (DWTs), is listed in Table 2.1. Tankers and bulk carriers constitute a majority of the world fleet.

Table 2.1
World Fleet Size by Type of Vessel, 1998
(deadweight tons)

Vessel Type	Fleet Size	Percentage
Oil tankers	279,509	35.4
Bulk carriers	275,519	34.9
General cargo	101,259	12.8
Container vessels	61,147	7.8
Other	71,147	9.0
World total	788,581	100

Source: Data from United Nations Conference on Trade and Development (UNCTAD), *Review of Maritime Transport 1999* (New York and Geneva: United Nations, 1999), p.16.

Container vessels make up only a small fraction of the world merchant fleet, but since 1980 the number of container ships has increased fivefold and has grown to 8 percent of the world fleet.[2] The process of "containerization" has revolutionized the marine transport industry with automation of loading and unloading. Goods that were previously carried by bulk vessels or general-cargo vessels are now more quickly loaded and unloaded with gantry cranes and specialized lifters. These same containers can then be loaded directly onto rail or truck chassis, further facilitating intermodal transport. Efficient cargo transfer also allows transshipment. Transshipment is the transfer of cargo from one ship to another in a hub-and-spoke style of operation between ports. The advantage of transshipment is that larger vessels, benefiting from economies of scale, deliver cargo to a region; and then smaller feeder vessels deliver the cargo to its final destination. Transshipment will be discussed in greater detail later in this chapter.

Trade and Maritime Metrics

The most common metric, or unit of measurement, for reporting trade is value, typically given in U.S. dollars. Shipping companies, however, primarily consider trade volume. Ships are filled with a physical quantity of goods. In contrast to countries, a trade imbalance always refers to volume rather than value and is always unfavorable. If the volume of trade is favored in one direction, then the shipping line is often forced to make the return trip with empty space. Carriers can only charge for goods carried, so empty space results in lost revenue while costs remain essentially the same. Trade volume is often reported in metric tons. This particular metric is useful because import tariffs also are often on a per-ton basis and because, for most forms of transport, maximum carrying capacity is stipulated in tons.

For the container shipping industry, volume is generally measured in twenty-foot equivalent units, or TEUs. A TEU refers to a standard twenty-foot container box. Other container box sizes exist, such as forty-foot containers (with a similar unit of measurement—the forty-foot equivalent unit, or FEU), but most trade volume in the container industry is reported in TEUs.

The second difference between analyzing trade and transport is the method of grouping. In trade, regions are grouped economically. Individual ports are subsets of individual countries; countries are subsets of trade blocs, and trade blocs are located typically within continents. Maritime trade routes are also grouped geographically, but the geography is water-based. Shipping companies are not as concerned about the economies in which they operate as they are about the physical path that their ships must take. In South America, for example, common regional groupings are the West Coast of South America (WCSA), the East Coast of South America (ECSA), and the North Coast of South America (NCSA). This classification scheme somewhat artificially divides trade blocs as well as individual countries (e.g., Colombia has ports on both the WCSA and ECSA), but the division is logical from the point of view of maritime trade.

Central Issues in the Containerized Liner Shipping Industry

Stability

The liner shipping industry is capital intensive. Even though the cost of building a new vessel has decreased in the last several years, the current cost of a new vessel still easily exceeds $20 million.[3] The shipping industry can reallocate vessels to different routes, but the total capacity is fixed in the short term. On the other hand, national trade, and its resultant transport requirements, can vary much more drastically. Shipping companies balance the desire to expand their fleets against the risk associated with having excess capacity.

Balance

The same vessels that carry goods in one direction are used on the return route. The voyage cost of an empty vessel is not significantly different from that of a fully loaded vessel. If the vessel must make a return voyage at less than full capacity, this lost revenue must be recuperated in the other direction. This problem is more significant in container shipping because it may mean that empty containers also will need to be transported, along with associated loading and discharging costs. Balanced traffic flows allow the shipper to charge reasonable rates and remain profitable. In addition, currency fluctuations are a particularly volatile factor in determining these trade balances. Balancing is particularly evident in north-south trade lanes along the ECSA and the NCSA routes where trade in one direction will subsidize trade in the other.

Port Efficiency

The daily operational costs of a vessel are high (as much as $7,000 per day for a 1,500- to 2,000-TEU vessel),[4] and every hour that a vessel is docked is an hour for which it cannot charge for the transportation of goods. Port efficiency will be discussed further in chapter 3, but it is important to recognize its impact on the establishment of scheduled routes.

Effects of Globalization

As in other areas of trade, globalization has had a major impact on the liner shipping industry. Globalization is "commercial interdependence among factors of production in different countries, which results from collective efforts to produce raw materials and components, as well as to provide assembly and distribution services for goods that will be sold throughout the world."[5] The major result of globalization in the shipping industry has been industry concentration. Concentration itself has affected everything from ship size to number of port calls to changes in shipping services offered. On the supply side of liner shipping, concentration is both a cause and a result of containerization.[6] The overall degree of containerization, currently about 60 percent of general-cargo traffic, is expected to reach 70 percent or higher by the year 2010. Total container traffic now exceeds 200 million TEUs per year.[7]

The rate of increase in liner shipping capacity has far exceeded the corresponding increases in world output and trade. Between 1991 and 2000, container shipping capacity increased at an average annual rate of 10.5 percent, compared to 2.5 percent in worldwide gross domestic product (GDP), 6.5 percent in international trade, and 2.1 percent in world merchant fleet.[8] The relative costs of transport have decreased because of increased efficiency and because transport volume (i.e., tonnage) has not grown as much as the value of traded goods.[9] Maritime transport is generally less expensive and slower than alternative transport and therefore is used to haul relatively low-value, high-volume goods. Hence, maritime transport's share of the volume of world trade is larger than its share of the value of world trade.[10]

The demand for goods being carried has a direct effect on the demand for transport services in the liner shipping industry, and companies compete with one another to win contracts. This competition, and the demand for carrier services, is affected by the technologies, routes, frequencies, and prices offered by liner operators. Acquiring advanced technology, avoiding protectionism and subsidies that distort competition, and improving the quality of goods and services are ways that shipping companies attempt to keep their market share in the global economy.[11]

Changes in shipping services have come about as shippers have begun to expect higher quality services, including shorter transit times, more direct services, guaranteed delivery times, door-to-door services, low incidence of damage, and the use of electronic communications and systems that have received ISO 9000 certification.[12] Identical services are offered to all clients because scale economies have made it difficult to sell different services to different clients. Similarly, traditional price differentiation has given way to FAK (freight all kinds) freight rates.[13]

Globalization has affected both trade direction and volume, blurring the distinction between north-south and east-west trades. Reliance on transshipment means that a portion of the north-south trade is transported by east-west carriers for part of the journey. In addition, seasonal cycles, trade imbalances, and route differences add to the difficulty in defining trade directions.[14]

The trade-off between scale economies and just-in-time delivery has greatly affected costs. Reduced costs resulting from the use of larger ships are often less important than the frequency of liner shipping services and the ability to control all the logistics from the supplier to the consumer. Liner vessels' carrying capacities will most likely continue to increase until longer port stays result in higher costs for transport services.[15]

Conferences, Alliances, Mergers, and Acquisitions

Shipping conferences are composed of vessel operators joined together for the purpose of establishing freight rates and have been used to enhance profits rather than to reduce costs. Historically, conferences were the best means through which shipping companies could operate in the midst of high operating costs and volatile freight rates. The combination of greater economies of scale due to increased vessel size and maritime deregulation has made conferences ineffectual.

Recently, there has been a move toward stronger alliances and mergers. Unlike conferences, the major goal of an alliance is to reduce the cost of transport. While keeping their individual corporate identities, alliances allow liner shipping companies to combine cargo volumes, increase service frequencies, and increase vessel use through vessel sharing agreements (VSAs). Similarly, terminals, equipment, and containers are shared, and companies are able to use their collective financial strength in order to procure and replace long-term assets.[16] While it is true that market share of alliances has increased, they are often unstable and are likely to be replaced by mergers.

The 20 largest container carriers are listed in Table 2.2. Presently, no single shipping line controls more than 6 percent of the world's total slot capacity; approximately 30 companies hold a share of about 1 percent each.[17] It is expected, however, that the number of global lines will decrease as vessel size increases. Eventually, there may be a total of ten major carriers, plus niche operators. Eleven of the twenty major carriers are based in Asia: NYK-Line, Mitsui OSK-Line, and K-Line of Japan; Janjin Shipping, Hyundai Merchant Marine, and Cho Yang Shipping of Korea; OOCL of Hong Kong; Evergreen and Yangming of Taiwan; NOL of Singapore; and COSCO of China.

Large shipping lines tend to expand into new markets, increasing competition on many individual trade routes. Meanwhile, barriers to entry have increased. As a result, new carriers are only entering the market as part of existing alliances.[18] There are now fewer operators than in the past. On most individual trade routes, however, the number of lines competing for cargo has increased.[19] Asian lines have entered the North Atlantic trade, east-west lines are entering north-south markets, and the feeder services of large lines are competing with traditional regional lines.[20]

Governmental Regulation

One major goal of governmental regulation is to increase trade through fast, reliable, and affordable maritime transport. In addition, regulation may aim to protect and promote employment and increase taxable income in maritime industries. Ratifying international conventions and including them in national regulation may reduce environmental costs and protect human lives at sea.[21]

Table 2.2
Top 20 Container Carriers

Rank	Company	Total TEUs	Total Vessels	TEUs on Order	Vessels on Order
1	Maersk Sealand	617,785	246	117,368	29
2	P&O Nedlloyd	324,268	129	71,791	18
3	MSC	259,228	142	71,690	11
4	APL	228,257	84	64,250	15
5	Cosco	217,144	123	38,932	9
6	Evergreen	199,458	59	19,500	3
7	Hanjin	178,460	48	34,502	7
8	NYK	145,639	66	68,200	11
9	CMA CGM	141,606	64	86,507	19
10	OOCL	136,298	46	40,762	9
11	Zim	131,019	71	38,580	8
12	K-Line	130,666	56	66,600	12
13	MOL	130,533	58	47,222	8
14	Yangming	129,865	51	33,306	6
15	Hapag-Lloyd	118,023	32	28,800	4
16	HMM	114,817	34	25,200	4
17	Senator	111,980	35		
18	CSCL	104,993	62	124,362	27
19	Lloyd Triestino	79,307	20	24,304	4
20	UASC	70,250	44		
	World fleet	6,685,81	7,026	1,561,313	508

Source: Data from *Containerisation International*. Online. Available: http://www.ci-online.co.uk/fleetstatistics/default.asp?currentRec=20. Accessed: February 27, 2001.

The question of governmental regulation with regard to liner conferences, alliances, and mergers is attracting increased attention. The primary purpose of a liner conference is to set rates on a specific trade route. Cooperation is used to increase income and only to a lesser extent to reduce costs. Through liner conferences, discussion agreements, alliances, and mergers, liner shipping companies strive to achieve scale economies and reduce costs.[22] Competition is the best mechanism for reducing costs and avoiding oligopolies. The enforcement of antimonopoly laws and the prohibition of mergers by national or regional cartel offices might help to ensure the continuation of competitive practices.

Economies of scale cannot be realized if too many lines operate individually. Similarly, an increased number of liners operating in the market could lead to overcompetition and duplication of efforts, where no single line has sufficient cargo to justify the use of large vessels or gantry cranes in its own terminal. Such overcompetition could lead to higher unit costs and higher freight rates.[23]

The move away from protectionism has been evident throughout Latin America. Less protection of national carriers allows new participants to enter the market, where more carriers compete on individual routes. As a reaction, alliances and mergers are formed to avoid overcompetition. Meanwhile, the abolition of cargo reservation and introduction of port reform have led to declining freight rates.[24] While fewer workers may be needed in the ports themselves because of advanced, capital-intensive technologies, long-term employment may be created in industries that are dependent on foreign trade.[25]

Vessel Size

The most widely used large container vessels are presently Panamax vessels. These vessels have the maximum dimensions to pass through the Panama Canal with a maximum beam of 32.3 meters and a length of 290 meters. The largest Panamax ship carries up to 4,442 TEUs with approximately 60,000 DWTs.[26] Liner shipping concentration has led to the development of the post-Panamax vessel, the largest of which carries more than 6,000 TEUs (feasibly up to 7,500 TEUs) or 40-50 percent more TEUs than a Panamax vessel.[27] Post-Panamax vessels are wider than Panamax vessels, reducing the need to take the weight of individual containers into account when loading cargo.

The development of large-capacity double-stack container railway systems in the United States and greater political stability in the Middle East and Suez Canal have facilitated the introduction of larger ships. Sixty percent of the orders for container slots in 1997 were for post-Panamax ships. By end of that year, 50 were in operation and 40 were on order.[28] Post-Panamax vessels presently operate on only two routes: transpacific (i.e., U.S. West Coast-Asia) and between Europe and the Far East. No post-Panamax ships call at Latin American or Caribbean ports.

Technology and natural limits of the port environment, as well as dis-economies of scale, may not permit vessels to be bigger than 8,000 TEUs. Limiting factors include port water depths, outreach of cranes, and the quantity of containers to be moved in a short time.[29]

The use of larger vessels has led to a reduction in the number of port calls. While the additional costs for feeder and intermodal connections remain lower than the amount saved by decreasing the number of port calls, the number of port calls by post-Panamax

41

vessels will continue to decline. This reduction leads to more transshipment, further concentration of port traffic in fewer and larger ports, and the development of hub ports.[30] Alliances may have a strong impact on the development of hub ports by suspending services to certain ports because of low production or by initiating terminal-sharing agreements. Therefore, the private sector through alliances and consolidation among liner companies and terminal operators may ultimately be choosing the winning ports that become transshipment hubs.

Costs

Fixed costs are increasing because of the use of more and larger gantry cranes in ports, bigger and more-expensive ships, increased investments in technology, more-expensive but fuel-efficient ship engines, and electronic communications. Increasing fixed costs as a proportion of total cost leads to decreasing variable costs and fewer operators in the market.[31]

Unlike fixed costs, variable costs have reached historically low levels. Despite holding average unit cost constant, increasing fixed costs and decreasing variable costs have led to an increased optimum volume per company and have forced smaller companies out of the market.[32] Ships need to be full to achieve economies of scale and decrease unit cost. Similarly, alliances must be stable in order to achieve desired efficiency gains. Initial merger costs must be lower than the resulting long-term cost savings.[33] Scale economies are reached when costs are reduced, not when sales are increased.

Increased earnings are an indicator of cost-effectiveness and are not solely dependent on the freight rates of individual carriers.[34] Carriers use cost reduction from technological progress and scale economies to increase their market share. Combined with the forces of a free market, such cost reductions are bound to lead to lower freight rates. Freight rates have also decreased because of technological progress, economies of scale, and competition.

Shipbuilding, Seafarers, and Vertical Integration

Concentration has developed in other maritime areas, such as shipbuilding, seafarers, and vertical integration, as well. With respect to new orders for shipbuilding as of April 1998, 37.7 million DWTs were being built in Japan and 32.6 million DWTs in Korea, with all other countries only producing 23.6 million DWTs. Thus, Japan and Korea produce 75 percent of the world's DWTs (up from 61 percent in 1991).[35]

Forty percent of the world fleet DWT is registered under one of the world's four open registries in Panama, Liberia, Cyprus, and the Bahamas.[36] These so-called flags of convenience (FOC) are less stringent with respect to maritime safety and the protection of the marine environment and are used to reduce labor costs with employment of foreign seafarers. In fact, in 1995, 39 percent of the world's seafarers and officers came from four nations: Philippines, Indonesia, China, and Turkey. This figure is expected to increase to 48 percent by 2005, largely because it is safer for individual ships to employ fewer nationalities to avoid misunderstandings during emergencies.[37]

Vertical integration is still unusual within the shipping industry, although there are some examples. Vertical integration takes many forms and occurs, for example, when a shipping line acquires a container leasing company, a freight forwarder buys a shipping company, an international port operator merges with a shipping line, or an international investor purchases a shipyard and shipping line.[38] Some liner companies operate their own ports (Evergreen in Panama) or are assigned dedicated terminals (Maersk in Rotterdam).[39]

Transshipment

Transshipment refers to cargo that is transferred from one ship to another, leading to increased port container moves and fewer ship miles. Transshipment has developed as a result of expanded economies of scale and the consolidation of carriers and is expected to increase as ship sizes increase. Transshipment reduces unit cost through the use of larger vessels, increasing services per week per port and the number of port calls. In addition, it has changed the relationship between vessels and ports by creating the hub-and-spoke port system (see chapters 3 and 4).

Increased transshipment will increase the demand for feeder services since few ports have sufficient cargo to fully load a 4,000- to 6,000-TEU ship. Similarly, the use of larger vessels ensures faster delivery for the majority of the cargo's journey, offsetting the additional cost of transshipment and resulting in shorter delivery times. The cost of transshipment is likely to decrease as technological progress continues. Containerization will also increase the percentage of cargo transshipped since containers are easier to transfer than other nonuniform cargo.[40] Other shippers are likely to use a transshipment service once it is established. Overall, transshipment benefits shippers through increased competition, greater choice due to transshipment options, and lower freight rates deriving from increased productivity and scale economies.[41]

Technology

Technology is a direct factor regarding services provided and cost under a given economic and regulatory framework.[42] New technology has changed the relationship between fixed and variable costs. Fixed costs are increasing with the advent of bigger gantry cranes in ports, larger ships, computers, fuel-efficient ship engines, and electronic communication.[43] Because of better communication technology, clients are more informed and better able to compare different transport options,[44] thus increasing competition among shipping companies and forcing them to provide a greater number of services at the lowest price possible.

Overcapacity

Liner shipping capacity is presently increasing more rapidly than corresponding increases in world output and trade. Although liner trade is expected to increase fairly rapidly, overcapacity remains a problem and likely to affect freight rates.[45] Overcapacity is a result of irregularity of service frequency and of east-west trade imbalances and resulting decreases in the industry's profitability.[46] Weaker conferences are less able to control shipping supplies and set common rates. This inability to sell space at certain rates artificially creates overcapacity. In addition, it spurs increased competition among liners. Because liner companies use the same technology (i.e., containers), they must compete on the basis of price rather than product differentiation and quality.[47]

Higher fixed costs in relation to variable costs raise the importance of using full capacity. Opportunity costs are extremely high for ships that are not fully loaded. Economies of scale can lead to a vicious cycle whereby increases in capacity lead to lower freight rates, which in turn cause increases in capacity in order to reduce unit costs in response to lower freight rates.[48] As long as the marginal costs are covered, liners operating with overcapacity will lower freight rates to earn as much income as possible.

Freight Rates in Latin America and the Caribbean

The setting of freight rates encompasses the consideration of many different variables, including the products being shipped, distance, container size, value of merchandise, volume, economies of scale, and balance of commerce.[49] Interestingly, distance itself plays a smaller role than one may believe. For instance, the United Nations reports that shipping containerized cargo from Miami to Buenos Aires is less expensive than shipping to the WCSA and the Caribbean.[50] How can this fact be explained, and what are the consequences for freight rates in general? Competition and vessel size are among the factors usually advanced to explain the above phenomenon. The ECSA exhibits greater competition and uses larger ships than do other Latin American regions.[51]

The actual cost of shipping items has gone down. However, the value of the commodities shipped has increased, resulting in rising inventory and insurance costs.[52] Moreover, within the maritime industry, conferences have weakened and, in some cases, disappeared. Consequently, where liners would have normally coordinated capacity along a trade route, market competition and overcapacity are now major factors.[53] The trend of greater competition is also occurring within an environment of lower demand for services. At the end of 1999, despite the continued growth in the volumes of containers being moved (now averaging 7-8 percent), margins remained low.[54] Profits were comparatively low because of the lingering effects of the 1998 Asian financial crisis and worldwide directional imbalances between capacity supply and demand within trade routes. The combination of lower freight rates, increased competition, and overcapacity have led to growing industry concentration on all routes. This concentration allows large players to reduce costs through economies of scale, thus producing a profit.[55]

Freight Rate Trends: ECNA to ECSA

In 1998, freight rates between the East Coast of North America (ECNA) and the ECSA were very low. It is estimated that all the lines operating on the ECSA trade lane collectively lost $500 million in that year.[56] Moreover, since 1997, more than 16 regional ECSA players have either folded, left the market, or went under new ownership.[57] Recently, this trade route experienced entry by large-scale operators, such as Evergreen, P&O Nedlloyd, and APL, through joint service, VSAs, and acquired ownership. Consequently, the entry of global players in the trade route increased the surplus of ships servicing the trading lane. The end result of this increased competition was the effective oversaturation of the lane with supply, thus placing a downward pressure on rates and decreasing all carriers' profitability along the route.

During the same period, the route experienced significant changes in trade flows. In the first quarter of 1998, northbound container volumes were 58,767 TEUs versus southbound volumes of 102,750 TEUs.[58] This imbalance reversed itself after the January 13, 1999, devaluation of the Brazilian real. In the first quarter of 1999, northbound container volumes rose to 73,629 TEUs, while southbound volumes fell to 66,822 TEUs.[59] Hence, the currency devaluation increased U.S. demand for Brazilian exports and, correspondingly, reduced Brazilian demand for U.S. exports. Liner shipping profits dissipated as a result of these changes in trade flows and the added costs of repositioning containers.

Efforts to increase profits took the form of reducing capacity and imposing equipment imbalance surcharges. APL, for instance, reduced its capacity along the route by dropping one of its seven vessels from its VSA with Crowley, Libra, and Lykes.[60] Other carriers applied surcharges ranging from $250 per TEU and $500 per FEU from Santos, Buenos Aires, and Rio de Janeiro to a hefty $400 per TEU and $700 per FEU from all other ports on the ECSA.[61] The average freight rate per TEU after the imposition of the surcharges was 40 percent higher than the rate before the Brazilian devaluation.[62]

Additional solutions included terminal handling charges, peak season charges, and the Bunker Adjustment Factor. For instance, the cost of fuel enters into the price setting of freight rate through a mechanism called the Bunker Adjustment Factor, whereby carriers recover fuel expenses by charging customers a fee. A recent general rate increase on the ECNA and Gulf lanes to South America and the Caribbean resulted in an increase in early 2001 to $108 and $285 for 20- and 40-foot containers, respectively.[63] This rise in the Bunker Adjustment Factor reflects the real costs of marine diesel oil and intermediate fuel oil to container shippers. *Containerisation International* reported in August 2000 that the worldwide average bunker price per ton was at $250 for marine diesel oil and more than $150 for intermediate fuel oil.[64] Both prices mirror a rising worldwide trend in the cost of fuel. Specifically, the impact of increased fuel costs is demonstrated by the fact that in January 1999, the world average monthly bunker price per ton was about $145 for marine diesel oil and about $60 for intermediate fuel oil.[65] Unfortunately, the 67 percent increase in marine diesel oil and more than 100 percent increase in intermediate fuel oil costs are expected to continue rising in 2001 because of OPEC fuel production restrictions.

Freight Rates Today: ECNA to ECSA

Most recently, the ECNA-to-ECSA trade route has reached an equilibrium of sorts where northbound and southbound container flows are more balanced.[66] However, freight rates are still increasing from their early 1999 low of $400 per TEU for both northbound and southbound freight.[67] A large part of the rate recovery occurred through the withdrawing of capacity from the route. Evergreen Marine Corporation, for example, removed more than 100,000 TEUs in 1999 and 60,000 TEUs in January 2000 from the route.[68] This withdrawal reverses the aforementioned expansion of large international players in the route on account of loss registered due to overcapacity and low demand from 1998 to 1999.[69]

Liner Services in Latin America and the Caribbean

In this section, the current state of liner activity in LAC will be summarized, identifying how goods are transported from one area to another and comparing vessel deployment and carrying capacity on major trade routes within LAC and between LAC and its major trading partners.

Deployment figures presented in the following pages include the number of scheduled services on major trade routes, the total number of vessels operating on those routes, the aggregate carrying capacity of those vessels (total TEUs), the average capacity of those vessels (average TEUs), and the capacity of the largest vessel (max TEUs). It is important to recognize that the number of scheduled services differs from the number of companies because of VSAs, in which several companies may share space on a given ship. Carrying capacity, measured in TEUs per week or per year, is the key metric to compare with trade volume to identify how goods are shipped from one region to another.

As noted earlier in the chapter, the economic groupings used to analyze international trade differ from those used for analyzing maritime transport. The present analysis will use geographic groupings commonly employed in the maritime industry with some modifications useful for identifying the flow of goods. For LAC, these groupings are listed in Table 1.3, along with the key ports in each of the regions. Because Panama conducts a large amount of transshipment and acts as a gateway between the Atlantic and Pacific Oceans, it will be considered as a separate region, to help identify the related trade flows.

With regard to liner activity within each of these regions, this analysis uses data collected from the *Containerisation International* (CI) Website.[70] The data include more than 600 ships with a total capacity of nearly one million TEUs. While this is not an exhaustive list, it is believed to be representative of the industry as a whole. Because CI updates this information on a regular basis, the data are current as of the week of March 16-23, 2001.

Activity within LAC

The largest vessel in the data set approaches 5,000 TEUs, while the average size is only 1,540 TEUs. Vessel ages range from 30 years to less than one year, with an average age of 10 years. Fully cellular vessels account for nearly two-thirds of the ships and more than 80 percent of the total capacity, an indication of the importance of the containerized shipping industry.

Table 1.4 compares the number of containerships in LAC with the world fleet. Vessels deployed in LAC account for approximately 10 percent of the world container fleet in vessel count and approximately 15 percent of the total capacity.

Table 2.3
Geographic Groupings of Major Latin American and Caribbean Ports

Region	Country	Major Ports
WCSA	Chile	San Antonio
(West Coast of South America)	Chile	Valparaíso
	Colombia	Buenaventura
	Ecuador	Guayaquil
	Peru	Callao
ECSA	Argentina	Buenos Aires
(East Coast of South America)	Brazil	Santos
	Brazil	Rio Grande
	Brazil	Rio de Janeiro
	Brazil	Paranagua
	Brazil	Recife
	Uruguay	Montevideo
NCSA	Colombia	Cartagena
(North Coast of South America)	Venezuela	Puerto Cabello
	Venezuela	La Guaira
CARIB	Bahamas	Freeport
(Caribbean)	Jamaica	Kingston
	Puerto Rico	San Juan
	Trinidad & Tobago	Port of Spain
WMEX	Mexico	Ensenada
(West Coast of Mexico)	Mexico	Manzanillo
EMEX	Mexico	Veracruz
(East Coast of Mexico)	Mexico	Tampico
PAN	Panama	Balboa
(Panama)	Panama	Coco Solo
	Panama	Cristóbal
	Panama	Puerto Manzanillo
CAM	Belize	Belize City
(Central America)	Costa Rica	Puerto Limón
	Guatemala	Santo Tomas de Castilla
	Honduras	Puerto Cortes

Source: Data from *Containerisation International*. Online. Available: http://www.ci-online.co.uk/.
Accessed: February 27, 2001.

Table 2.4
Containership Service in LAC

	LAC	Percentage of World	World
No. of vessels	640	9	7,049
Total KTEUs*	983	15	6,720
Average TEU	1,537	-	953

*KTEU represents 1,000 TEUs.

Source: Data from *Containerisation International*. Online. Available: http://www.ci-online.co.uk/.
Accessed: March 26, 2001.

The regional deployment figures are listed in Table 2.5. Because a given vessel may operate in more than one LAC region, the aggregated number of vessels listed in Table 2.5 is 80 percent greater than the total number of LAC vessels listed in Table 2.4. The cause could be either vessels that operate within only one region or between one LAC region and other parts of the world.

Table 2.5
Regional Summary of Containership Service in LAC

Region	Vessels	Total TEUs	Average TEUs	Max. TEUs
PAN	165	382,314	2,317	4,890
ECSA	206	320,470	1,556	3,428
CARIB	219	249,547	1,155	3,429
NCSA	177	204,803	1,177	2,698
WMEX	92	197,250	2,144	4,437
WCSA	129	175,908	1,364	2,474
EMEX	84	108,501	1,292	3,424
CAM	79	67,036	849	2,080

Source: Data from *Containerisation International*. Online. Available: http://www.ci-online.co.uk/.
Accessed: March 26, 2001.

In terms of the number of vessels, the Caribbean (CARIB) and the ECSA have the greatest vessel deployment within LAC. Each of these regions is served by more than 200 vessels, or approximately one-third of the total deployment within LAC. The region with the smallest deployment is Central America (CAM), with only 7 percent of the vessels operating within LAC.

Panama is the third largest in number of vessels and the largest in total capacity. The 382 KTEUs (thousand TEUs) account for nearly 40 percent of total LAC deployment. The regions of the ECSA and CARIB are second and third in total deployment, with 320 KTEUs (33 percent) and 250 KTEUs (25 percent), respectively. CAM remains the smallest, with only 67 KTEUs (7 percent).

These comparisons are summarized in Figure 2.1, which shows deployment in terms of total number of vessels and total capacity. Note that these comparisons do not directly correlate with the volumes of trade being carried out by each of these regions, only with the shipping activity. Differences can be due either to goods passing through a region or being discharged or to transshipment.

Figure 2.1
Regional Deployment within LAC

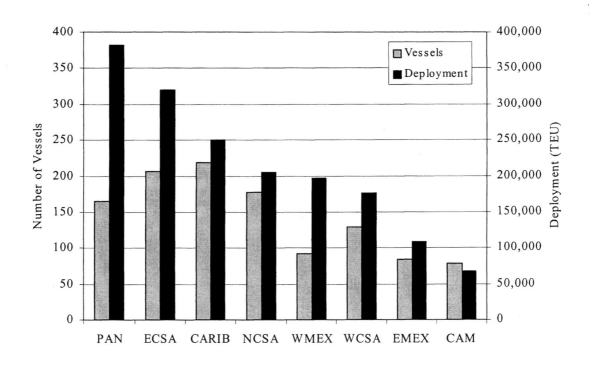

Source: Adapted from *Containerisation International*. Online. Available: http://www.ci-online.co.uk/. Accessed: March 26, 2001.

Another important deployment statistic is vessel size. The average and maximum vessel sizes operating in each of the regions are listed in Table 2.5 and shown in Figure 2.2. As stated earlier, the average vessel size deployed in LAC is 1,540 TEUs. Panama is served by the largest vessel—nearly 5,000 TEUs—and has the largest average vessel size— 2,300 TEUs, or 50 percent greater than the average. The West Coast of Mexico (WMEX) is also served by vessels significantly above the average, although many of these are on routes that also serve Panama. The other region served by above-average-size vessels is the ECSA. The average for all other regions is below the average, with CAM being the smallest. The average vessel size in this region is less than 900 TEUs, or only about 60 percent of the LAC average.

Figure 2.2
Vessel Size Operating within LAC

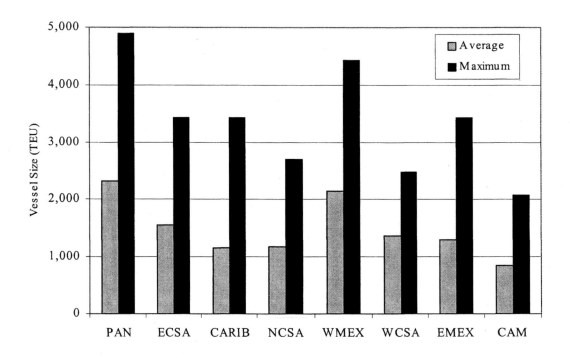

Source: Adapted from *Containerisation International*. Online. Available: http://www.ci-online.co.uk/. Accessed: March 26, 2001.

Intraregional Service

An intraregional service, as defined here, is a carrier that has port calls in two or more of the LAC regions listed in Table 2.3, whether or not they continue on to other parts of the world. However, services that operate only within LAC account for just 10 percent of LAC deployment. Nearly one-quarter of all containerized maritime trade in LAC occurs with other countries in LAC,[71] which implies that a majority of intraregional trade is carried by vessels that will continue on to other parts of the globe.

Table 2.6 summarizes fleet deployment of intraregional services and lists the number of vessels and their total capacity that connect any two of these regions. For example, nine vessels, with a total capacity of 6,600 TEUs, make port calls along the ECSA and in CAM. Quantities listed along the diagonal of this table (e.g., CAM-CAM) represent the total deployment calling on ports in that region. Because vessels may visit more than two regions, the values listed in this table cannot be aggregated to calculate total deployment within LAC.

Table 2.6
Intraregional Vessel Deployment in LAC

Region	Services	Vessels	Total TEUs	TEUs/week
ECSA and CAM	5	9	6,597	1,844
ECSA and WMEX	-	-	-	-
ECSA and EMEX	8	26	34,880	7,365
ECSA and PAN	4	4	5,033	400
ECSA and CARIB	14	25	30,738	7,415
ECSA and WCSA	7	12	13,042	1,307
ECSA and NCSA	24	47	73,922	24,554
NCSA and CAM	18	34	35,925	9,541
NCSA and WMEX	6	14	21,906	4,631
NCSA and EMEX	18	49	48,497	13,445
NCSA and PAN	20	39	59,285	9,799
NCSA and CARIB	43	97	85,994	23,273
NCSA and WCSA	16	40	55,513	7,846
WCSA and CAM	3	8	7,652	1,044
WCSA and	11	36	54,694	10,480
WCSA and EMEX	1	2	1,296	302
WCSA and PAN	19	57	100,417	17,023
WCSA and CARIB	9	22	31,523	3,906
CARIB and PAN	19	40	67,553	13,104
CARIB and	2	9	11,368	2,102
CARIB and EMEX	13	53	57,901	12,055
CARIB and CAM	16	38	35,242	9,539
PAN and CAM	12	10	8,979	5,146
PAN and WMEX	15	59	148,141	20,688
PAN and EMEX	5	1	132	66
WMEX and CAM	7	11	11,967	4,095
WMEX and	3	4	4,491	2,233
EMEX and CAM	9	20	15,368	4,543

Source: Data from *Containerisation International*. Online. Available: http://www.ci-online.com.uk/. Accessed: March 26, 2001.

As noted in the previous section, Panama has the largest deployment in terms of total TEUs of service. Of the intraregional routes considered, Panama also has the largest deployment, with connections to the WMEX and the WCSA occupying the top two spots of the routes listed in Table 2.6. Approximately 150 KTEUs operate on the route connecting Panama to the WMEX, more than 15 percent of the total deployment within LAC and nearly 40 percent of the deployment calling on Panama. More than 100 KTEUs operate on the route connecting Panama to the WCSA, approximately 10 percent of the total deployment within LAC and 25 percent of the deployment stopping in Panama.

Service between the NCSA and the CARIB (NCSA-CARIB) has the greatest number of vessels—nearly 100—and significantly more than any of the other lanes. However, the average vessel size in this trade lane is relatively small (less than 1,000 TEUs), making it only the third largest in terms of TEUs deployed.

A significant determinant of trade flows is vessel carrying capacity. Carrying capacity is based on the total deployment and the frequency of port visits. As used here, carrying capacity will be expressed in thousands of TEUs per week (KTEUs/week). As with deployment figures, carrying capacity does not equate to trade volume. A trade lane with large carrying capacity may have a significant amount of trade volume pass through without being discharged at any of the ports along that lane.

Table 2.7
Most Active Intraregional Trade Lanes

		Vessels	Total TEUs	Services	TEUs/week
NCSA	ECSA	47	73,922	24	24,554
NCSA	CARIB	97	85,994	43	23,273
PAN	WMEX	59	148,141	15	20,688
PAN	WCSA	57	100,417	19	17,023
NCSA	EMEX	49	48,497	18	13,445
PAN	CARIB	40	67,553	19	13,104
EMEX	CARIB	53	57,901	13	12,055
WCSA	WMEX	36	54,694	11	10,480
NCSA	PAN	39	59,285	20	9,799
NCSA	CAM	34	35,925	18	9,541

Source: Data from *Containerisation International*. Online. Available: http://www.ci-online.co.uk/. Accessed: March 26, 2001.

Trade lanes that include the NCSA are some of the most active routes in all of LAC in terms of carrying capacity. This activity is emphasized in Table 2.7, which lists the most active intraregional trade lanes in terms of TEUs per week, and shown in Figure 2.3. The NCSA occupies three of the top five spots, with the most active destinations being the ECSA, the CARIB, and the EMEX. This activity occurs despite the fact that this region has only a moderate level of total deployment (200 KTEUs, only the fourth greatest in LAC and nearly equal to the fifth greatest, WMEX). Presumably this activity results from its central location between large traders of Brazil, located in the ECSA, and the CARIB.

Collectively, Panama is the LAC region with the most active carrying capacity of intraregional trade. Trade lanes to the WMEX and the WCSA are the third and fourth most active within LAC, with carrying capacities of 21 KTEUs/week and 17 KTEUs/week, respectively.

Figure 2.3
Most Active Trade Lanes within LAC

Source: Adapted from *Containerisation International*. Online. Available: http://www.ci-online.co.uk/. Accessed: February 27, 2001.

Service between LAC and the World

The major trading partners of LAC are North America, Europe, and Asia/Pacific. Of the 9.6 million TEUs traded by LAC in 2000 (imports and exports combined), approximately 60 percent was evenly split between North America and Europe and 15 percent was with Asia/Pacific. Africa constituted a meager 2 percent of the trade, with the remaining 23 percent occurring within LAC. Table 2.8 summarizes this information.

Table 2.8
Liner Trade between LAC and the World, 2000
(in thousands of TEUs)

World Region	Exports	Imports	Total	% of Total
Asia/Pacific	698	736	1,434	15
Europe	1,780	1,080	2,860	30
North America	1,515	1,475	2,989	31
Africa	91	66	157	2
LAC	1,102	1,102	2,204	23
Total	5,187	4,458	9,644	100

Source: Data from WEFA/ECLAC, Maritime Profile database, "Containerized Latin American and Caribbean Trade" (Economic Commission for Latin American and the Caribbean, Santiago, Chile, March 2001), printout.

Focusing on the three largest trading partners, Europe, Asia, and North America, Table 2.9 lists deployment and carrying capacity between LAC and these three regions. All have approximately the same level of deployment, about half a million TEUs. Trade with North America has the greatest number of vessels, indicating a smaller average vessel size. The average vessel size operating between LAC and North America is 1,750 TEUs. Conversely, the least number of vessels travel across the Pacific Ocean, and the average vessel size on this trade route is more than 2,400 TEUs. Vessels deployed on the LAC-Europe trade route have an intermediate number of vessels and a more moderate vessel size, about 2,000 TEUs. This trend is consistent with the logic that the benefits of economies of scale are greatest on the longest routes.

Considering the carrying capacity on these routes, however, there is a discrepancy with the trade data listed in Table 2.8. The carrying capacity operating between LAC and North America is about 125 KTEUs per week, or 6.5 million TEUs per year. This value is twice that of the carrying capacity on the trade lane with Europe, even though annual trade with these two regions is approximately equal. The reason for this discrepancy is not clear, but one possibility is that many of the vessels traveling to Europe stop first in North America before continuing on across the Atlantic. Similarly, the carrying capacities operating to Europe and to Asia are approximately equal, even though twice as much trade occurs with Europe. The discrepancy could also occur because vessels stop in North America before continuing on across the ocean.

Table 2.9
Service between LAC and the World

	Vessels	Total TEUs	Services	TEUs/week
Europe/Mediterranean	260	500,777	77	63,315
Asia/Pacific	195	471,468	41	62,264
North America	340	594,577	134	124,246
Africa	61	104,329	22	18,537

Source: Data from *Containerisation International*. Online. Available: http://www.ci-online.co.uk/. Accessed: March 26, 2001.

Table 2.10
Major Ports in North America

Region	Country	Major Ports
WCNA West Coast North America (excluding Mexico)	U.S./Canada	Long Beach San Francisco Seattle Vancouver
ECNA East Coast North America (excluding Mexico)	U.S./Canada	Miami Charleston Savannah Norfolk New York
GCNA Gulf Coast North America (excluding Mexico)	U.S.	Jacksonville New Orleans Houston

Source: Data from *Containerisation International*. Online. Available: http://www.ci-online.co.uk/. Accessed: February 27, 2001.

Table 2.11
Vessel Deployment between LAC and the World

Region	Services	Vessels	Total TEUs	TEUs/week
ECSA and Asia/Pacific	13	56	100,436	25,697
ECSA and Europe	27	78	119,280	16,961
ECSA and WCNA	1	-	-	-
ECSA and GCNA	10	21	30,440	5,854
ECSA and ECNA	25	28	46,975	24,454
NCSA and Asia/Pacific	1	-	-	-
NCSA and Europe	20	67	72,200	11,463
NCSA and WCNA	2	9	16,284	1,267
NCSA and GCNA	21	38	39,849	11,266
NCSA and ECNA	32	49	72,825	25,547
WCSA and Asia/Pacific	12	44	69,041	12,294
WCSA and Europe	13	34	44,388	5,021
WCSA and WCNA	11	38	56,514	11,390
WCSA and GCNA	3	2	1,296	302
WCSA and ECNA	7	23	35,834	5,090
CARIB and Asia/Pacific	3	22	66,259	8,316
CARIB and Europe	33	108	158,645	21,848
CARIB and WCNA	1	15	48,635	3,242
CARIB and GCNA	16	47	60,611	11,069
CARIB and ECNA	37	92	129,928	26,173
PAN and Asia/Pacific	21	100	285,520	38,304
PAN and Europe	16	80	228,608	25,042
PAN and WCNA	14	77	221,826	25,046
PAN and GCNA	9	25	41,062	4,047
PAN and ECNA	19	92	263,740	35,248
EMEX and Europe	9	37	60,349	10,586
EMEX and GCNA	19	63	95,321	19,175
EMEX and ECNA	7	31	56,395	8,816
WMEX and Asia/Pacific	16	64	156,794	24,026
WMEX and Europe	8	34	109,358	14,949
WMEX and WCNA	18	72	166,296	26,550
WMEX and GCNA	5	13	15,875	4,351
WMEX and ECNA	9	34	104,458	15,800
CAM and Asia/Pacific	2	6	6,356	742
CAM and Europe	7	29	26,949	4,765
CAM and WCNA	1	6	6,356	742
CAM and GCNA	15	26	19,818	9,247
CAM and ECNA	11	24	16,846	9,914

Source: Data from *Containerisation International*. Online. Available: http://www.ci-online.co.uk.
Accessed: March 26, 2001.

In order to discuss the trade lanes from within LAC to North America, we will subdivide North America into three regions: West Coast, Gulf Coast, and East Coast. The major ports in these three regions are listed in Table 2.10. This division is essential to obtain a better understanding of the trade lanes because there are significant differences in the routes depending on the location of the port in the United States. Direct connections from the various regions within LAC to the world are listed in Table 2.11.

In terms of total deployment, Panama's connections to the world dominate LAC. Routes connecting this small Central American country to Europe, Asia, and both the ECNA and WCNA all have deployments significantly exceeding 200,000 TEUs. The routes with the next largest deployment totals are those in which many of the vessels also stop in Panama; for example, the WMEX to the WCNA, the WMEX to Asia, and the CARIB to Europe. All these routes have average vessel sizes approaching or exceeding 3,000 TEUs, significantly larger than the average within LAC.

Table 2.12
Most Active Trade Lanes between LAC and the World

LAC Region	World Region	Services	Vessels	Total TEUs	TEUs/week
PAN	Asia/Pacific	21	100	285,520	38,304
PAN	ECNA	19	92	263,740	35,248
WMEX	WCNA	18	72	166,296	26,550
CARIB	ECNA	37	92	129,928	26,173
NCSA	ECNA	32	49	72,825	25,547
PAN	WCNA	14	77	221,826	25,046
PAN	Europe	16	80	228,608	25,042
ECSA	ECNA	25	28	46,975	24,454
WMEX	Asia/Pacific	16	64	156,794	24,026
CARIB	Europe	33	108	158,645	21,848

Source: Data from *Containerisation International*. Online. Available: http://www.ci-online.co.uk/. Accessed: March 25, 2001.

In terms of carrying capacity, Panama also leads the other regions, although its dominance is not quite so significant. The major trade lanes connecting LAC to the rest of the world, in rank of carrying capacity, are summarized in Table 2.12. The top five of these trade lanes are shown in Figure 2.4. The two connections with the greatest carrying capacity are Panama to Asia and Panama to the ECNA, both with more than 35,000 TEUs per week, or 1.8 million TEUs per year. These two routes have significantly more carrying capacity than the next three largest, which have approximately 25,000 TEUs per week. These routes are the WMEX to the WCNA, the NCSA to the ECNA, and the CARIB to the ECNA. These last two trade lanes, however, are filled by many of the same services traveling between the NCSA and ECNA and stopping in the CARIB along the way.

Another method of considering liner activity is the number of services in operation. With regards to this metric, Panama ranks fairly low, with some of the smaller trade lanes having the greatest number of services in operation. The top five trade lanes in terms of services offered connect the LAC regions of the CARIB and the NCSA and ECSA with either the ECNA or with Europe. The implication is that trade lanes with fewer trade flows are not necessarily served by fewer services. On the contrary, these lanes have some of the greatest liner activity but with smaller vessels.

The Effect of Concentration in Latin America and the Caribbean

Transport itself is becoming more relevant in LAC, and high surface transport costs have made maritime transportation the most cost-effective means of transporting goods. Transport costs are decreasing relative to the value of the goods shipped but are assuming an increasing share of the total costs within the production process. Traded volume is also increasing and, in fact, growing faster than the world's output. The share of containerized transport is also growing. LAC shipping lines responded to the region's economic reforms and the resulting high economic growth rates by either adding capacity or entering the market. Latin American shippers benefit from increased transshipment because it allows them to provide more services per week per destination. Freight rates may decrease because of increased competition for the service to and from Panama.[72]

Internationally, the liner industry is dominated by the top 20 companies listed in Table 2.2 as of February 2001.[73] These companies alone account for 3,569,596 TEUs of the total worldwide TEU capacity of 6,685,811, which represents more than 50 percent of worldwide TEU capacity. Similarly, these 20 companies have a total of 1,001,876 TEUs on order from a total 1,561,313 worldwide TEUs on order, more than 60 percent of total worldwide TEUs on order. However, collectively these companies represent only 21 percent of total worldwide ships. The smaller percentage of actual ships versus the large TEU capacity shared by these companies indicates the use of extremely large vessels when compared to the entire worldwide fleet. Moreover, the fact that these carriers account for 40 percent of total ships on order corroborates predictions of larger vessel use along international trade routes.

Figure 2.4
Most Active Trade Lanes between LAC and the World

WMEX -WCNA
72 vessels
166 KTEUs
27 KTEUs/week

PAN -ASIA
100 vessels
286 KTEUs
38 KTEUs/week

PAN -ECNA
92 vessels
264 KTEUs
35 KTEUs/week

CARIB -ECNA
92 vessels
130 KTEUs
26 KTEUs/week

NCSA -ECNA
49 vessels
73 KTEUs
26 KTEUs/week

Source: Adapted from *Containerisation International*. Online. Available: http://www.ci-online.co.uk/.
Accessed: February 27, 2001.

Table 2.13 shows that many of the top international carriers differ in their LAC rankings compared to their world rankings (Table 2.2). In total, these top 20 operators in LAC maintain 381 ships, or 35 percent of their total world fleet in LAC. Moreover, they have a combined 770,000 TEUs, representing 31 percent of the total world TEUs held by these companies as deployed in LAC. Of particular note are Hapag-Lloyd, Zim, Evergreen, WWL, NYK, Italia, CCNI, Kien Hung, Lykes, TMM, Hamburg Süd, and Cho Yang, with more than 30 percent of their worldwide fleet deployed in LAC.

Table 2.13
Top 20 LAC Container Carriers

LAC Rank	World Rank	Company	LAC Vessels	World Vessels	% of Fleet	LAC TEUs	World TEUs	% of Fleet
1	1	Maersk Sealand	64	246	26	137,177	624,582	22
2	2	P&O Nedlloyd	34	129	26	74,874	327,848	23
3	15	Hapag-Lloyd	18	32	56	60,132	118,023	51
4	11	Zim	23	71	32	59,159	130,842	45
5	22	CSAV	32	35	91	54,419	59,601	91
6	3	MSC	24	142	17	53,599	256,739	21
7	6	Evergreen	19	59	31	35,276	204,053	17
8	9	CMA/CGM	17	64	28	29,667	135,123	22
9	36	WWL	13	14	93	26,854	28,222	95
10	8	NYK	22	65	34	25,842	143,836	18
11	40	Italia	16	17	94	25,223	26,523	95
12	37	CCNI	15	17	88	24,354	28,689	85
13	17	Senator	8	35	24	24,052	109,636	22
14	13	MOL	14	58	24	22,306	136,165	16
15	45	Aliança	12	14	86	21,780	24,462	89
16	31	Kien Hung	15	26	58	21,674	33,783	64
17	25	Lykes	11	26	42	21,270	49,044	43
18	47	TMM	9	9	10	18,940	18,940	100
19	46	Hamburg Süd	10	12	83	16,527	19,214	86
20	34	Cho Yang	5	16	31	15,877	29,722	53

Source: Data from *Containerisation International*. Online. Available: http://www.ci-online.co.uk/fleetstatistics/default.asp?currentRec=20. Accessed: March 25, 2001.

Case Studies

The following case studies of particular routes provide illustrative examples of how several maritime companies operating in Latin America are dealing with the issues of increased globalization discussed throughout the chapter. The studies include a transoceanic route, an intraregional route, and a coastal route.

Transoceanic Case Study: Hamburg Süd

Background

Hamburg Süd is one of the oldest and largest privately owned shipping companies in Germany, competing in the international shipping industry for more than 125 years. The company's main office is located in Hamburg, where it boasts one of the largest container facilities in Europe. Currently operating about 100 vessels, Hamburg Süd's fleet includes modern container ships, gas tankers, and reefer and tramp ships. In 1999, the company handled a total cargo volume of 517,000 TEUs.[74] Since its inception, the company serviced South America and particularly Brazil, either for passenger travel or for the transportation of goods.

In 1980, Hamburg Süd inaugurated its first full container service from Europe to the ECSA. The company became known as a carrier of frozen products. Today, all the vessels on this service are container ships and carry both dry and reefer cargo.

Company Demographics

Although Hamburg Süd operates numerous services in South America, the focus of this case study is on the transoceanic trade between the ECSA and Europe. On this route, Hamburg Süd transports poultry and meat from southern Brazil and fruit from northern Brazil. The company currently utilizes 20-foot containers on the route, but as the container trade continues to expand and shippers are more willing to work with 40-foot containers, the strategy is to revise vessels and containers. In addition, the company has plans to increase reefer capacity, decrease the number of insulated container spaces, and increase the number of reefer plugs for integrated containers.

Generally, cargo from South America is heavy compared to that coming from Europe. Therefore, from Brazil and Argentina, the company finds that it must pay more attention to weight rather than filling capacity. Because of the fluctuations in the market, occasional unpredictability, and for purposes of insuring stability, the company aims to diversify cargo as much as possible. Further, high-paying cargo is not very abundant.[75] During the first months of 2001, two of Hamburg Süd's regular commodities, coffee and juice, took the company by surprise. Shippers were not ready to export the goods until several months later than normal. Therefore, the company found itself sailing with too much open space.

After a "very weak" year in 2000, as described by marketing agents for the ECSA-to-Europe route, the company is optimistic that in 2001-02, there will be increases in commodities such as beef and chicken. At the end of 2000, the agents observe that mad cow disease seems to be strengthening the export market for these commodities from Latin America to Europe. They also speculate that the euro may increase the total number of exports.[76]

Port Rotation and Routes

The service operates on a fixed-day weekly schedule and, on the European side, serves the following ports: Rotterdam, Hampton, Felixstowe, L'Havre, and Antwerp.
On the ECSA, Hamburg Süd works with two slings. Sling one calls are to Buenos Aires, Rio Grande, São Francisco do Sul, and Santos. Sling two calls are to Rio de Janeiro, Paranaguá, Santos, and Salvador, which alternates with Suape. Hamburg Süd has a joint service on this route with CMA/CGM and Aliança. Also on sling two, Hamburg Süd

provides an additional service with Maersk, and in 2000, the company began a slot charter with MSC.

Sling two was created to ensure frequency and to increase the amount of space available.[77] The company was having to limit bookings for the service. Now, with the new slings on a fixed-day schedule, reliability has led to an increase in customer satisfaction. The route now operates with a total of six vessels on sling one and five vessels on sling two. Previously, a total of only six vessels serviced the route. All vessels in sling two are larger than before its creation. The sling one ships have a capacity of 1,250 TEUs, and sling two ships are 1,850 TEUs each. Figure 2.5 depicts the two slings on a map.

Freight Rates, Prices, and Profits

During the year 2000, Hamburg Süd and others on the route chose to reduce their total tonnage. As the year progressed, all the companies on the service were able to maintain a satisfactory level of performance. However, all of them then needed to improve services to create competition, and in order to do this, all companies, particularly Hamburg Süd, felt that it was necessary to try to increase their rates. Additionally, competition had decreased significantly in the last several years, and all carriers had hoped that this alone would allow each of them to increase their rates.

Hamburg Süd expected to go through a process of rate restoration by the end of the year.[78] However, the company found itself unable to do this in 2000 and even projected that it would be difficult in the near future. The challenge was multifaceted. First, since at least September 2000, global prices were falling and all markets were depressed during the year. In Buenos Aires, the economy was and continues to be particularly depressed. All companies were being forced to sell at lower prices. Relative to its neighbors, the Brazilian economy was better but still not good enough to sustain the price increases. Also, the situation became so dire that some of the companies involved in a VSA with Hamburg Süd on this route found that they had to undercut prices just to fulfill their part of the agreement. This VSA regards only volume, not prices, and, therefore, one carrier can theoretically undercut another. Undercutting prices was not standard protocol, however, for the service or the agreement.[79] Unlike the other companies in the VSA who are more focused on fulfilling their portions of the agreement, Hamburg Süd has a policy emphasizing profit, which made the company unable to increase rates because of its own fixed costs and the factors mentioned.[80]

For this phenomenon to actually change, the company projects that total tonnage must increase. Under the agreement, a company may maintain its cargo for one extra week so as to avoid giving it to another carrier. Such behavior decreases customer satisfaction, further decreasing demand.

Further, all the companies on the route must compete with prices in the Asian markets. Finally, any major changes in the route require that all VSA partners agree, making rapid response to price fluctuations more difficult.

Figure 2.5
Hamburg Süd ECSA-to-Europe Sailing Schedule

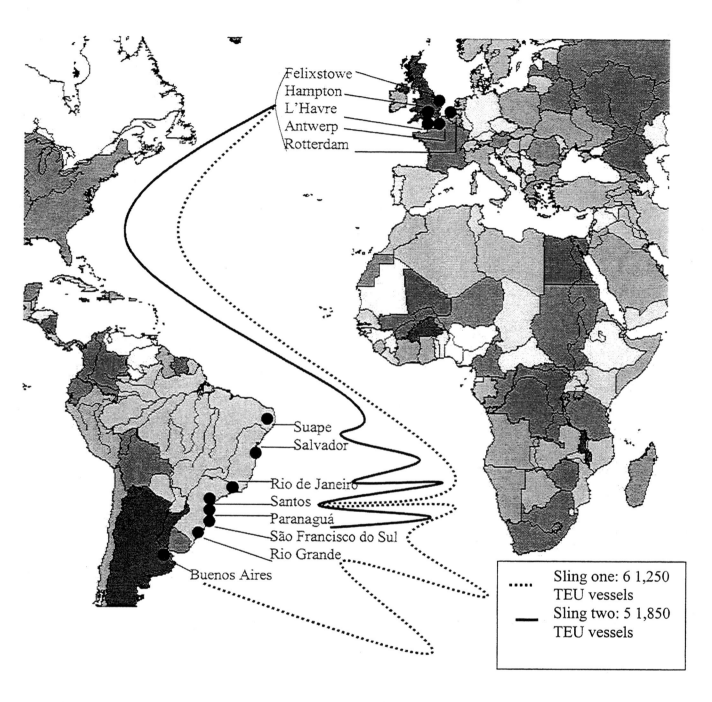

Source: Information compiled from interview with Vanessa Deeke, Marketing Agent, Hamburg Süd Brasil, Ltda., São Paulo, Brazil, January 22, 2001.

Competitors

Initially, the service started without Maersk, but Maersk was added because, with additional carriers, total costs were lowered for all concerned. Also Maersk was very familiar with reefers because of significant experience in exporting fruit. At the same time, however, Hamburg Süd's main competitors are those with reefer capacity, which particularly includes Maersk and also CSAV.[81]

Because of these cooperative arrangements and despite the price difficulties, Hamburg Süd sees no long-term negative aspects of the VSA.[82] Its recent merger with Aliança and other agreements has actually allowed Hamburg Süd a much greater exchange of information about markets, and it notes that this is possibly the most important advantage.[83] In fact, Hapag-Lloyd and NYK will be joining the service this year, using the same vessels presently operating on the service.[84]

Vessel Capacity

Although this service is transoceanic, Hamburg Süd explains that larger vessels are not necessarily the answer. Instead, Hamburg Süd has opted for a fixed-day, reliable service that it recently created with its second sling.[85]

Technology

Like many other large companies, Internet technology has truly revolutionized the way Hamburg Süd does business with its customers. In addition, new crane technologies in Brazil and Europe are influencing which ports are called. Given the current economic situation, the main factor in determining which ports will be called remains the simple principal of finding those ports that have cargo.[86]

Transshipment

Since its merger with Aliança, Hamburg Süd has greatly increased its involvement in Brazilian transshipment–not so much in its own capacity but as Aliança's partner.

Points of Interest on the Transoceanic Route

Hamburg Süd currently continues on from Europe to Hong Kong, but in the near future it is considering a route with a shorter time frame. It remains to be seen what this change will bring on its ECSA-to-Europe route.[87]

Intraregional Shipping Case Study: Antillean Marine Shipping Corporation

Background

Antillean Marine Shipping Corporation (Antillean) is representative of small- to medium-sized independent firms servicing Caribbean markets from the southeastern United States. Launched in 1960, Antillean has remained a family-owned and -operated business with an operating scope largely limited to the Dominican Republic, Haiti, and

Turks and Caicos.[88] Antillean's Miami, Florida, headquarters allows the corporation to partake in the voluminous trade in both bulk and containerized cargo passing through the Port of Miami and its private terminals.[89]

Antillean services breakbulk, heavy equipment, and containerized cargo. The company specializes in 807 apparel and textile cut goods for assembly overseas.[90] Consequently, the U.S. garment industry is a large user of the company's services.[91] Approximately, 60 percent of Antillean's container moves to the Dominican Republic and Haiti consist of cut goods for the apparel industry, with the remaining 40 percent composed of general cargo.[92] Service to the Dominican Republic consisted specifically of 17,500 TEUs of cut goods and 11,500 TEUs of general cargo during 2000.[93] Antillean's Haiti services handled 9,500 TEUs of cut goods and 6,500 TEUs of general cargo in 2000.[94] The total volume of general cargos serviced by the company has not had a significant increase since 1998 because of stagnation in foreign demand.[95] However, U.S. garment and apparel industry exports have increased substantially in the last three years, and Antillean foresees this trend continuing.[96]

Company Demographics

Antillean owns and operates three terminals along the Miami River servicing its 13 vessels. Two of the terminals allow for simultaneous direct loading and unloading of three vessels at a time. The company's main terminal contains 50,000 square feet of warehouse capacity and more than 1 million square feet of open space for container storage, heavy equipment operations, and breakbulk cargo.[97] Additionally, intermodal service to most U.S. locations is facilitated through 2,000 feet of dockage space and CSX long-haul railroad access.[98] Antillean's other terminals maintain 800,000 square feet of open space and 25,000 square feet of supplementary warehousing space.[99]

Internationally, the company maintains two terminals in the Dominican Republic. Antillean's northern terminal is located in Santiago de los Caballeros, providing more than 300,000 square feet of container storage, chassis, and repair.[100] The second terminal is located at Santo Domingo outside the Port of Rio Haina, providing more than 260,000 square feet of container storage and facilitating terminal operations for the central and southern regions of Antillean's operations in the Dominican Republic.[101]

Antillean's total container fleet exceeds 15,000 TEUs, which are all maintained and serviced at facilities and subsidiaries of the corporation.[102] The company has an extensive fleet of 20-, 40-, and 45-foot containers and chassis, including a variety of specialized equipment, such as ventilated, insulated, and refrigerated containers; high cube, open top, garment-on-hanger containers; flat tracks; and custom built 10-foot containers for the apparel industry.

Antillean's shipping fleet comprises 13 vessels with a total of 41,507 DWTs.[103] This tonnage represents an average of 3,193 DWTs per vessel, with a maximum of 4,245 DWTs. Total fleet capacity is 1,888 TEUs at an average of 145 TEUs per vessel.[104] The maximum amount of vessel TEUs registers at 213 TEUs.[105] Antillean's fleet travels at an average 11.69 knots, with a maximum 12.50 knots.[106] Antillean recently acquired four general container vessels in order to meet export demand to the Dominican Republic and Haiti. These acquisitions represented a 44 percent increase in Antillean's overall fleet size, making the company one of the largest shipping lines operating on the Miami River.[107]

Thirty-one percent of the company's fleet is five years old or younger. Eight percent of the fleet is between six and ten years of age. An additional 31 percent is within a range of 11 to 15 years old. Moreover, 62 percent, or eight vessels, sail under the Panamanian flag. The remaining vessels sail under the flag of Antigua and Barbados. Furthermore, 62 percent of the vessels are registered in Panama, with the remaining five vessels registered in either Neermoor or St. Johns. Antillean's container and general-cargo vessels represent 84 percent of its fleet, with the remaining 16 percent divided between landing craft and dual bulk/container carriers.

Port Rotation and Routes

Antillean offers six routes from Miami to the Caribbean, as indicated in Figure 2.6. The Dominican Republic is the largest area of operation for the corporation, representing the majority of calls for the shipping line. The company calls twice weekly on the ports of Puerto Plata, Rio Haina, and Boca Chica for a combined 3,173 TEUs per month from Miami. Antillean additionally calls twice monthly on the Port of La Romana for a total of 136 TEUs. Turks and Caicos is second to the Dominican Republic in the amount of TEUs serviced by the corporation and in terms of potential capacity. The Port of Providenciales is called on weekly for a total of 260 TEUs per month, and the Port of South Caicos is called on twice monthly for a total of 136 TEUs per month. Haiti represents Antillean's smallest country of call in terms of total potential capacity, with a total of 260 TEUs per month going from Miami to Port-au-Prince, for twice weekly service.

Freight Rates, Prices, and Profits

Antillean contends that most global freight rates have been depressed for the past few years. It notes that along some trade routes such as the Far East, carriers have succeeded in raising rates. However, Antillean believes that freight rates on the Americas and the Caribbean trade routes have remained substantially lower than those in other regions on account of the Brazilian devaluation and trade imbalances. Consequently, most regional carriers operating along these trade routes are currently operating at a loss. The most visible effect of the low freight rates has been the consolidation and rationalization of services along the routes. One recent example of a consolidation is the purchase of Crowley's South American operations by Hamburg Süd.

Freight rate fluctuations have affected Antillean negatively during the past few years. Along the Caribbean trade route, Antillean experienced downward fluctuations in freight rates while operational costs rose on account of increased fuel and port expenses. However, currently Antillean is experiencing a positive trend. The corporation foresees significant increases in the export of apparel and garments for foreign assembly during the next three to five years because of the resolution of "parity" with regard to NAFTA during 2000. The parity agreement grants Caribbean Basin Initiative (CBI) nations preferential import duties and quotas, which Antillean believes will spur demand for its services. The corporation predicts a 5-10 percent increase in the movement of these goods.

Figure 2.6
Antillean Marine Shipping Corporation Sailing Schedule

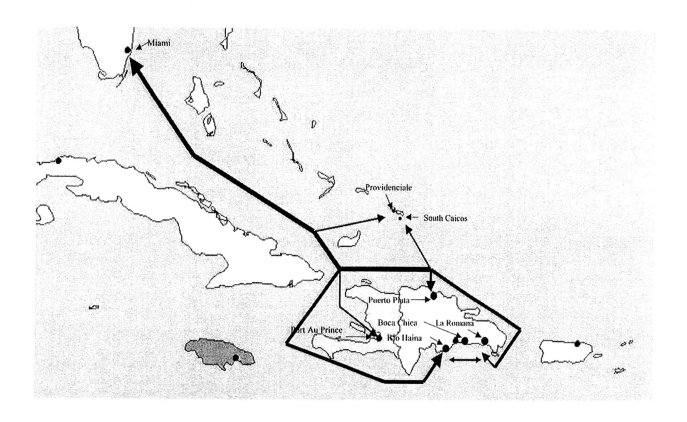

Source : Information compiled from correspondence with Joe Naranjo, Operations Manager, Antillean Marine Shipping Corporation, March 2, 2001.

Additionally, Antillean recently joined the Hispaniola Discussion Agreement as a means to openly discuss openly trade issues affecting other carriers servicing the Dominican Republic and Haiti. In this forum, issues such as the increased operational costs due to rising fuel prices have been dealt with collectively by discussion and agreement among members. For instance, bunker surcharges have risen on 20-foot containers from $75 to $100 and for 40-foot containers from $100 to $180 to cover added fuel costs. Moreover, carriers have issued a new chassis charge (wheel charge) of $40 for intermodal and $10 for local use against shippers without equipment to move containers. This new charge is a cost minimization recovery technique employed in other regions but has just been implemented on the Haiti and Dominican Republic trade route.

Nevertheless, though the trade and freight rate trend is improving along the routes served by Antillean, the company is still recovering from years of depressed returns along the route. The company is currently pursuing a competitive pricing strategy to increase its participation along its major routes. However, Antillean does not wish to go the way of other regional carriers by consolidating and/or rationing its services. The company understands that these steps may increase its profitability in the short term, but in the long term Antillean feels that its markets do not lend themselves to service consolidations or rationing.

Vessel Capacity

Antillean has not been affected by global increases in vessel sizes because of restrictions in its home port along the Miami River. River depth restrictions prevent the use of vessels exceeding 200 TEUs. Moreover, market demand for larger vessels along Antillean's trading routes is not sufficient to operate vessels in the post-Panamax range.

Technology

Antillean's investment in technology and specifically e-business has made the company more competitive and efficient. Currently, the company offers real-time online tracking of cargo in addition to rate requests to customers. Antillean has recorded a decline in the number of telephone inquiries made by customers and believes further investment in advancing its electronic data and information systems will be of great benefit to the company. Particularly, Antillean is researching the possibility of offering an electronic filing and documentation retrieval system.

Transshipment

Antillean has had limited experienced with transshipment cargo. The company recently expanded its services to provide customers with new opportunities to trade with companies outside Antillean's direct service areas. Through the introduction of direct calls at Turks and Caicos, the company has witnessed an increased number of customer inquiries and shipper offerings to sustain entry into the trade route. However, the company is seeking to further expand its reach by offering global carriers its services through connecting carrier agreements and transshipment agreements. Antillean believes that it is poised to facilitate the movement of transshipment cargo to and from Caribbean hub ports.

Points of Interest in the Caribbean

Antillean is deeply concerned with social and political stability in Haiti. Recently, the company's services to Port-au-Prince have suffered on account of Haiti's political instability and economic woes. Freight rate levels have deteriorated greatly, and the overall number of TEUs moving through Haiti has not increased substantially during the past few years. Antillean believes that its route from Miami to Port-au-Prince may improve if the new Haitian government administration under Jean Bertrand Aristide is able to deliver promises made to the business community. However, if Aristide cannot change Haiti's status quo, Antillean expects no considerable growth or demand for increased services to the Haitian market.

The company also wishes to see the expansion of free-trade zones in both of its major markets, the Dominican Republic and Haiti. Antillean believes that the respective governments on Hispaniola realize the importance of free-trade zones to their national economies. Antillean estimates that hundreds of thousands of workers who would otherwise be unemployed find employment in free-trade zones.

Finally, Antillean has a balanced view of restricted entry into cabotage trade in the Caribbean. The company believes that protection of the national transportation infrastructures is a meritorious goal, yet Antillean believes that in most instances these laws restrict to national economic progress. Antillean predicts that liberalization of cabotage laws will have a positive effect on its operations given that it services four ports in the Dominican Republic alone.

Coastal Case Study: Cabotage in Brazil

Background

Two shipping companies provide the great majority of Brazil's cabotage service today: Aliança Navegação e Logística Ltda. and Docenave-Navegação Vale do Rio Doce S.A. Currently each company claims about 50 percent of the market share on the service.[108] Transroll, a third smaller company that actually began the first cabotage service in 1996, has now pulled out of the service almost entirely. Today, this company operates only one service from Buenos Aires through Montevideo to Salvador.

Company Demographics

Aliança has been in Brazil since 1951, when it was established by the German emigrant Carl Fischer. Beginning as a coastal shipping operation, the company expanded its operations over time to the ECSA and northern Europe. When the Brazilian shipping industry was deregulated in 1991, the company then opened a service to the ECNA. In 1998, the company was purchased by the Oetker Group of Germany, who maintained Aliança's Brazilian flag. As a result, Aliança now joins the Oetker Group's other holdings, such as Crowley and Columbus Line, and cooperates most extensively with Hamburg Süd, which also has a historic presence in Brazil. The company began providing cabotage service in September 1999.

Docenave has been in Brazil since 1962. The company is headquartered in Rio de Janeiro and, unlike Aliança, maintains Brazilian ownership.[109] Docenave is among the ten largest international shipping companies in the world today. Although over the years Docenave has been known in Brazil as a carrier of bulk cargo, in 1999 it entered the container trade on the cabotage service.

Port Rotation and Routes

For Aliança, two dedicated container vessels run fortnightly through the following ports: Rio Grande, São Francisco do Sul, Santos, Suape, Fortaleza, and Manaus. The vessels carry 1,500 TEUs each, and one of them is chartered from Transroll.

For Docenave, five multipurpose vessels chartered from Frota Oceanica & Amazonica run fortnightly on two separate slings through the following ports: on the first sling—Buenos Aires, Montevideo, Rio Grande, São Francisco do Sul, Santos, Recife, Fortaleza, Natal, Maceio, Salvador, Sepetiba, and on the second sling—Sepetiba and Manaus. Two of the vessels are 1,254 TEUs each, and three of the vessels carry 666 TEUs each. Figure 2.7 depicts the two services on a single map.

Freight Rates, Prices, and Profits

From the beginning of 1996 until the end of 2000, the cabotage service in Brazil sustained almost entirely net financial losses. Transroll, as a family-owned company, was unwilling to suffer continuing losses on the service and finally chartered out all of its ships. However, one of Transroll's original ships is still operating on the cabotage service and is now chartered out by Aliança. Despite the losses, both Aliança and Docenave are very optimistic about the service's future potential. They both report exponential growth on the service: Aliança explained that it has doubled its lifting every four months since the inception of the service, and Docenave reported its first profit of $200,000 in December 2000.[110] As of the publication of this report, Docenave was experiencing continuous monthly profits since March 2001.

Entering the market in September 1999 and December 1999, respectively, Aliança and Docenave now face the challenge of continuing to garner profits from the cabotage service and proving the viability of the service.

In an increasingly competitive market with high fixed costs, both companies find themselves struggling with the same challenge as many larger international companies: how to lower variable costs as much as possible while increasing profits. Aliança is perhaps more fortunate on this front. As part of the Oetker Group, the company may be more capable than Docenave of sustaining losses in the short run.

Figure 2.7
Cabotage in Brazil: Aliança and Docenave Shipping Schedules

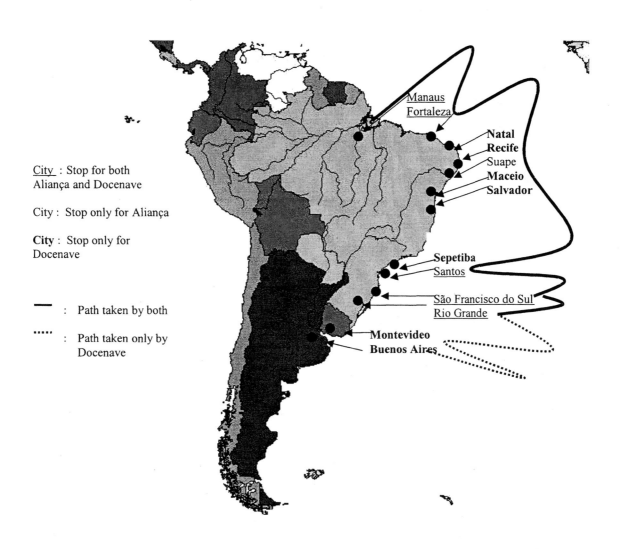

City : Stop for both
Aliança and Docenave

City : Stop only for Aliança

City : Stop only for
Docenave

— : Path taken by both

····· : Path taken only by
Docenave

Manaus
Fortaleza
Natal
Recife
Suape
Maceio
Salvador
Sepetiba
Santos
São Francisco do Sul
Rio Grande
Montevideo
Buenos Aires

Sources: Information for Docenave compiled from interview with Docenave, Rio de Janeiro, Brazil, January 24, 2001. Information for Aliança compiled from Aliança.com. Online. Available: http://www.Aliança.com.br. Accessed: March 21, 2001

Competition

Protected by the Brazilian cabotage laws for what appears to be an indefinite period, both companies' greatest competitor will be the trucking industry rather than other large shipping lines. To any onlooker, the strength of the truckers seems unusual given that Brazil has more than 4,500 miles of coastline[111] and that 80 percent of Brazil's population lives within 100 miles of the Brazilian coast.[112] The logic lies in the country's tumultuous inflation during the 1980s and slow movement through Brazil's ports.

Inflation meant that goods needed to arrive as quickly as possible before prices changed dramatically and sellers lost profits. Sea freight movement was too slow. In addition, many of Brazil's ports were inefficient, heavily unionized, and lacking in modern equipment.[113] Since the Real Plan was implemented in 1994, Brazil's currency has stabilized, and, as a result, according to Paulo Augusto Camello of Aliança, "a feeling of security seems to pervade business matters."[114] Further, port reform and modernization are slowly improving prospects for increases in cabotage services. Nonetheless, shipping companies must first struggle to revise such public habits as favoring the time efficiency of trucks over the cost and environmental efficiency of ships.

For the moment, relatively higher shipping prices also inhibit the change in behavior. Higher prices are also influenced by the state of the ports. Directors for cabotage service at both companies predict dramatic changes in these behaviors and prices within three to five years.

Customer Service

In addition to price, customer service is increasingly the way that companies distinguish themselves from each other. However with the trucking industry as their key competitor in the short run, it has become imperative that Aliança and Docenave attempt to cooperate on improvements for customers. Currently, the companies both operate a fixed-day service, often serving the same ports, but customers sometimes find that they will be without a ship for two weeks, and then suddenly two ships from the different companies will arrive at the same time. Responding to customer complaints about such irregularities of the service, Aliança and Docenave have tried to come to an agreement that would provide regular fixed-day service. So far these discussions have been unsuccessful. Docenave's general cargo and containers' manager explains the lack of agreement: "There is one major distinction between Aliança and Docenave. Aliança belongs to the Hamburg Süd group and therefore they have an interest in feeder services and port calls that are strictly for Hamburg Süd. Of course, it would be much better for clients if our ships did not arrive at the same ports on the same day for example. Aliança has an interest in attending to Hamburg Süd cargo which simply is not the interest of Docenave."[115] Company representatives both expressed interest in continuing the attempt to establish a joint service. However, until there are more vessels in the service, which is currently limited by the Brazilian cabotage laws, or unless cabotage and feeder operations are separated in the system, then it may be difficult.

Vessel Capacity

Although the global trend has been to increase vessel size, cabotage services in Brazil diverge from this trend. Docenave and Aliança are most concerned about providing fixed-day services to their clients, which inherently implies the use of smaller vessels in the short run. The key to short-term success is to be able to fill existing vessels, convince more customers to choose cabotage over trucking, and finally to pull a profit.

Technology

Despite the fact that technological advances could cause the wealthier and larger German-owned company to surpass the smaller Brazilian-owned company, the reality is that improvements in technology have made it somewhat easier for the smaller company to compete. Both companies explain that the Internet has made a huge positive difference in the quality of customer service that can be provided.

Aliança has been able to make one huge long-term investment savings: with the help of a German shipbuilding project, they now use "one-man bridge ships," ships that can be entirely operated by only one person.[116] Meanwhile, Docenave is having to continue to upgrade their ships that were built for mixed cargo rather than containers.

Transshipment

One new development in Brazil that may greatly affect transshipment and the cabotage trade is the emergence of the Sepetiba port, a modernized, megacapacity port. In the short run, the port will not be used extensively as it lacks sufficient intermodal connections. However, if the Brazilian federal government and the private sector continue as they have been—which is to favor the development of infrastructure around this port—Docenave may find itself suddenly propelled into a very strong new transshipment market. Docenave is owned by the industrial giant that built the port and is currently using the port despite its relatively low turnover of containers.

In the short run, for Docenave and Aliança, the transshipment trend poses no major changes to the routes or schedules of either company.

Points of Interest in the Brazilian Cabotage Services

The cabotage services offered by these two companies are unlikely to change significantly in the next several years. The federal government remains strongly in support of the cabotage laws that keep these Brazilian companies and their cabotage services strong.

Notes

[1] Martin Stopford, *Maritime Economics* (London: Rutledge, 1997), p. 366.

[2] United Nations Conference on Trade and Development (UNCTAD), *Review of Maritime Transport 1999* (New York and Geneva: United Nations, 1999), p. 94.

[3] Drewery Shipping Consultants, *Ship Costs: Issues, Developments, and Prospects to 2003* (London, May 1999), p.13.

[4] Ibid., p. 5.

[5] Economic Commission for Latin America and the Caribbean (ECLAC), *Concentration in Liner Shipping: Its Causes and Impacts for Ports and Shipping Services in Developing Regions*, by Jan Hoffmann (Santiago, Chile, August 17, 1998), p. 26.

[6] "The Impact of Structural Changes in Liner Shipping on Caribbean Ports," *FAL Bulletin*, 142 (April 1988). Online. Available: http://www.eclac.cl/English/news/Falbulletin/fal142en.htm. Accessed: March 8, 2000.

[7] H. E. Haralambides, "A Second Scenario on the Future of the Hub-and-Spoke System in Liner Shipping" (paper presented to the Latin Ports & Shipping 2000 Conference & Exhibition, Miami, Fla., n.d.), p. 2.

[8] Ibid.

[9] ECLAC, *Concentration in Liner Shipping*, p. 25.

[10] Ibid., p. 28.

[11] Ibid.

[12] Ibid., p. 32; and "The Impact of Structural Changes."

[13] ECLAC, *Concentration in Liner Shipping*, p. 26.

[14] Ibid., p. 33.

[15] Ibid.

[16] Ibid., p. 12.

[17] Ibid.

[18] Philip Damas, "U.S./Brazil Trade Returns to Stability," *American Shipper* (November 2000), p. 70.

[19] ECLAC, *Concentration in Liner Shipping*, p. 11.

[20] Ibid.

[21] Ibid., p. 45.

[22] Ibid., p. 46.

[23] Ibid., p. 47.

[24] Ibid., p. 48.

[25] Ibid.

[26] Ibid., p. 6.

[27] Ibid., p. 51.

[28] Ibid., p. 7.

[29] Ibid.

[30] Ibid., p. 14.

[31] Ibid., p. 52.

[32] Ibid.

[33] Ibid., p. 55.

[34] Ibid., p. 57.

[35] Ibid., p. 20.

[36] Ibid., p. 21.

[37] Ibid.

[38] Ibid., p. 22.

[39] Ibid.

[40] Speech by Jan Hoffmann to the seminar "Avance en la Tecnología Portuaria y Maritima Mundial su Relevancia en Chile," Santiago, Chile, May 14-15, 1997.

[41] ECLAC, *Concentration in Liner Shipping*, p. 84.

[42] Ibid., p. 50.

[43] Ibid., p. 51.

[44] Jan Hoffmann, "Concentration in Liner Shipping," *FAL Bulletin*, 147 (October 1988). Online. Available: http:www.eclac.cl/English/news/Falbulletin/bol147/FAL147.HTM . Accessed: March 8, 2000.

[45] ECLAC, *Concentration in Liner Shipping*, p. 63.

[46] Haralambides, "A Second Scenario," p. 2.

[47] ECLAC, *Concentration in Liner Shipping*, p. 64.

[48] Ibid., p. 66.

[49] ECLAC, "Tendencias en el transporte marítimo internacional y sus implicaciones para América Latina y el Caribe," by Jan Hoffmann, September 2000, p. 15.

[50] Ibid., p. 14.

[51] ECLAC, "El potencial de puertos pivotes en la costa del Pacífico sudamericano," by Jan Hoffmann, n.d. p. 17.

[52] ECLAC, "Cabotage and Liner Shipping in Mercosur—The Fear of Foreign Competition," by Jan Hoffmann, April 2000, p. 17.

[53] Ibid.

[54] Jane Boyes, "Ups and Downs in Liner Shipping," *Containerisation International Yearbook 2000*, ed. Jane Degerlund (London: Black Bear Press Ltd., 2000).

[55] ECLAC, "Cabotage and Liner Shipping," p. 17.

[56] Robert Ward, "A Flipping Hell," *Containerisation International* (June 1999), p. 45.

[57] Ibid.

[58] Ibid., p. 46.

[59] Ibid.

[60] Ibid., p. 47.

[61] Ibid.

[62] Ibid.

[63] Telephone interview by Ricky Garcia with Gonzalo Garcia, Jr., Account Executive, Farovi Shipping, January 15, 2001.

[64] "Key Numbers," *Containerisation International* (August 2000), p. 7.

[65] Ibid.

[66] Robert Ward, "Rollercoaster Ride," *Containerisation International* (July 2000), p. 39.

[67] Ibid.

[68] Ibid.

[69] Ibid., p. 40.

[70] *Containerisation International.* Online. Available: http://www.ci-online.co.uk. Accessed: March 16-23, 2001.

[71] "WEFA/CEPAL Maritime Profile March 2001." Online. Available: http://www.ECLAC.cl. Obtained from Dr. Jan Hoffmann, Maritime Economist, International Trade, Financing and Transport Division, United Nations Economic Commission for Latin America and the Caribbean, Santiago, Chile April 2001.

[72] Ibid., p. 79.

[73] "World Ranking" (Fleet Statistics) *Containerisation International.* Online. Available: http://www.ci-online.co.uk. Accessed: February 27, 2001.

[74] Hamburg Süd. Online. Available: http://www.hamburg-sued.com/Company.htm. Accessed: March 2, 2001.

[75] Interview by Cara Dougherty with André Freire Bittencourt, Marketing Manager, Hamburg Süd Brasil, Ltda., São Paulo, Brazil, January 22, 2001.

[76] Ibid.

[77] Interview by Cara Dougherty with Vanessa Deeke, Marketing Agent for East Coast South America to Europe Route, Hamburg Süd Brasil, Ltda., São Paulo, Brazil, January 22, 2001.

[78] Ibid.

[79] Interview by Cara Dougherty with Dalton Seiji Honda, Marketing Agent for East Coast South America to North America Route, Hamburg Süd Brasil, Ltda., São Paulo, Brazil, January 22, 2001.

[80] Ibid.

[81] Deeke interview.

[82] Bittencourt interview.

[83] Honda interview.

[84] Bittencourt interview.

[85] Ibid.

[86] Deeke interview.

[87] Honda interview.

[88] Antillean Marine Shipping Corporation. Online. Available: http://www.antillean.com. Accessed: March 1, 2001.

[89] Ibid.

[90] Telephone interview by Ricky Garcia with Mireya Babún García, Vice President, Equipment and Operations, Antillean Marine Shipping Corporation, March 1, 2001.

[91] Ibid.

[92] Joe Naranjo, General Manager, Antillean Marine Shipping Corporation, response to second liner shipping questionnaire, February 25, 2001.

[93] Ibid.

[94] Ibid.

[95] Babún García interview.

[96] Naranjo response to second liner shipping questionnaire.

[97] Antillean Marine Shipping Corporation (online).

[98] Ibid.

[99] Ibid.

[100] Ibid.

[101] Ibid.

[102] Ibid.

[103] Letter from Mireya Babún García, Vice President, Equipment and Operations, "Shipping Fleet," to Ricky Garcia, February 12, 2001.

[104] Ibid.

[105] Ibid.

[106] Ibid.

[107] Antillean Marine Shipping Corporation (online).

[108] The only noncommercial source for this information is the Brazilian Merchant Marine, which has not yet compiled its 2000 statistics. It has also decided that the 1999 statistics will not be published because of a severe backlog of unpublished figures. Officials from Docenave estimate that they operate 60% of the traffic as a percentage of total TEUs on the cabotage service, and officials from Aliança estimate that they operate 50% of the traffic.

[109] Navegação Vale do Rio Doce S.A.—Docenave. Online. Available: http://www.docenave.com.br/. Accessed: February 1, 2001.

[110] Interview by Cara Dougherty with José Carlos da Rocha Ramos, General Cargo and Containers Manager, Navegação Vale do Rio Doce S.A.—Docenave, Rio de Janeiro, Brazil, January 24, 2001.

[111] Julian Thomas, "Multiple Routes Serve Shippers' Varied Needs," *Journal of Commerce Week*, Special Advertising Supplement (December 11-17, 2000), p. 6A.

[112] Ibid., p. 2A.

[113] Robert Ward, "Coastal Haven," *Containerisation International* (July 1999), pp. 44-45.

[114] Interview by Cara Dougherty with Paulo Augusto Camello, Cabotage Operation Centre, Aliança Navegação e Logística, Rio de Janeiro, Brazil, January 23, 2001.

[115] Ramos interview.

[116] Camello interview.

Chapter 3. Ports and Port Reform

Introduction

Latin America was characterized by models of centralized governance and heavy state intervention in the economy for much of the 20th century. With the advent of global trade liberalization and economic integration, it became clear to most Latin American governments that these models were inhibiting domestic economic growth rather than stimulating development. Port reform has become a part of the overall process of deregulation and privatization as state-run industries have sought to adjust to changing times.

This chapter examines port reform in Latin America and the Caribbean (LAC). It begins with an overview of different types of port reform that have occurred in the hemisphere. The remainder of the chapter presents case studies of the reform processes that have been undertaken at 11 LAC ports and the Panama Canal. The case studies were selected from a spectrum of port administration models, levels of traffic, types of markets served, and levels of development. Each case study discusses port infrastructure, operations, strategic plans, labor issues, economic impacts, competition with other ports, and lessons learned from port reform.

Levels of Port Privatization and Organization

The most common trend in privatization is the "landlord port." In this model the port authority (oftentimes the government) owns the port infrastructure and is also in charge of its management. The port authorities serve as concessionaires, as they contract out services to private firms. These firms own the assets of the port superstructure and equipment and perform the services that are needed. The "landlord port" model is one followed by many large ports.[1] Examples of this type are Buenos Aires, Argentina, and Colón, Panama.

A second type of organization is a "tool port," with which the government has more participation than it does with the landlord model. Port authorities are the owners of the infrastructure, but they also own the superstructure (such as the buildings) and the equipment. Private firms rent these assets through concessions or licenses.[2] Two examples of this model are Antwerp (Belgium) and Seattle (United States).

A third type of model is a "service port," in which port authorities are solely responsible for all activities. Service ports own both the infrastructure and the superstructure, hire employees, and provide services directly.[3] The best example of this type of port is Singapore, although it, too, is moving toward privatization.

As can be observed, the trend of privatization is a worldwide phenomenon in varying degrees. The United Kingdom is the only nation to have fully privatized its ports. Ports are generally adopting the landlord port model because it allows the port authorities to retain some ownership and to avoid the risk of monopolization of some assets by private firms.

Case Studies of Port Reform

The LAC ports chosen for case studies are as follows:

- Buenos Aires, Argentina

- Puerto Cabello, Venezuela

- Kingston, Jamaica

- Limón/Moín, Costa Rica

- Rio Haina, Dominican Republic

- San Antonio, Chile

- Santos, Brazil

- Veracruz, Mexico

- Willemstad, Curaçao, Netherlands Antilles

- Colón and Balboa, Panama (and the Panama Canal)

These ports vary according to geographical location, performance levels, and both type and degree of reform. The case of Panama is treated separately because of its unique position in the world market. Analysis of each port is based on information obtained from published statistics, government documents, and personal interviews with government officials, terminal operators, port clientele, labor officials, freight forwarders, and other individuals associated with ports. Table 3.1 presents salient port characteristics.

Buenos Aires, Argentina

Background

The Port of Buenos Aires is located at the mouth of the Río de la Plata on the Atlantic Coast of South America. Buenos Aires is the capital and largest city in Argentina, with a population of around 12 million people in the greater metropolitan area, which includes both the city and the province of Buenos Aires. The port is accessed via an access canal dredged in the riverbed leading out into the Atlantic Ocean.

The Port of Buenos Aires has historically been of great importance for the Southern Cone region as well as the premier port of Argentina. The port handles 90 percent of the

Table 3.1 Comparative Port Characteristics

Name of Port	Type of Port Organization	Year of Reform/ Type of Reform	Length of Concession Contracts (terminal)	Number of Concessionaires (terminal)	Presence of Labor Unions	Governmental Level of Port Authority (state, national)	Availability of Strategic Plan/Action Plan	TEU Volume 1999 or 2000	Percentage of National Container Traffic
Buenos Aires	Landlord	1995 Privatization	20 years	4 now, 5 originally	Yes/company	National/provincial	Yes	1,126,712 (2000)	90
Curaçao	Tool	1980 De-privatization	10 years	1	Yes/local	National/Municipal	Yes	76,105 (2000)	100
Kingston	Tool	1974 Transshipment only	Contract expires 2001	1	Yes	National	Yes	894,779 (2000)	
Panama	Landlord	1994 Privatization	20-25 years	4	Yes/private	National	Yes	1,353,727 (2000)	100
Puerto Cabello	Landlord	1991 Privatization	2-10 years	1	Minimal	State	No	496,315 (2000)	70
Limón/Moín	Service	1972 Stevedores	N/A	None	Yes	National/Provincial	Yes	571,957 (2000)	100
Rio Haina	Tool	1970 Restructuring	Varies up to 10 years	1	Yes/local	National	No	415,629 (1999)	90
San Antonio	Landlord/tool	1981-97 privatization	20 years	2	Yes/multi-user port	Municipal	Yes	374,474 (1999)	47
Santos	Landlord/tool	1993 Privatization	25 years	2	Yes/state	National/state	Yes	987,708 (2000)	55
Veracruz	Landlord	1993 Privatization	20 years	5	Yes/each terminal operator	National/state	Yes	570,000 (2000)	45

container traffic for all Argentina, amounting to 40 percent of the entire external trade for the country.[4]

In the year 2000, Buenos Aires surpassed Santos, Brazil, as the leading port in terms of TEUs handled in South America, reaching the 1,126,712-TEU mark, second only to Colón, Panama, in all Latin America.[5] The Port of Buenos Aires has experienced rapid growth in container traffic since privatization in 1995, which was expedited by the commencement of operations at the Exolgan terminal in the Dock Sud area in 1997.[6]

Infrastructure

The port consists of two main areas: the Puerto Nuevo area inside the city limits and the Dock Sud area, located just south of the city limits in the province of Buenos Aires. The Puerto Nuevo area is divided into six terminals, of which Terminals 1, 2, 3, and 5 are equipped to handle significant container traffic.

Terminals 1 and 2 are operated by a consortium headed by London P&O Steam Navigation Company known as Terminales Río de la Plata (TRP). TRP has historically been the leader in container handling in the Puerto Nuevo area, peaking in 1998 with more than 400,000 TEUs handled—over half of the total for Puerto Nuevo that year.[7] TRP consists of two docks with seven berths and a total berthing area of 1,813 meters, with a draft of 32 feet.[8] It is serviced by five Panamax-sized gantry cranes and 11 rubber-tired gantries (RTGs) and has a total operating area of 28.5 hectares.[9] It has a maximum capacity of 1 million TEUs and has 120 reefer plugs.[10]

Terminal 3 is operated by a joint venture between Quatro Invest, LANCO, and the International Finance Corporation, known as Terminales Portuarias Argentinas (TPA).[11] It has six berths, serviced by two Panamax-sized gantries and two RTGs, with a total dockside area of 1,397 meters and a service area of 15 hectares.[12] There are a total of 140 reefer plugs available in the terminal.[13]

Terminal 5 is operated by a joint venture between Bemberg Inversiones S.A. (BISA) of Argentina and International Container Terminal Services Inc. (ICTSI) headquartered in the Phillipines, known as Buenos Aires Container Terminal Services S.A. (BACTSSA).[14] BACTSSA has two berths with a total length of 885 meters and a maximum draft of 32 feet.[15] BACTSSA is serviced by four Panamax-sized gantry cranes and nine RTGs, as well as two 80-ton Gottwald cranes.[16] The total surface area of BACTSSA is 250,000 square meters. It has an estimated 450,000-TEU capacity in its 180,000-square-meter stacking area, and it has 480 reefer plugs.[17]

Exolgan is operated by a consortium headed by International Trade Logistics, S.A. (81 percent ownership), the German Bank of Investment (4 percent), and the Port of Hamburg (15 percent).[18] It has a total operating area of 450,000 square meters, with 1,000 meters of berthing space and five berths.[19] It is serviced by three Panamax-sized gantry cranes, one post-Panamax-sized gantry crane, 15 RTGs, and 500 reefer plugs.[20]

Operations

The port offers service 24 hours a day, 365 days a year. Since the 1995 privatization, the port has seen a steady increase in the amount of container traffic, from 504,600 TEUs in 1995 to 1,126,712 TEUs in 2000.[21] From 1995 to 1998, the growth rate for container traffic in terms of TEUs was 21.3 percent, third in relation to both the leading Asian and European ports.[22] Crane operation averages 23-25 containers/hour, with five-person gangs, an increase from the pre-privatization average of 8-10 containers/hour.[23] Because of the increased competition at the port, the average turnaround time has decreased from around three days before privatization to 12 hours maximum currently.[24]

Organization

The Port of Buenos Aires has separate organizational structures for the Puerto Nuevo and Dock Sud terminals. The terminals in Puerto Nuevo fall under the administration of the Administración General de Puertos (AGP), the successor to the defunct national agency that formerly controlled all port operations. The AGP collects the fees charged to each concessionaire, as well as the general port fees charged to all ships entering the port. The AGP in turn provides services to all the common areas of the port, including dredging, security for the warehouses, lighting, maintenance of the gates, and maintenance of buoys.[25]

Dock Sud is under the administration of the Administración Portuaria Bonaerense (APB), an agency within the government of the province of Buenos Aires. The creation of provincial-level port authorities was a key element of the Argentine port reform process. This structure has allowed for increased local control and cooperation with local authorities. It has also allowed the Exolgan terminal a certain advantage vis-à-vis the Puerto Nuevo ports, as Exolgan's relationship with the provincial government has been much more cooperative because of the competitive position of the provincial government with the AGP in terms of capturing market share.

Reform Process

Before 1989, the Argentine port system was under the centralized control of the Autoridad General de Puertos (AGP S.E. E.L.), a state-run enterprise created in 1956 that controlled all port planning and operations from the national office in Buenos Aires.[26] The AGP S.E. E.L. was in charge of administrating almost 100 ports, the national railroad system, and the national agency in charge of roads and bridges. The legacy of the AGP S.E. E.L. administration of the transportation infrastructure is very negative; it was a period of insufficient investment that was often badly planned, inadequate, or expensive.[27] In the case of ports, there were often times when the consulting and administrative fees for new infrastructure cost more than the actual construction.[28] During the 1980s, stagnant economic growth led to decreasing investment in the port facilities, reaching a low of $200,000 for all Argentine ports in 1989.[29]

Cargo-handling operations were conducted by approximately 30 private firms that shared the dock space in the terminals. The firms provided their own mobile equipment but were barred from investing in any permanent infrastructure. Much of the infrastructure provided by the port was built before the 1920s and had become obsolete. Lacking sufficient funding from the national government, and without any investment from the private sector, the Port of Buenos Aires fell into a state of disrepair.

The deficiency in investment resulted in poor operations in the Port of Buenos Aires. During the 1980s it had gained notoriety as a *puerto sucio*, or "dirty port," because of the hidden fees charged by the port administration and the port workers' union, organized under the powerful Sindicato Unidos Portuarios Argentinos (SUPA).[30] The port had excessive personnel and regulations, both from the AGP S.E. E.L. and from the SUPA, which made labor and administrative costs extremely expensive. An official report from the General Union of Public Industries (known by its Spanish acronym, SIGEP) in 1990 stated that the structure of the personnel of the AGP S.E. E.L. included many more managers than actual employees and that the majority of the employees were concentrated in the Buenos Aires area, leaving other areas of the country severely understaffed.[31]

At the same time, ordinary port workers were often poorly trained. They were employed on a part-time, rotating basis, and gang sizes and work hours were completely controlled by the unions.

The central planning conducted by the AGP S.E. E.L., instead of providing efficiency and economies of scale as envisioned, was the source of inefficient distribution of resources and regulation that stifled productivity.[32] The political forces that influenced the policy and administration of the AGP S.E. E.L. were its own institutional survival, coupled with appeasement of port labor unions. It ignored the needs of port users, port operators, and Argentine consumers, because governmental economic policy until the early 1990s was inward looking and closed. Argentina was not focused on developing an export-based economy or providing its citizens access to cheap imported goods. While countries concerned with their global market opportunities focused on port development as a strategic area of transportation infrastructure, Argentina was following a model of development that did not place a priority on developing transportation links to the rest of the globe.

Consequently, as the rest of the world began to adjust to the structural transformation of the shipping industry that containerization represented, the limits placed on Argentina's ports by lack of investment and dependence on manual labor left Buenos Aires in a disadvantageous position in relation to its competitors worldwide.

The Argentine port reform process began in 1992, as part of an overall economic restructuring process initiated by then newly elected President Carlos Menem and his secretary of the economy, Domingo Cavallo. Their strong political will was necessary to force the restructuring that included the port reform program.[33] The objectives outlined in the port reform laws were clear and their enforcement was strict. Martin Sgut identifies the seven goals of the Argentine transportation reform program:

- Improve efficiency and investment in the transportation system

- Increase trade

- Increase the productivity of the port system

- Make Argentine ports competitive, particularly the port of Buenos Aires

- Remove the planning and state control functions from national port administration

- Promote free trade

- Terminate the large deficits of state-owned industries, such as Ferrocarriles Argentinos and Aerolineas Argentinas[34]

Menem and Cavallo were determined to break the power of the SUPA over port operations and to privatize operations by offering terminal concessions. For the Puerto Nuevo area, the concessions were going to be made to private operators at each of the six terminals in an open international bid process. In the Dock Sud area, the port was going to be handed over to the provincial government of Buenos Aires to administer.

The concession process was designed to meet the needs of port users, which meant safeguarding concentration of terminal ownership in an oligopoly of port operators.[35] Additionally, the concession process would build in a safeguard against price-fixing by terminal operators by enabling the port administration to set a maximum port tariff.[36] Transparency would be ensured by publication of port tariffs, so as to guarantee that the concessionaires would be basing their rates on actual costs and not abusing the concession they received to operate in a public space to receive undue rents.[37]

The effort to reform the labor structure at the port was arguably the most important objective and accomplishment of the port reform of 1992. The labor reform had three objectives: elimination of restrictive labor practices, such as the labor registry, and strict separation of the port labor between ship and shore-based workers; promotion of stable labor relations between port workers and private firms; and reduction of port workers while minimizing the social impact.[38] Because the reform process promised to bring in new technology, eliminate the strict separation of port duties and qualification, and was focused on reducing costs, the elimination of many port jobs was unavoidable.

The port restructuring would have to minimize the impact that this loss of employment would cause in order to make the reform politically feasible. A system of incentives was created in 1984 to encourage stevedores to retire voluntarily. This system created a fund from surcharges to the port tariff to indemnify those who participated in the program. This program was able to reduce the total amount of stevedores from 5,100 in 1984 to 1,150 by 1994.[39] The AGP S.E. E.L. also implemented a program of voluntary retirement that reduced the total amount of laborers from 5,000 in 1989 to 400 in 1994.[40] These reductions were necessary precursors to the drastic reforms that were soon to follow. As a condition of acquiring a concession, the government was able to place 1,150 stevedores from the old stevedore registry and 300 former workers of the AGP S.E. E.L. in jobs with the new private operators of the Port of Buenos Aires.[41]

The reform process was commenced through three legislative acts: Decree No. 2694/91, Decree No. 817/92, and the Port Law No. 24.093. Decree No. 2694/91 mandated deregulation of the pilot industry for ships coming into the Argentine ports. Decree No. 817/92 eliminated the labor allocation system by dissolving all prior labor agreements between the AGP S.E. E.L. and port unions.[42] This act broke union control over port laborers by allowing private cargo handlers to contract directly with their workers. Port Law No. 24.093 restructured the AGP S.E. E.L., eliminating its status as a state-owned corporation and transforming it into an administrative agency in charge of administering the Port of Buenos Aires in the interim until the new municipal port authority could be formed.[43] The law also established the legal framework necessary for the concession process. The restructuring meant that the AGP would have a reduced role in the operations of the port, meaning that it would no longer be the direct employer of many of the port workers.[44] It also meant that the nature of the port workers' relationship to their employees would no longer be the realm of the stricter standards established for government employees in the administrative codes, but their rights would be guaranteed as any other laborer in the private industry under the labor code.

The devolution of control to provincial authorities created an atmosphere of competition between the ports in the Buenos Aires region, especially since the port of Dock Sud was assigned to the control of the province of Buenos Aires rather than remaining under the control of the national port authority. It was this condition that allowed the development of Exolgan at Dock Sud in 1995, immediately increasing the container capacity of the Port of Buenos Aires by 300,000 TEUs. On a national level, the AGP S.E. E.L. was replaced by the Argentine Port Council (Consejo Portuario Argentino, or CPA), whose focus is to coordinate and promote the efforts of all ports toward further development. The CPA draws its leadership from the administrators of all Argentine ports and is currently headed by an official from the APB.[45]

The success of the port reform process in Buenos Aires is due to the lack of preference given to any of the sectors affected by the port reform process. The impartiality of the process gave the government legitimacy and showed solidarity in its action.[46]

Labor

The labor situation in the Port of Buenos Aires has changed dramatically since the reform effort began in 1992. The effect of the initial reform mandated by Decree No. 817/92, wrested control of port employment from the SUPA and allowed port workers to contract with private operators on a full-time basis. The effect of this legislation was to reduce the amount of port workers from more than 6,000 employees under the AGP administration, to around 1,200 in the concessioned terminals by the end of 1998.[47]

As indicated above, part of the reform process mandated indemnities to be paid directly to these displaced workers, in an effort to offset the social impact that this restructuring had on the port labor community. The total cost of indemnifying the 2,820 displaced employees from the AGP and the 5,403 displaced stevedores is estimated to be $120 million, with an average indemnity award of $15,000 per employee. As indicated above, this process was undertaken over a period of ten years for the stevedores, and six years for the AGP workers, well before the concessions were made. The program was established via negotiations between the government, the labor unions, and port operations companies. It was through these negotiations that the surcharge on port user fees was instituted to finance the indemnity fund.[48]

Whereas port workers under the AGP administration were characterized by their inefficient work performance, poor training, militancy, and predatory nature toward port users, under the concession scheme, the workers contracted at the port are well paid and have permanent jobs with salaries above the minimum wage.[49] Workers tend to be better trained and receive bonuses based on performance.

Nevertheless, because of a precarious economic situation, the level of unemployment in Argentina has consistently been in the double digits since the port reform process began. Although the level of employment at the port since 1994 has not decreased dramatically, from 3,250 in 1994 to 2,600 in 1998, the social impact may be aggravated by the persistent economic slump.[50]

Criticism of the privatization of ports will point to the persistent unemployment as an indicator of the negative tradeoff that society must make in order to pursue a liberal macroeconomic policy. Port privatization only produces fewer jobs and more profits for the (often international) companies that are using resources and infrastructure originally paid for by tax dollars. The correct method of evaluating the port employment situation in Argentina is to compare the net benefits of port employees' contributions to the economy versus the net economic gains to all other sectors. In the previous state-controlled regime, port employees may have garnered a larger share of the revenues generated by the port, but their benefits were attained at the costs of port users and Argentine consumers. This type of situation is also inequitable and detrimental to the economy, as it places all jobs dependent on exports at a disadvantage relative to goods produced in countries whose ports are more efficient and less expensive. If organized labor loses leverage in the port, it is not at the expense of all laborers in the Argentine economy—it may, in fact, benefit others.

Overall, business/labor relations are cooperative rather than conflictual. Skilled labor has replaced the scores of unskilled stevedores that previously controlled the cargo-handling operations in the past, in accordance with global trends toward capital-intensive port services. Most important, however, is to note that the port-restructuring process dealt with the problem of excess labor at the nascent stage of reform—which allowed significant time for displaced workers to adjust, as well as for all the affected sectors to create a solution to the adverse social impact that these displaced workers create. Cooperation and negotiation provided for a solution that was equitable to all parties, leaving minimal political conflict and resentment by disaffected sectors.

Performance

The Port of Buenos Aires has improved its container-handling capacity since the port reform process began. Most notable has been the development of the Exolgan terminal in Dock Sud, which has increased the container capacity of the entire port by more than

300,000 TEUs annually since 1997. Table 3.2 illustrates how container movement for the entire port has almost doubled since 1994. While the port experienced an overall decrease in container traffic after 1998, growth at Exolgan has been steady.

Table 3.2
Port of Buenos Aires Container Movement (TEUs), 1994-99

	1994	1995	1996	1997	1998	1999
Puerto Nuevo	532,000	505,000	530,000	720,000	818,000	727,969
Dock Sud	8,000	136,000	214,000	303,000	322,000	348,133
Total Buenos Aires	540,000	641,000	744,000	1,023,000	1,140,000	1,076,102

Source: Data from Administración General de Puertos Sociedad del Estado, *Estadistica Del Movimiento Portuario Ano 1999*, Buenos Aires, 2000, Grafico No. 3.

These trends show how the competition between the terminals increased the amount of container traffic, especially in the Exolgan terminal. At the same time, the leveling off of the growth trend shows that the capacity for containers in the port has been reached. Any growth in container traffic at any one terminal will come at the expense of the others. This uneven growth may prove detrimental to the concessionaires who have yet to reap the profits of their capital investment, causing some to question the viability of the Argentine model for achieving investment goals in the long run.

Competition

Intraport

As illustrated above, Buenos Aires has intense interterminal competition both within the Puerto Nuevo terminals and between the terminals at Puerto Nuevo and Dock Sud.[51] As mentioned above, the two ports are situated beneath two distinct port administrative entities, with each rival port authority promoting the virtues of its market position relative to the other.

Before Exolgan came online in 1995, almost all the container traffic for the city of Buenos Aires passed through the Puerto Nuevo terminals, as it had under the old centralized system. After the development at Exolgan, port users had a choice to circumvent the congestion and regulatory barriers presented by the AGP in the Puerto Nuevo area. The monopoly position in this lucrative market was broken, giving rise to stiff competition not only between the container terminals at Puerto Nuevo but also extending out to the nearby province.[52]

As far as interterminal competition is concerned, there has been no problem guaranteeing a competitive atmosphere in Puerto Nuevo. When the concession plan was originally conceived, there was concern over market abuses by terminal operators who consolidated the operations of more than one of the terminals.[53] This concern soon gave way to grievances by terminal operators about the existence of a state of hypercompetition, because too many concessionaires were operating in the port, driving prices lower and dividing a finite amount of traffic.

The grievances were set aside, as terminal operators sought a method of consolidating their position or leaving the market.[54] Flexibility in the port law allowed for an amendment to the original port reform act, which had prohibited horizontal integration, in favor of consolidation subject to approval from the national antitrust board.[55]

Interport

The Port of Buenos Aires sees itself as being the major port in the Southern Cone, a port that captures market share from other ports in the region, such as Montevideo, Uruguay, and Santos, Brazil.[56] Buenos Aires surpassed Santos in 1999 as the number one port in South America in terms of TEUs handled.[57]

Unfortunately, the competitive position of Buenos Aires is undermined by the shallow draft of the access canal that leads into the port. The 32-foot draft of the canal prevents fully loaded post-Panamax ships from calling on the port. Nevertheless, the port is still competitive in capturing cargo flows from other Argentine ports as well as from Montevideo, because of its superior efficiency in operations. [58]

Future Developments

Strategic Plans

The Port of Buenos Aires will continue to be the principal port of Argentina. Although the concentration of maritime traffic will no longer be exclusive to Buenos Aires, the performance and competitiveness of its terminals will ensure it continues to receive most of the traffic of the Greater Buenos Aires metropolitan area. Nevertheless, the growth of each area within the port will vary because of the different port authorities that govern Puerto Nuevo and Dock Sud.

At Puerto Nuevo, the AGP will soon be phased out in favor of a new port administrative entity that will be directed by a board of directors that will consist of representatives from the municipal government, the terminal operators, and port users.[59] This intended change has been part of the modernization plan since its inception in 1993, but the AGP has been slow to concede its role and has delayed the creation of the new administrative entity.[60] This delay has been a source of concern for private operators who question the need for the AGP and its staff of 400 employees five years after the privatization process began.

The weakening of central control has meant more competition for the Puerto Nuevo terminals, because the central government can no longer control which ports will develop container capacity and the central government no longer has a vested interest in ensuring that port traffic flow through terminals it no longer operates. Therefore, the viability of forming a strategic plan to be coordinated among all the terminal operators is strictly reduced. However, the overall liberalization of Argentine economic policy signals a dedication to increasing the participation of Argentina in the world economy. The Port of Buenos Aires is Argentina's main commercial point of contact to the world, which implies that it has achieved a new level of importance to the national economy. Lower port costs decrease the overall costs of Argentine exports, thus making them more competitive in the world markets.[61]

At the same time, the port operators share a common interest in seeing the port traffic in Buenos Aires increase. The role that the port authority will play in attending to the operators' needs is still important. The area that would be of primary concern for all the port operators is the access canal to the port. If the access canal were deepened, then larger ships with greater capacity would be able to call on the port.

Since the relaxation of the port law that allows for multiple terminal ownership by one operator, there is a good chance that Puerto Nuevo will soon experience mergers among port operators, leaving fewer operators in the port. The recent acquisition by Maersk of Terminal 4 signals the entry of this multinational operator into the port operations at Puerto Nuevo and further increases the probability of conglomerates forming among the terminal operators there.

Need for Reform

Buenos Aires is very advanced in its reform process. Once the AGP is transformed into the new Buenos Aires port authority, the administrative reform process should be complete. The next challenge for port administrators is to improve the access infrastructure to the port. The decision to deepen the access channel will require a great deal of capital for the initial work as well as for maintenance. Land-side access to the port also requires attention in order to decrease the congestion and the cost that port users suffer while moving goods in and out of the port.[62] Improvements in the rail access are particularly important because of the poor condition of the rail lines presently and the location of rail lines in high-density, high-traffic areas in the city.[63]

The potential of the port reform will not be fulfilled on a national level until container ports are developed to serve the hinterlands that lie outside the province of Buenos Aires. Plans are currently underway for the development of a large container port at Zarate, 100 kilometers northwest of Buenos Aires, that will service the traditional industrial belt of Argentina with less congestion and cost than Buenos Aires.[64] Development of container ports in the provincial Argentine hinterland will allow Argentine products cheaper and easier access to export markets. Without growth in this area, the overall cost of Argentine exports will continue to be higher than it should be, causing a deterioration of its market position.

Lessons Learned

The Port of Buenos Aires has successfully reformed its port administration, reaching a level of investment and productivity comparable to any port in Europe or North America.

From a port that was notoriously expensive and slow with limited modern infrastructure confined to one container terminal at the beginning of the decade, it has become the premier port in the region, with modern gantry cranes present in four terminals.

Perhaps not as significant for the Port of Buenos Aires but of significance for the rest of the Argentine Republic is the decentralization of port administration to the provincial government. This restructuring has allowed for the development of regional ports that will be better able to handle regional traffic than the congested infrastructure in the Buenos Aires region. Creation of economic opportunities for the provinces will decrease the burden placed on the infrastructure of Buenos Aires, as well as its environment.

Although port labor has lost significant control, the workers remaining in the port are better trained and better paid than their AGP counterparts. When weighing the costs and benefits of labor restructuring, it is important to note the improved services that the terminal operators provide. The growth in container traffic is indicative of the multiplier effect on the economy as goods become cheaper to transport, and Argentine exports are no longer subject to the export barrier of high port costs.

The transformation of the Argentine economy from the closed, import-substitution model to the liberal, free-market model demands an efficient and low-cost portal to global markets in order to reap the benefits that are an obvious result of the privatization of port operations. Criticism of the privatization process is of an unanticipated nature: instead of the dangers of oligopoly control, there is fear that there is too much competition for cargo in the Buenos Aires area. Overcompetition, while a legitimate fear, brings benefits to port users and consumers in the form of lower prices and eliminates the need for vigilance of port operators by regulatory authorities because the market regulates the operators.

When the AGP finally concedes control over the operations at the Port of Buenos Aires, the structural transformation of the port sector will be complete. The only objective left will be the long-term goal of decentralization. The Argentine model has proved to be successful in the short term; only time will tell whether it can be sustainable over the long term.

Puerto Cabello, Venezuela

Background

Puerto Cabello is located on the western half of Venezuela's Caribbean coastline. The most recent major expansion occurred in the 1980s with the construction of Area VI. These berths were designed to handle the growing traffic in containerized and bulk cargo.

Currently, Puerto Cabello is the largest commercial port in Venezuela and one of the largest in LAC. It receives more than 3,000 vessel calls annually with trade volumes approaching 10 million tons.[65] In 1998, nearly 500,000 TEUs passed through Puerto Cabello, making it the fifth largest in LAC.[66]

Infrastructure

Five kilometers of wharfage have been built in Puerto Cabello's natural harbor. Although all the wharfage is available for public use, not all of it is available for containerized traffic. The port also handles a variety of other cargo—dry bulk, breakbulk, liquid chemical, and vehicles. Dry bulk and liquid chemical goods are unloaded at specialized terminals with dedicated transfer equipment and storage facilities.

The rated capacity of the port is 10.5 meters (34 feet), even though not all the berths are 10.5 meters deep. There are no specific restrictions on maximum length or breadth. A dredging program was completed in 1998. This program was intended to provide a depth of 12.2 meters (40 feet), but the official rating has not yet been increased.

Loading and unloading of containers are accomplished with RTGs or ship-based cranes. The port's strategic plan calls for the installation of fixed gantry cranes, but this has not yet occurred. The five 40-ton RTGs are complemented with 64 toplifters, 36 reachstackers, 79 terminal trucks, and various other lifters of varying capacity.

All container traffic is handled by private companies operating on concessions. The nine key terminal operators for container traffic have a combined yard area of 332,000 square meters with storage capacity of more than 25,000 TEUs and plugs for 550 reefer containers.[67] Intermodal connections to Puerto Cabello include both rail and highway facilities.

Operations

Container activity at Puerto Cabello has grown significantly over the last decade. In 1991, when port reform was instituted, annual container traffic was less than 100,000 TEUs. In the first few subsequent years, traffic increased steadily. The biggest jump occurred between 1996 and 1997, when container moves jumped from 245,000 to 385,000 TEUs, or nearly 60 percent. The most recent statistics, for 1999, list 496,000 TEUs, making Puerto Cabello the fifth most active container port in LAC, which is also becoming increasingly important as a transshipment point. Of the nearly half a million TEUs handled in 1999, nearly 30 percent (145,000 TEUs) were transshipped containers.

Port operations are becoming increasingly modernized. Terminal port operators, for example, have recently implemented the NAVSYS computerized tracking system to organize loading and unloading operations. Five new travel lifts have been installed in the storage yard, allowing containers to be stacked six wide and six high.[68]

Customs operations have not yet been computerized and remain a very labor-intensive process. Vessel sharing agreements (VSAs) provide stability for the shipping industry but complicate processing of cargo. Each shipper must separately submit a shipping manifest and other related documents and forms. Even containers bound for transshipment must clear customs, a process that often takes as much as a week.[69]

Organization

Puerto Cabello is a landlord port, in which the bulk of services are performed by private operators working under concession contracts. The port authority, Instituto Puerto Autonomo de Puerto Cabello (Autonomous Port Institute of Puerto Cabello, or IPAPC) is a state agency that acts only as the administrative body of the port. The permanent infrastructure of the port (docks, wharfs, etc.) is owned by the IPAPC, but all other equipment is owned by the concessionaires. The port authority is also responsible for maintenance of the port infrastructure.

The port authority generates income from the rent charged to the concessionaires (discussed in greater detail below), from direct vessel charges, and from tariffs for loading and discharging cargo. All these rates are set by the legislature and were most recently updated in 1997.[70] Concessionaires are free to set their rates.

Vessel charges include port entry fees, dockage fees, pilot fees, and any special charges, for example, fees for dangerous cargo. Cargo fees are $1.75/ton for bulk cargo, either loading or discharging. Container fees are charged per container, whether 20- or 40-foot. Laden containers are taxed $45 per container; empty containers, $6; and those bound for transshipment, $31.

Reform Process

Venezuela initiated port reform in 1991, eliminating the Instituto Nacional de Puertos (National Ports Institute, or INP) and turning over to each state the responsibility for administration and operations of the ports within its borders. Only the roles of regulation, security, and pilotage remain with the national government, under the Ministry of Transport and Communications.

Under its new role as operator of the port, the state of Carabobo established the IPAPC. This institute had the responsibility of port organization, operations, and management. In its first year of existence, it reduced the port staff from 5,300 employees to only 170. The displaced workers were given severance packages in the form of one or two lump-sum payments, while those who continued working were hired by private companies. The total number of workers currently employed indirectly by the port is approximately 3,000.

The immediate results from the privatization process were impressive. According to one operator who experienced the transition firsthand, port productivity jumped virtually overnight: "Vessels that were supposed to be here five days got off in one or two days."[71] By 1993, the port was showing a profit and has continued to do so.

Port services are provided by private operators through concession contracts. The operators pay an application fee, a deposit, and a monthly rental for use of land that they are allocated. The land rental rate varies from $1.00 to $1.50 per square meter per month, depending on which region of the port the rented land is on. Operators must additionally pay tariffs for cargo or containers transferred. All these rates are set by the national legislature.

Criticisms of the concession system include the duration of the contracts and the tariff rates, especially from the smaller operators, whose concession contracts are relatively short, ranging from two to three years. Larger operators can obtain longer-term contracts. Operators must purchase their own equipment, and short-term contracts make it difficult to amortize the costs. Furthermore, a number of clauses in the contract allow the port authority to terminate the contract unilaterally. There is no record that this right has been executed in the past, but the possibility exists.

On the other hand, Puerto Cabello is just completing its first decade of operation under port reform. One official noted that the initial concession contracts were relatively short but have increased in length since that first round.[72] The port seems to be attempting to balance the desire to attract outside investment while protecting the value of their assets. Committing to a long-term contract before the potential of the port is fully realized could also cost the port in the long run.

Operators are free to charge what they like for their services but, in practice, are limited by the tariffs imposed by the port authority. These tariffs, it is argued, are too high, as much as half what the stevedoring company charges its customers. But there may be some justification for these high tariffs in this case. It is estimated that as much as 60 percent of the port income is returned to the state to be spent on projects other than port maintenance or development of the port infrastructure. While this implies that the port is charging more than it needs to and increasing the cost of shipping to Puerto Cabello, much of this money may be going to long-term investment in local industry that will ultimately increase use of the port.

Labor

The port reforms of 1991 essentially brought an end to organized labor in Puerto Cabello. Some individual unions remain, but there is no large union of any significant strength. As such, the operators have complete control over assignment of labor and the gang sizes. For the major container operators, relatively small gang sizes are chosen. Terminal Port Services, for example, reports using six workers on each of two cranes, about one dozen truckers to transport containers to the storage area, and five coordinators to oversee the operation.

The fraction of casual workers used is also chosen by the operators, which appears to be related to the skill level required. Companies that require less skilled labor, for example, to unload breakbulk goods, report the use of nearly 75 percent for casual workers. Operators that use more technologically advanced equipment, such as the larger companies for container operation, report only 10 to 15 percent for casual workers.

The absence of organized labor leads to relatively low pay rates. Skilled labor can earn more than $1,000 per month, but the pay for the typical longshoreman is only $11-15 per day, or $200-400 per month, depending on the number of days worked.

The absence of organized labor also contributes to poor working conditions for unskilled labor. One operator, for example, noted that the dust and pollution in some areas made for hazardous working conditions, but there was no recourse for either the company affected or for the workers employed under these conditions.

Representative Costs

The total costs of loading or discharging a vessel at Puerto Cabello vary widely, depending on factors such as the vessel size and type, contracts between the shipper and the stevedoring company, and the amount of goods loaded or discharged. Nevertheless, an estimate of the typical costs involved may be obtained by choosing a representative vessel and typical load.

The representative vessel chosen has a weight of 28,550 DWTs and an overall length of 190 meters. It is assumed that 600 containers will be transferred, 150 of which are empty. The costs provided are courtesy of H. L. Boulton and Company, the parent company of Terminal Port Services.

The vessel charges are listed in Table 3.3. These costs include port access and docking charges paid to the port authority and pilotage and other charges paid to the port captain. Note that for this representative vessel, these are fixed charges irrespective of the amount of containers loaded or discharged. The largest fraction of these costs is docking charges, which consist primarily of line handling charges.

Table 3.3
Representative Vessel Costs

Authority	Charge Type	Cost	Fraction of Vessel Costs
IPAPC	Port access	$1,876	10%
IPAPC	Dock time	$1,140	6%
Port Cap.	Docking and inspection	$13,102	70%
Pilot	Pilot charges	$2,543	14%
	Total vessel cost	$18,661	100%

Source: Data from H. L. Boulton and Company, Puerto Cabello, Venezuela.

Because the liner service must include these costs in the rates it charges its customers, it is useful to consider this fixed cost as a "per container cost" dependent on the number of containers transferred. The representative vessel chosen has a capacity of approximately 1,500 TEUs, or 750 40-foot containers. The maximum possible number of containers transferred is 1,500 40-foot containers (750 discharged and 750 loaded). Table 3.4 lists the vessel costs per container for several quantities of containers transferred up through a maximum of 1,000. For the assumptions made, this implies one-third of the vessel capacity is discharged and an equal amount is loaded. The implications of this table will be discussed below in terms of the loading/discharging costs.

The discharge or loading of containers involves two costs: the port tariff and the stevedoring charge. The first, discussed above, is charged by the IPAPC and depends on whether the container is loaded, empty, or bound for transshipment. These charges are set by the legislature and independent of the concessionaire and the shipping line. The first row of Table 3.5 lists these tariffs, including the 15 percent value-added tax charged by the state. The second cost is that charged by the stevedoring company (i.e., the terminal operator) to cover its labor costs, overhead, and profit. These charges are set by contract between the operator and the shipping line and can vary widely. Representative costs are listed in the second row of Table 3.4. The net cost of transferring a container is given in the third row of Table 3.5, ranging from approximately $75 for an empty container to $115 for a laden container, with a transshipment container falling between the two. As seen inTable 3.4, the vessel costs can be a significant fraction of the transfer costs if few containers are transferred. For our example of 600 containers, the vessel cost of $31 is approximately 30 percent of the transfer cost.

Table 3.4
Representative Vessel Costs per Container

Containers Transferred	Fraction of Capacity	Cost per Container
50	3%	$373
100	7%	$187
300	20%	$62
600	40%	$31
1,000	67%	$19

Note: Assumes 1,500-TEU vessel and equal number of 40-foot containers loaded and unloaded.

Table 3.5
Loading/Discharging Costs per Container

	Full	Empty	Transshipment
H. L. Boulton	$63.53	$69.30	$59.80
IPAPC	$51.98	$6.93	$35.88
Total	$115.50	$76.23	$95.68

Note: Includes 15% value-added tax; costs are based on Table 3.3 and Table 3.4.

Economic Impact

No specific information on the economic impact of Puerto Cabello was obtained, although it can be surmised that the impact has been significant. The only major employers in Puerto Cabello are the port authority and the concessionaires. Moreover, approximately 70 percent of Venezuelan maritime trade passes through this port, and it is located in the state of Carabobo, one of the most heavily industrialized states in Venezuela. Its 1.5 million inhabitants (8 percent of the Venezuelan population) produce 30 percent of the country's gross domestic product (GDP). It contains more than 60 industrial parks. Seventy percent of the factories of the state are located in Valencia, the state capital, lying 40 kilometers to the south of Puerto Cabello.[73]

Competition

There is extensive competition in the Venezuelan port system. Within the port, there are numerous concessionaires competing for business. Including the smallest, there are more than 30 terminal operators with the largest handling less than one-third of the container traffic and the top four handling less than 70 percent of the cargo.[74] There is extensive competition in the other services as well. The 1999-2000 port handbook lists 12 warehousing companies, 10 companies offering general services, 15 trucking companies, nine ship suppliers, and three tug operators.

There is also extensive competition between Venezuelan ports. For container traffic, the two major ports are La Guaira, located to the east and very near the country capital of Caracas, and Maracaibo, located to the west. When the national port authority was dissolved in 1991, each of the states was free to establish its own system of port management. There is control by each of the states as to the direction of development that the ports in their state take, but La Guaira and Maracaibo are in different states and hence free to compete against one another.

Future Developments

Despite the success of reform in ports such as Puerto Cabello, there is movement to reverse the trend of deregulation. This trend comes in two forms. First, cabotage law was recently reactivated. Cabotage restrictions existed previously, but exemptions were not difficult to obtain. However, in July 2000, President Hugo Chavez Frias signed the "Ley de Reactivacion," calling for reactivation of a national commercial fleet and more stringent enforcement of restrictions on foreign vessel use for domestic transport. It is still too early to tell the full effects of this law.

The second form of the trend back toward regulation is a proposed national port law. There is growing sentiment that there may be too much competition at the national level, that complete freedom of development may result in multiple Venezuelan ports developing major facilities without a sufficient potential business base. For this reason, a national port law is under consideration. As currently discussed (a draft has been written but not yet submitted to the legislature), this law would establish a national port authority to coordinate port development.[75] This body would establish a strategic development plan at the national level, and its approval would be required for ports to implement infrastructure improvements. Operation and management responsibilities would remain at the state level.

Implementation of a national port law could affect Puerto Cabello's plans for a major new container facility. As proposed, this facility would ultimately have the capacity of handling 1.6 million TEUs annually, more than three times the current level of container activity. A feasibility study, partially funded by the U.S. Trade Development Agency, has been completed, but construction has not yet started. It is not clear whether or not this project will be started, or when, especially since container berths currently have a 50 percent occupancy rate.

Finally, despite the significant progress made to date, the port lacks a formal strategic plan. The port authority has worked to modernize and upgrade the capacity of the port, including the recently completed dredging program and the proposed new container facility, but a strategic plan would assist in providing a long-term view for port development.

Lessons Learned

Puerto Cabello is one of the success stories of port privatization. From a large, inefficient organization it has transformed itself into one of the major ports in Latin America and one that has shown consistent profitability for the better part of the last decade.

Nevertheless, there are many possibilities for improvement. Longer duration concession contracts would encourage further infrastructure investment. Also, the port authority has been criticized for not reinvesting a sufficient amount of its profits in further development of the port.

The income generated from these fees is used for maintenance and port development. Major infrastructure purchases are left to the concessionaires, but an example of port development is the recently completed dredging program costing approximately $4 million. Nevertheless, the port has been criticized for not spending enough of its income on further development of the port but, instead, directing the income to other state development projects.

Kingston, Jamaica

Background

Jamaica is the third largest of the Caribbean islands with a size of 4,411 square miles. It lies 600 miles south of Florida, 100 miles southwest of Haiti, and 90 miles south of Cuba. Jamaica has several ports along its coast; however, this study will focus on the Port of Kingston, which handles approximately two-thirds of the vessels visiting Jamaica's ports and 87 percent of the container traffic through the island.[76] The Port of Kingston boasts the world's seventh-largest natural harbor and is located at the intersection of two major international trade routes. Kingston is only 32 miles from the main north-south and east-west shipping lanes that converge through the Panama Canal and reportedly has access to 32 countries and can easily serve more than 100 ports.[77] The port consists of three terminals, two of which are exclusively dedicated to container traffic and are collectively known as Kingston Container Terminal. The third terminal, known as Kingston Wharves, is a general-cargo facility offering both container and bulk cargo services. This study focuses primarily on Kingston Container Terminal, as it is the island's primary transshipment facility.

Organization

The Port of Kingston is divided into Kingston Container Terminal and Kingston Wharves and can be described as two separate ports, as they function independently of each other. The Port Authority of Jamaica (PAJ) owns the Kingston Container Terminal, which includes the land and the equipment. However, all assets are managed and operated by third-party companies under contract. As such, Kingston may be called a "tool port."

The PAJ is the island's principal maritime agency responsible for public ports. It has two primary roles, the development and the regulation of Jamaica's port and shipping industry. In its developmental role, the PAJ is "responsible for fostering the commercial development of ports and allied services island wide." The PAJ reinvests any profit accrued from pilotage dues, handling fees, and rents. In its regulatory capacity, the PAJ is "responsible for the safe navigation of vessels in Jamaica's ports and harbors as well as the setting of wharfage tariffs by way of public hearings."[78] The management of the PAJ works closely with various organizations to ensure that client needs are met and to maintain port efficiency. These "partner" organizations include the Shipping Association of Jamaica (SAJ), the Jamaica Maritime Institute, and Jamaica's Export and Investment Promotions Agency.[79]

The PAJ also conducts marketing activities geared toward promoting the use of the Port of Kingston as the primary transshipment center in the Caribbean and asserting itself as a competitive player in the global arena.

Infrastructure

The infrastructure available at the Port of Kingston includes four Panamax and six post-Panamax ship-to-shore gantry cranes. In addition, the PAJ has placed on order four super post-Panamax cranes, which can reach more than 22 rows of containers.[80] The port also has 38 straddle carriers, 54 hectares available for storage space, 1,250 meters of berth, 446 reefer plugs, and two harbor tugs.

The port underwent a process of upgrading through the 1980s and doubled its capacity in the 1990s. A major expansion in the mid-1990s led to an 800,000-TEU throughput capability, but the PAJ anticipates that Kingston Container Terminal will have exceeded its current capacity by the end of March 2001. In preparation for the anticipated demand, the PAJ has made plans to accommodate the expected increase in container throughput. A third phase of expansion will leave the port with a capacity of 1,200,000 TEUs by the end of 2002.[81]

Ongoing expansion includes new cranes on order and an expansion of the terminal itself to include an additional 11 hectares of storage space. Additional equipment due by 2002 includes 12 straddle carriers and 542 meters of berthing space. Furthermore, the PAJ also expects to receive tenders in April 2001 for dredging of the harbor to 14.5 meters. The PAJ expects to accommodate new businesses by June 2001 and complete the current phase of expansion by the end of 2001. According to PAJ estimates, by 2004, transshipment at the Port of Kingston will have increased by approximately 26 percent. The PAJ believes that this is a "conservative figure" and that the actual increase may be substantially higher. In addition, the PAJ expects an increase in cargo to 1.3 million TEUs. It also anticipates initiating another phase of expansion in 2004-05, as it currently has provision to develop 1,000 acres.[82]

Operations

While the PAJ owns the port and assets, the port itself is managed and operated by Kingston Terminal Operators Ltd. (KTO). KTO holds the only management contract at the Kingston Container Terminal, which is due for renewal in July 2001.[83] KTO is a private enterprise stevedoring company and is a wholly owned subsidiary of Kingston Wharves, the management company for the Kingston Wharves Terminal, which is the general/bulk cargo facility at the Port of Kingston. Kingston Container Terminal is an exclusive container terminal that functions primarily as a transshipment facility, while Kingston Wharves is a multipurpose facility that also offers container services.[84]

The Kingston Container Terminal services several international shipping lines and has been the main hub for ZIM Container Service for several years. Kingston is a port of call for mainline services and also offers feeder services to other ports within the region. The Kingston Container Terminal is further subdivided into two terminals: a North Terminal—Bustamante, which handles domestic cargo, and a South Terminal—Gordon Cay, which is used primarily for transshipment. However, KTO asserts that "the two terminals are managed and operated as one integrated terminal" and reports that transshipment accounts for almost 90 percent of container activity at the Kingston Container Terminal.[85]

The port is operational 365 days a year, 24 hours a day, and is fully equipped with modern facilities and equipment. On average, 107 container vessels per month call at the Port of Kingston. Kingston Container Terminal also performs an average of 48,000 container moves per month (approx. 81,700 TEUs).[86] Vessel arrivals are planned at least seven days in advance, and more than 95 percent of container movements are prenotified by lines and agents using Electronic Data Interchange (EDI). KTO employs advanced computer technology in the daily management of port operation activities. The COSMOS software system that is used has four modules: SHIPS for vessel planning, SPACE for yard management, TRAFFIC for straddle carrier management, and SIGNAL for EDI connectivity. Computerizing the coordination and assignment of port activities enabled more efficient handling of cargo at the terminal and optimal use of resources.[87]

The PAJ attributes the success of the Kingston Container Terminal to sound management, a skilled workforce, and careful planning. The infrastructure is also described as impressive because of modern handling equipment along with a full range of support services. KTO finds that average port productivity is around 20 container moves per hour. However, KTO notes that up to 26 moves per hour are often realized because of improved performance.[88]

KTO has recently hired crane operators and persuaded the SAJ to negotiate severance pay for discharged employees and pensions for those who retired. KTO reports that it has employed 44 of the 50 reassigned workers and that the South Terminal has attained productivity levels of 25-26 moves/hour, while the North Terminal lags behind with 17 moves/hour.[89]

Though the PAJ reportedly received fewer vessels in 1999, the volume of cargo handled increased. Nearly two-thirds of all vessel activity in Jamaica is focused on the busy container and general-cargo terminals at the Port of Kingston. The dominant sector at the Port of Kingston is the increasingly active transshipment trade. The Port of Kingston handled 5.2 million tons of transshipped cargo in 1999, which denotes an 11 percent increase from the previous year.[90]

Reform Process

The driving forces that initiated port reform in Jamaica were the container revolution and developments within the maritime industry in general. The same forces, which also led to the evolution of the transshipment industry, prompted the Port of Kingston to tailor its development projects toward capturing the potential trade the transshipment industry would offer.

In 1974, the governing party decided to become more involved not just in port ownership but also in port operations as it recognized the important role transshipment would come to play in the maritime industry.[91] The Jamaican government used its resources to restructure and invest in the Port of Kingston. The government, however, issued management contracts to Kingston Wharves and Western Terminals (to operate the new container facility), a group that later consolidated and formed KTO as a limited liability company. In addition, the government decided to restructure the maritime authority and authorized the additional functions (developmental) of the PAJ, whose prior role had been primarily regulatory. The PAJ's mandate was to build modern port facilities to support other sectors of the economy. Thus, for the first time, the government built a container port and invited tenders for port operations.[92]

In that first year (1975), the port handled less than 40,000 TEUs. More recently (2000), that figure rose to 871,000 TEUs, which denotes a steady increase of 15-20 percent annually. The Kingston Container Terminal prides itself in having been the first port in the region built and developed to facilitate transshipment. Despite the rapid and remarkable growth of transshipment at the Bahamas port, Freeport, the PAJ believes that no business has been lost to this newcomer. In fact, the PAJ reported a 26 percent increase in container throughput between 1999 and 2000. Regarding growth and performance, the PAJ thinks that it has performed well, in realizing overall growth of 336 percent during the 1990s.[93]

The Labor Accord of 1966 facilitated the mechanization of port operations that resulted in a reduction of the labor force, from a 5,000 strong workforce down to 2,000. Because of the link between waterfront trade unions and political forces, port developments have been at the forefront of the political process. The Labor Accord also abolished the gang system, and port labor was mostly derived from casual port workers.[94] Therefore, by the 1970s, port modernization already had a foundation for reform and mechanization.

Labor

The SAJ is a registered trade union of employers formed following a period of "general instability in 1939, which resulted in upheaval" and the formation of 20 or more independent employers, each with separate labor requirements.[95] The SAJ has now grown to comprise 62 members. Its role is to negotiate on behalf of owners with employees' trade unions and to maintain a pool of labor assigned to different shipping lines. Negotiations have resulted in guaranteed pay for workers for five shifts a week composed of 40 hours. Labor rates are determined according to category and specialization. The size of the workforce has been reduced to 205 casual workers.

Before the recent negotiation process (between SAJ, KTO, and PAJ), a gang consisted of 18-20 persons, which was negotiated down to 8 persons. In addition, three flexible start times were introduced to correspond with the new eight-hour shifts, noting a change from seven-hour shifts. The work year previously consisted of 361 days; the changes enabled a 365-day work year. The conditions regarding workweek were also changed; workers could now work any five of seven days, constituting their workweek. Subsequently, the premium charge associated with weekend work was abolished. Labor changes enabled an increase in productivity; workers' earnings also increased. Currently, the ratio of casual to permanent workers is 1:2 (60:120). The port charges flat rates for port workers.

There is a mechanism for addressing labor concerns before they fester into issues. This process is through the Joint Industrial Council, which consists of (1) Bustamante, (2) trade unions, and (3) United Port Workers & Seamen's Unit. The Joint Industrial Council and the SAJ hold monthly meetings between negotiations. The SAJ is glad to acknowledge that there have been no strikes in the past several years.[96]

The SAJ affirms that technological change is welcome and emphasizes that training is available to maintain skills and encourage productivity but that there is minimal cross-training of port workers. The SAJ explains that labor is assigned in two different ways, by the recruiting assignment center or by electronic assignment. The SAJ also serves as a lobby group, presenting labor concerns to the Jamaican government. Labor is authorized by two-year contracts between the SAJ and employees unions, which are renewed once any pending issues have been resolved. Following resolution of, say, workers' compensation concerns, any resultant increase in pay would be paid out as back pay in the event that the resolution did not occur before the contract renewal date.[97]

Performance

The Port of Kingston has witnessed remarkable growth in its transshipment business compared to the growth of domestic cargo. In 1975, Kingston transshipped 6,000 TEUs and handled 50,000 TEUs of domestic cargo. Over the years, the transshipment sector has increased remarkably, consistent with changes in the maritime industry in general. Meanwhile, domestic cargo has witnessed modest growth. In 2000, Kingston transshipped 643,000 TEUs and handled 218,000 TEUs of domestic cargo. The growth of transshipment in Kingston reached its peak in the 1990s when an increase of more than 700 percent was realized in the ten-year period from 1990 to 2000. On the other hand, growth of domestic cargo has been modest, with a 137 percent increase over the same ten-year period.[98]

Kingston Container Terminal has a set target berth occupancy rate of 55 percent and had attained this level by May 2000 but dropped down to 48 percent by November of the same year. In terms of container moves, port efficiency is tracked by the number of moves per gang hour. Class A vessels enjoy the highest moves, at a rate of 21.5 per hour. Classes B and C observe moves of 19 and 18 per hour, respectively. Multipurpose vessels are handled at a rate of 17 moves per hour. On average for the three classes of vessels (A, B, and C), KTO handles approximately 19.5 moves per hour, just below its target rate of 20 moves per hour.[99]

Port tariffs are determined by agreement between the PAJ and individual lines each year. In addition, the PAJ guarantees port productivity each year for the lines, and Kingston Terminal is under obligation to respect the agreement. As such, the PAJ and KTO are constantly revising their operations and looking for ways to increase productivity and efficiency. An example of port tariffs at Kingston is $105.70 cess for a 20-foot container. The $105.70 is the sum of two components, $86.00 for cargo cess and $19.70 for security cess. The word "cess" is the charge that the Shipping Association of Jamaica collects on cargoes coming into Jamaica to cover vacation time, medical expenses, ad overtime pay. Likewise, for a 40-foot container, the charges are $132.00 cess, comprised of $106.50 for cargo cess and $25.50 for security cess.[100]

The port also charges $314 and $537 per 20-foot and 40-foot container, respectively. These charges are assessed primarily on domestic cargo and are for stripping and stuffing. Other related charges include $0.92 per linear meter for berthing and $0.14 per ton for a harbor fee.[101]

Economic Impact

Kingston Free Zone (KFZ): The idea mirrors a similar process (export-processing zone) in Colón, Panama. It was believed that an export-processing zone would attract light manufacturing to spur growth of domestic cargo. The KFZ has been successful. However, it was greatly affected by a downturn in the economy due to the Asian economic crisis and the signing of NAFTA. Consequently, the KFZ is being phased out, and the government is now focusing on information technology and has plans to develop an industrial park along those lines.[102] The selected site is in Portmore, to the west of Kingston, approximately 20 minutes from the airport.

Tourist Centers: Over the past 30 years, the public sector "has triumphed over the development of ports." The private sector was run down and bankrupt. The PAJ purchased the Port of Montego Bay in 1986 and within eight months had accomplished a major turnaround and was realizing a profit. The PAJ also envisions a profit center at Port Antonio by developing it for a specific clientele base, along the lines of exclusive resort areas and cruises.[103]

PAJ: Its mandate is to build modern port facilities to support other sectors of the economy. Cruises earn approximately 15 percent of tourism, which is the country's largest foreign exchange earner.[104] Ocho-Rios is the major cruise port and has a certain level of privatization. The PAJ is contemplating retaining the services of Global Terminal Operators to oversee port operations. The PAJ feels that the local managers have done what they can; however, "efficiency is the bottom line" and will be pursued with vigor, even if it entails trying different approaches. Thus, there are ongoing initiatives to increase efficiency, which may include further restructuring or outsourcing of port activities. The current management contract expires in mid-2001. The PAJ realizes that it is involved in an extremely competitive industry and, to some extent, loyalty plays an important role, so that if ZIM Container Service were to ask for a 30 percent increase in capacity, the PAJ must accommodate the request. The PAJ cites as its current needs: capital, expertise, and networking.

Future Developments

As stated earlier, the PAJ works with "partner" organizations in assessing future needs and leveraging resources to ensure continued success of the port and in meeting the goals of its mission statement "to maintain the position of the Kingston Container Terminal as the leading container transshipment port within the North American region, while utilizing this facility as a catalyst for the development of allied business services and world class standards in port operations."[105]

In its annual report, the PAJ highlights its achievements and details its short-term to medium-term strategic plans. These include the following:

- developing a comprehensive plan for a new phase of expansion of the Kingston Container Terminal over the next two years;

- capitalizing on the increased capacity made available from the earlier expansion program completed in 1996-97 by maximizing container volumes and improving service quality;

- laying the groundwork for future expansion of the container terminal, such as securing appropriate land requirements and developing options for greater private-sector involvement in port operations;

- increasing shareholder value by implementing strategies to increase output, productivity, and efficiency of all the commercial activities of the PAJ;

- expanding the use of information technology to drive all aspects of the PAJ's business; and

- improving the safety of navigation in ports and harbors and updating the regulatory framework to ensure that their policies and programs are supported by the appropriate legislation. [106]

Progress is already underway to realize the goals of its mission statement: a planned expansion of the terminal to include approximately 30-45 more acres. In addition, an estimated $80 million has been invested in the South Terminal expansion project, which involves the construction of 271 meters of quay. In a later phase, another 271 meters will be added. At the same time, new equipment is on order, and there is ongoing training at the Jamaica Maritime Institute, which offers world-class courses.

Lessons Learned

In Kingston, the reform process began as early as 1974, which witnessed governmental intervention in a previously private operation. The subsequent success of the port is attributed to the visionary leadership at that time and to the early investment into what has today become a critical component of port operations—container facilities and transshipment. In 1986, the government intervened once again in a private operation that encountered trouble and rescued the Port of Montego Bay. The PAJ reports having taken over operations at Montego Bay, which was losing money, and turning that venture into a profit-realizing center within only eight months.

Realizing that the industry is a volatile one, the PAJ continues to strive for excellence, as it carves its niche as a major transshipment center in the region. The PAJ has retained the services of Singaporean professionals in the pursuit of increased port productivity and efficiency. In addition, there has been continued investment in the port facilities and search for new customers. As the Port of Kingston approaches the crossroads in its venture, one may wonder whether today's leadership will mirror the business acumen of its predecessors of two and a half decades ago. The current arrangement involves the use of one terminal operator. Will Kingston be further subdivided so that operations are split between the North and South Terminals, along domestic versus transshipment lines? There has been talk of inviting a global terminal operator. Perhaps a different sort of management structure will emerge, with a partnership, so to speak, between local and foreign management companies. The port has compared itself to Singapore and may emulate the developments in the East.

There is some level of uncertainty in Kingston for the moment. What can be said, however, is that Kingston will continue to strive to play the important role that it plays in the region, for maritime trade in general but for transshipment in particular. Furthermore, Kingston is conveniently located to serve as a transshipment center for Cuban cargo, unless of course Havana itself emerges as a competitor, once that lucrative market is opened to the global community. In the meantime, however, what Kingston must focus on is ensuring that port productivity and efficiency remain high, so that it can leverage its resources to propel the port to greater heights. Kingston also stands to gain from diversifying its portfolio as it has done in the past, more so now than before, as the alternate sources of income will be crucial.

Limón-Moín Complex, Costa Rica

Background

The Port of Limón-Moín Complex (the official name of the Port of Limón and the Port of Moín) is a public service port and is the largest of six ports in the Central American country of Costa Rica. Located on the Caribbean coast, the ports are 6 kilometers apart but operate as a single port complex.

Infrastructure

The Port of Limón was constructed in 1904 by the Compañía de Ferrocarriles (National Railroad Company) for the exportation of bananas. It realized subsequent improvements and investment as a multipurpose port in 1968 after the central government became its sole proprietor and committed to a joint venture with the German government to modernize the port.[107] The Port of Moín was constructed in the 1980s as a petroleum terminal and gradually realized variation in its cargo movement by 1984.

The total storage area of the Port of Limón-Moín Complex is 126,800 square meters, of which 7.9 percent is covered and 13.4 percent is used for general cargo. The remainder of storage area is used for containers in transshipment. It is able to accommodate 1,500 TEUs in rows of three and 80 intakes for containers that need refrigeration. The majority of containers that come to Costa Rica are shipped directly to private storage yards that are outside the port area because the port does not have sufficient infrastructure to accommodate the amount of containers that it moves. Therefore, those containers that are housed in the port area are primarily intended for transshipment. The total container area located outside the port complex is 1,800,000 square meters.

Limón

Limón consists of more than 775 meters of docks and 550 meters of breakwaters. The port has a depth ranging from 8 to 10 meters and five moorings for vessels at approximately 1,245 meters in length.[108] The total storage area for Limón is 62,300 square meters, of which 37,800 square meters is allocated for containers.[109] The remaining storage areas are considered for general usage or other types of cargo.

Moín

Moín has more than 550 meters of docks and 210 meters of breakwaters. Its depth ranges from 12 to 13 meters. There are four moorings for vessels at approximately 760 meters in length. The total storage area for Moín is 91,500 square meters, of which 89,000 square meters is used for containers.[110]

Equipment

The Port of Limón-Moín Complex currently operates with one gantry crane and the other equipment listed in Table 3.6.

Table 3.6
Limón-Moín Equipment

Type of Equipment	Amount
Cranes	1
Tugboats	3
Motorboats for pilots	2
Straddle carriers	6
Top-lifters	5
Container forklifts of 2.5 tons	42
Container forklifts of 4.5 tons	11
Container forklifts of 10.0 tons	2
Container forklifts of 15.0 tons	1

Source: Data from Secretaría de Integración Económica de Centro America (SEICA), "Central American Transport Study," Guatemala, November 2000 (draft), n.p.

Operations

Limón has three main docks. The first is the Muelle Alemàn (German Dock), named after its financier. This dock has been in operation since 1982 and is the most modern part of the entire port complex. It consists of two parts: the container terminal and the "Ro-Ro" (roll-on/roll-off) ramp. The cargo area terminal covers approximately 7.5 hectares and has 450 meters of docks. This dock is used primarily for containers, general cargo on pallets, bananas, and some cruise ships. The second dock is the Muelle Setenta (70s Dock), named for the year it was constructed. It is 325 meters long and 71 meters wide and is a multipurpose dock, used primarily for general cargo and occasionally for cruise ships. In general, however, this dock is hardly used because of its inefficiencies. The Ro-Ro ramp and dock used for cruise ships are considered to be the third dock. Constructed in 1998, this dock is the most recent investment in the port's infrastructure. It was constructed primarily for the purpose of servicing cruise ships so that cruise visits would not interfere with the other operations and vessels using the ports.[111] However, the dock was built incorrectly for use as a cruise terminal, and, thus, cruise ships continue to share the part of the Muelle Alemàn with other vessels.[112]

Moín's two primary docks are used for petroleum, banana, and grain export. The petro-dock is equipped with a Ro-Ro ramp that is hardly used because of the newest ramp in Limón. Even though this dock was constructed primarily for petroleum export and import, it also facilitates shipment of bulk grains, fertilizers, general cargo, gravel, and some cruise ships. The other dock at Moín is used primarily for the export of bananas from Chiquita and Dole. This dock, or group of docks, has a length of 525 meters. Moín is currently undergoing a short-term project partially funded by the government of China that will increase its total dock length by 250 meters.[113]

The commodities flowing through the port complex are primarily bananas and other fruits, which constituted 33 percent of the cargo moved in 1998, followed by containerized cargo of textiles and other products, which made up 29 percent. The remainder consists of iron, gravel, petroleum, automobiles, fertilizers, and other general cargo.[114]

Organization

The Ministry of Public Works and Transportation (MOPT) governs the maritime sector of transportation with the general director of Port and River Works. Both public agencies administer policy in the sector and empower the port authorities to administer and operate the ports. In the past, lack of communication and politics caused resentment between the MOPT and the port authorities. Therefore, the National Council on Ports was established as a unified front for the betterment of Costa Rican ports. It comprises representation from the ministry, private companies, the private sector, and port laborers.[115]

The port complex is administrated and operated by JAPDEVA (Junta de Administración Portuaria y de Desarrollo Económico de la Vertiente Atlantico).[116] It was established by law in 1963 to function as the port authority for the Atlantic side of Costa Rica. JAPDEVA was also charged to assume the role of promoting the economical and social development of the areas under its jurisdiction. As a result, JAPDEVA consists of two main branches: the Port Authority and the Administration of Development.[117]

The Port Authority provides services for the development of port activities, such as port operations (i.e., dock assignments, pilots, and tugboats), personnel and budgeting, engineering and maintenance, planning, information and technological support, port security, and prevention of contamination.[118] Other actors in the port are the private stevedore companies and the shipping lines.

Labor

The port complex employs 3,380 people. Of this total, JAPDEVA employs a total of 1,118 direct employees. It does not have casual or seasonal workers. The remaining 2,262 workers are employed by private companies. Most of the port workers belong to the labor union for the Port of Limón, SINTRAJAP, Sindicato Trabajadores JAPDEVA (Union of JAPDEVA Employees). Those that do not belong to the union are employees that JAPDEVA calls "persons of confidence," or employees in managerial positions.

JAPDEVA negotiates labor agreements with SINTRAJAP as long as its demands are well within the scope of JAPDEVA's appropriated budget. Once the union's demands rise above JAPDEVA's budget, the disputes are resolved with the Costa Rican Ministry of Labor.[119] Costa Rica does not have a law prohibiting strikes; therefore, if the Ministry of Labor fails to resolve a dispute with the union, the workers usually go on strike. This has been a common practice over the past 10 to 15 years. There is usually one strike in the Port of Limón per year.[120]

Performance

This port complex ranks as the fifth-largest port in the region and moved a total of 571,957 TEUs in 2000.[121] In 1998, a total of 454,584 TEUs were moved. In 1999, the port realized an increase to 590,259 TEUs.[122] Together, these ports are responsible for almost 100 percent of the container traffic in Costa Rica and 90 percent of the country's total exports.[123] Moreover, Limón and Moín facilitate 80 percent of the country's total trade.[124]

Customs agents are not under the administration of JAPDEVA and thus are autonomous of the port. Similar to problems found in other Latin American ports, the customs officials in the Port of Limón pose problems for overall port efficiency and time. Port services are offered to vessels on a 24-hour basis, but customs officials make their services available only during regular business hours and close at 4 p.m. Therefore, shipping agents are forced to either employ the services of customs brokers or have their cargo wait in the port until the operating hours of the customs officials, which, at both points, is an additional cost for the shipping lines.

Competition

There is no competition between the Port of Limón and the other Costa Rican ports of Caldera, Punta Morales, Terminal de Fertica, Puntarenas, Quepos, and Golfito, which are located on the Pacific Coast. Intraport competition for operators is nonexistent because JAPDEVA is the only port authoritative body. Competition does exist among the private stevedore companies and is regulated by JAPDEVA.

Reform Process

The Port of Limón has not undergone a process of reform, but many officials are optimistic that it will realize the privatization process in the near future. As of the spring of 2001 and after the research for this case study was complete, the privatization process was initiated on the Pacific Coast of Costa Rica. It is predicted that similar initiatives will take place on the Caribbean coast before the end of the year.

The only services that are privatized in the port are the stevedoring services. The stevedores were privatized from the early 1970s. Gradually, the three main companies formed an oligopoly that kept tariffs high. In 1995, JAPDEVA broke the oligopoly by allowing other private companies to compete for clients. Tariffs were cut almost in half as gang sizes dropped from 96 persons to 40; service was also substantially improved.[125]

Today, there are 11 private stevedoring companies that operate in the Port of Limón. Tariffs and gang sizes are not fixed. Each company establishes its own tariffs with the approval of a national office called ARESEP, Autoridad Reguladora de los Servicios Publicos (Regulating Authority for Public Services), which also approves the tariffs of JAPDEVA. Additionally, the shipping clients also have to pay a tariff to JAPDEVA for the use of the port and the stevedoring services.

Because of long relationships between the stevedores and the various shipping lines and agents, formal contracts are rare, as in the case of Chiquita Brands.[126] With the absence of a formal contract, under law, Chiquita can contract with another stevedoring company, but for various social reasons and assuredness, it chooses to remain with its current service provider. Subsequent to the deregulation of the stevedoring services, some shipping lines have chosen to establish contracts. These contracts can be for six months to a year and are written for specific types of cargo. In addition to the individual contracts that the stevedores have with their clients, stevedores also have a contract to provide services in the port with JAPDEVA. These contracts are established through a bidding process in which each company has to present a plan of services to JAPDEVA. The Ministry of Transport and the Ministry of Labor handle all contract disputes.

Economic Impacts

The Port of Limón directly employs a total of 3,380 people. This number includes both JAPDEVA and private companies' employees. Furthermore, 70 percent of Limón's population are dependent on the port indirectly.[127] Therefore, the economical effects that port activities have on the local economy are significant. In addition, JAPDEVA sets aside 10 percent of the port's earnings to invest in the educational and social development of the local community.

The opposition to port privatization maintains that the change will thwart the social and educational investment that JAPDEVA currently undertakes in the community. However, the Plan for Regional Development that was produced by JAPDEVA forecasts that the Limón area will benefit immensely from a more efficient port. Subsequently, this increased investment in the port will spur investment in five other economic sectors: tourism, "agri-industry," environmental preservation (as subsidies from foreign governments), local infrastructure, and agriculture. This economic spillover is expected to increase the overall standard of living in Limón, thus improving the economic, social, and educational sectors of the community.

Future Developments

The strategic plan for the Port of Limón began in 1995 as a result of the exponential increase in the volume of cargo it was moving: especially container traffic and vessel visits. The governmental authorities of the port solicited the Japanese Institute for Foreign Coastal Development to conduct a study and analyze the situation of the ports and the development system in place in order to modernize the Costa Rican ports system. The result was a strategic plan to be accomplished over 15 years and be completed by 2010. The institute compiled recommendations for investment in infrastructure, purchase of equipment, change in the methods of port operations, and a reduction in the labor force. Some have called this recommendation a radical administrative reform proposition.[128]

The short-term goals of this plan are embedded in the obtainment of new equipment and investment in the port infrastructure. Currently, the Port of Limón is awaiting further investment to complete its cruise ship terminal, which is expected to cost 600 million colónes. JAPDEVA has been awaiting a Panamax crane that was ordered in 1995 at a cost of $5.3 million. It has also been awaiting three straddle carriers, 30 2.5-ton forklifts, and six toplifters.

Included in the plan of modernization is the reparation of the container storage yard at a cost of 60 million colónes, a new security system at 15 million colónes, the purchase of dock cranes at a cost of 20 million colónes, and channel dredging and maintenance for 150,000 cubic meters at a cost of $1.5 million.[129]

Current projects for the Port of Moín include the completion of an additional 250 meters of length on the Taiwanese dock, which has already been initiated and is expected to have a final cost of $8.203 million. A container yard for support of this dock is also envisioned at a cost of 670 million colónes. In addition, the port is expected to purchase a gantry crane and other necessary equipment needed to efficiently operate the Taiwanese dock as a container terminal. Plans of dredging to 12 meters in depth at a cost of $2 million and acquisition of land for port expansion, expected to cost 800 million colónes, are also part of the strategic plan for Moín.

Similar to the plans for the Port of Limón, establishment of a modern security system is also projected, along with facilities to house agents, customs officials, and JAPDEVA personnel to assist with various documentation needs. Moreover, Moín is expected to obtain a technologically advanced system of lighting and traffic signaling for a safer, more efficient way to load, unload, and transport cargo in the cargo yard. These three investments are expected to cost 1.75 billion colónes.[130] These projects have been in a stagnant stage since 1995 and have been awaiting political and financial support from the central government.

Operating with only one crane, the Port of Limón is in need of investment. Whether or not privatization is its panacea is still questionable. Opponents to privatization hold that the resulting economic impact would be detrimental to the local community, a result that can be cushioned by other means. Lying at the heart of this opposition, however, are historical sentiments and the fear of losing leverage with the national government.

The need for private investment is exhibited by the inactiveness on the part of the government with the strategic infrastructure plans for the port complex. In its initial stages, subsequent to the release of the study conducted by the Japanese consulting firm mentioned earlier, JAPDEVA requested a Panamax crane to alleviate the congestion caused by the increase in the volume of containers handled in the port. The crane was requested in 1995 and, to date, has not been purchased or delivered. The central government does not have sufficient capital to make the purchase order for the crane.[131]

Consequently, some JAPDEVA officials, along with many local shipping agents, see privatization as inevitable and the only means of obtaining the much-needed infrastructure to bring the Limón-Moín port complex to international levels of productivity.[132] In general, private shipping agents and shipping lines feel that JAPDEVA, although bureaucratic in culture and practice, has made strides toward improving the services of the port complex.[133]

Lessons Learned

The obstacles preventing reform are abstruse. Some have claimed that a lack of national leadership inhibits advancement in port reform, while others assert that the government has made many strides toward restructuring the port system and that the main opposition is found within the workers and the port officials. Barriers to port reform in Costa Rica, however, can be found on both sides of the bargaining table.

Lack of national leadership has been a stumbling block on the road to reform. In the past, legislation allowing privatization of public services was greatly opposed in the legislature, and executives distanced themselves from a topic they considered to be self-destructive. Because Costa Rica is a socialist country, the word *privatization*, alone, daunts politicians, not to mention the average citizen. Privatization connotes the "selling off of national land," which yields a presentiment of treachery in the eyes of many Costa Ricans. Therefore, privatizing any major public service has proved to be a challenge for the national government.[134] Other shortcomings of the government include lack of communication and confidence with the residents of Limón.

A continuing political debate is that the province of Limón receives less public investment than other provinces of equal or smaller size. Therefore, the residents of Limón, as employees of a port that is responsible for 90 percent of the national trade, have used the port as a tool to obtain what they believe to be equality. Actions of this nature primarily consist of port strikes to obtain more funding from the government for schools and other services provided by public funds.

The government's failures in fulfilling promises made to the province of Limón, such as better schools, roads, and clinics, have strengthened the role of the labor unions in the area. Because there is only one access road into Limón, workers and union members have found it quite easy to block off this road and literally put the Costa Rican economy on hold until they obtain the public services they feel they are due.

Opponents to reform in the port are also a barrier to privatization. Most of JAPDEVA's port officials and laborers acknowledge the need for privatization in their port. Others are more comfortable professing the necessity of investment in the port's infrastructure, while recognizing private capital as a means of obtaining the required venture. Their objections arise in the negative outcomes that privatization of the port will bring for the city of Limón. The primary concerns of these officials are the loss of jobs and a decrease of local investment that JAPDEVA currently provides in the town.[135]

The labor union of the Port of Limón, SINTRAJAP, constitutes a large part of opposition to reform. Opinion is divided regarding the role that the labor union will play once the process of reform begins. The unions view the transfer of the port over to private corporations as equivalent to a transfer of their political power in Costa Rica.

Some officials of JAPDEVA express remorse but accentuate that the economic misfortune of some port workers will be temporary. These officials maintain that increased efficiency and performance in the port will stimulate other forms of employment that will ultimately alleviate the burden caused by privatization.[136]

Rio Haina, Dominican Republic

Background

The Port of Haina, or Rio Haina as it is often called, sits at the mouth of the Haina River just west of the municipal limits of Santo Domingo. Santo Domingo, the capital city of the Dominican Republic, is a modern city of more than two million inhabitants. Rio Haina is the primary container port for the capital city and for the entire nation of seven million. The port benefits from its location on the southern shore of Hispaniola in the central part of the Caribbean very near the Panama-European trade lane and receives transshipment traffic because of its location. Rio Haina has averaged more than 400,000 TEU moves per year in recent years, making it one of the 15 most active ports in the LAC region. In the 1990s, the port saw a tremendous explosion in container traffic, a reported fivefold increase in TEU moves in ten years. This increase was the result of a rapidly growing economy, increased port infrastructure, and possibly better accounting of throughput. The port also serves as the primary entrance point for petroleum products into the country and as an important bulk port of agricultural products as well.

Infrastructure

The Port of Haina is made up of the two sides of the mouth of the Haina River. The sides, referred to as Rio Haina Oriental (East Haina) and Rio Haina Occidental (West Haina), are under the control of the Autoridad Portuaria Dominicana, the Dominican Port Authority. In Rio Haina Occidental, the west side of the river, CSX Corporation and Maersk/Sealand have a concession to manage the terminal. The terminal has two large gantry cranes, one 35-ton and one 40-ton, and a berth length of 450 meters with 9.7 meters of depth alongside. Rio Haina Oriental has two gantry cranes with 273 meters of berth length and a similar alongside depth. The port authority has concessions agreements with more than 15 private firms to conduct stevedoring activities in this half of the port. The terminal area for both sides of the river totals more than 10 hectares, with an overall storage area of more than 30 hectares. The port is not served by ship-to-shore computer technology or with computerized movement of land-side containers. And though many tariffs are figured from the number of tons moved, the port is without a functioning container scale, and charges are calculated by the weight ticket from the previous port. The level of technological advancement at the port is minimal, which contributes to the remaining high level of manual labor.

Operations

The compilation of statistics for the Port of Haina is the sole responsibility of the Dominican Port Authority. The authority provides yearly totals for all types of ship visits and tons moved in each of the ports in the country. Rio Haina Occidental, the CSX and Maersk side, saw 302 cargo ship visits in 1999, while the oriental side had 1,766 cargo ship visits during the same period. Total containerized metric tons moved in 1999 was 2,257,000. The occidental side accounted for 659,000 metric tons, while the oriental side moved 1,598,000 metric tons. These figures show that the CSX/Maersk port area moved an average of 2,180 metric tons/ship, while the oriental side moved an average of 905 metric tons/ship, reflecting that the oriental side is still used for the unloading of much breakbulk cargo and the occidental side concentrates on containers and handles very little "loose" cargo. The breakdown of tons moved is interesting and instructive to larger trends in the country. The two sides of the Port of Haina saw 1,786,000 metric tons of containerized imports, while total containerized exports were 470,000 metric tons. This 4:1 import-to-export ratio reflects the overall trade imbalance facing the nation.

Though container movements account for a great deal of the activity at the Port of Haina, it is not the port's principal activity. The port moves 2.4 million tons of products in breakbulk and loose grains. Additionally the port is the primary entrance point for liquid petroleum products into the country.

Accurate statistics for container movements in the Port of Haina are made difficult because of the fact that more than 15 companies have stevedoring contracts to work the docks. While the port authority is charged with the collection and compilation of these statistics, the movement totals have been, at best, confusing and, at worst, unavailable. During a visit to the port in December 2000, a member of the research team was unable to obtain information for container movements, partially attributable to the fact that most of the workers in the port authority had recently changed. A change in the national governance resulted in a change of all civil employees, including those of the ports. The new personnel placed in the ports were relatively unfamiliar with the functioning of the port. A quick survey of typical sources of historical yearly TEU movement data shows similar problems.[137]

For most ports, *Containerisation International* (CI) gives yearly TEU movements; however, for Rio Haina, the most recent numbers are for 1994, which are given only as estimates. CI lists Rio Haina's 1992 and 1994 TEU movements as 87,194 and 139,719, respectively.[138] In *Strategies for Global and Regional Ports,* the Policy Research Corporation of the Netherlands gives a 1992 value of 87,000 TEU movements, matching CI's. However, the Policy Research Corporation's number for 1994 TEU movements is 198,000,[139] 42 percent greater than CI's number. The difference cannot be explained by the counting of moves of empty containers, because the source for the smaller value, the CI Website, includes empty moves in its total. The ECLAC Webpage *Perfil Marítimo de América Latina y El Caribe* has the yearly TEU movements for many ports. Rio Haina has an entry only for 1999 with 415,629[140] movements, suggesting that between the years of 1992 and 1999, Rio Haina experienced a 25 percent average annual increase in container movements. Though the country's economy saw tremendous growth during this period, yearly increases this large seem unlikely and most likely are partially attributable to inaccurate data.

Organization

In December 1970, the National Congress passed Law No. 70 and created the Dominican Port Authority, which was given complete control of all activities in every port in the nation and responsibility for all infrastructure and superstructure at the ports. This law allows the port authority to continue to operate the Port of Haina as a tool port by signing concession agreements with different private corporations. The concession agreements are usually for three-year periods and are public documents. These agreements define the amount a company pays the port authority for the use of the cranes and also the amount of area a company may use for container storage. Historically, the Dominican Port Authority has been less powerful than a direct reading of the law would imply. The national government in the Dominican Republic has not been entirely stable in the last 30 years, though recently the country has made strides toward greater stability. This instability has caused frequent changes in the management of the port authority, leading to a lack of cohesive long-range plans for the country's ports. Because the port authority is directly under the control of the ruling party, it is used as a mechanism to deliver rewards to the party faithful. This favoritism leads to the possibility of making decisions based on political considerations and not on sound economic reasoning, which is easily seen in the number of ports on the island. Though the Dominican Republic has only seven million citizens living on the island, there are 11 functioning ports. Each port has governmental positions that must be filled and union workers who vote and riot when they become unhappy.

The stevedoring companies have formed a group called the Asociación de Naverios de la Republica Dominicana, or ANRD (Dominican Shippers Association). The association is made up of 19 private companies, the largest company being Maersk/Sealand. Though these companies are in direct competition, they work together when signing contracts with the various unions at the ports and also sponsor training sessions for the dock workers.

Reform Process

The laws governing port activity in the Dominican Republic have changed little in the 30 years since Law No. 70 was signed. It is generally agreed that the current legal structure makes it difficult to raise the required capital to improve the nation's ports. Concession agreements can be signed for only ten years at a time, a period far too short for a private company to recoup a large investment. A notable exemption to this law is the contract Sealand signed in the 1970s, under which it continues to the present to have exclusive operating rights to the cranes on the west bank of the port. The company apparently obtained a right of renewal in its contract, though the legal basis for this right is questionable. The contract reveals a problem in the process. Any large concession contract is taken up on an ad hoc basis with negotiations taking place at the highest levels of the Dominican government behind closed doors. The process was repeated recently in the obtaining of permission for two greenfield port developments near Santo Domingo. Two different projects, Puerto Caucedo and Puerto Tortuguero, have been approved by the government for construction by private corporations to build and later manage. The Caucedo project received approval in 1998, but construction had not yet begun in April 2001.

Labor

All the ports in the Dominican Republic are unionized. There are different unions for each port activity: the Port of Haina has the Sindicato de Arrimo (Union of Security, for safe container movements), Unión Sindical de Estibadores del Puerto de Haina (Port of Haina Stevedores Union), and Sindicato Unido del 3½ de Ambos Lados del Puerto de Haina (Union of the Two Sides of the Port of Rio Haina at 3½). These unions combine to form the Federación Regional Portuaria de Haina (Haina Regional Port Federation) at the local level and are associated with the Federación Dominicana de los Trabajabores Portuarios (Dominican Federation of Port Workers) at the national level. The Federación Regional is responsible for drafting labor contracts with the ANRD, which the union workers then approve. Each port has its own contract. The labor agreements are usually for periods of three years. Silvio Ureña Mendoza, the secretary general of the Federación Dominicana de los Trabajabores Portuarios, states there are no large labor issues with the ANRD. Historically, the contracts have been signed with few problems and strikes, which, when necessary, have been very short.[141]

The number of workers at the Port of Haina suggests a lack of technical advancement. Mendoza explains that the three unions of Rio Haina have a total of more than 1,300 full-time members. During the busiest times of the year the number can swell to more than 2,000 workers at the port.[142] Unfortunately, there are no port efficiency statistics kept by the port authority, but a quick estimate can be attempted. Rio Haina moves 415,629 TEUs in a year with around 1,300 full-time union employees, for an average of 300 TEU moves/year/employee.[143]

Performance

The current pricing system in the Port of Haina is not consistent and is not publicly stated. The port authority uses a public document issued by the president of the Dominican Republic setting the tariffs to be paid to the state for port services. Decree No. 572-99 lists the charges the authority sets for the users of the ports, and the section for container trade states the tariffs to be charged to members of the ANRD. The tariffs for imports in containers are set at $2.00 per metric ton; the tariffs for exports are set at one-quarter of the amount, $0.50 per metric ton. The document states charges for container entrance and exit fees, container storage fees, crane hire, and several others associated with the ship's entrance into the port. However, two issues surface when calculating the total costs of moving cargo in the port. First, the majority of the charges are set as a percentage of the bill paid to the private company completing the work. These private companies are very protective of their pricing systems as there is a great deal of competition for business. So the largest part of the bill is dependent on costs that are privately arrived at between the customer and the shipping agent. A second issue is that a large portion of the governmental charges are calculated on a metric-ton basis, yet the one scale at the port seldom works and is not often used.

All of this aside, the Port of Haina saw explosive growth throughout the 1990s and was generally thought to have very reasonable port costs. Rio Haina is the lowest-priced port for import/export tariffs on a 20-foot container at $280 per unit. The port was also very competitive on transshipment rates with a cost of $80 per container.[144] The low costs at the port are certainly in part caused by the great competition among the private shipping agents. However, low labor costs contribute as well. Of the ten ports included in the tariff study, the Dominican Republic also has the lowest national average earnings per worker.[145]

A hidden cost at the port is due to the lack of security. Federico Schad, the vice president of F. Schad Shipping Agents and former president of the ANRD, believes the largest current problem in the port is theft of merchandise. Additionally, he said that a large number of hours are lost each day because containers must be rearranged and placed so that the doors cannot be broken and items stolen.[146]

There are few studies available that examine the efficiency of the Port of Haina. One study conducted in December 1999 calculates the total tons of cargo moved in the port divided by the number of workers registered at the port. The port moves 4,083 tons per worker.[147]

Competition

Intraport

There is much competition inside the port. Though the members of the ANRD work together when signing contracts with the various labor unions and often stand united in discussions with the port authority, they are in direct pricing competition for container movements.

Interport

The Port of Haina is the most active port in the Dominican Republic, but it is not without competition from within the country. Ports at Santo Domingo and Puerto Plata also move large quantities. However, because all the ports are managed by one entity and the port authority can determine where a ship will dock, unfettered competition does not exist. Internationally, the competition is more fierce. It has been reported that transshipment accounted for 56 percent of the activity in the port in 1996.[148] The majority of this transshipment took place on the occidental side of the port. During this time, Sealand was conducting a great deal of its Caribbean transshipment on the island. However, with the construction of the large transshipment port at Freeport in the Bahamas, much of this activity has been lost. Transshipment quantities have fallen from a high in 1997 of 1,194,158 metric tons to 176,399 metric tons in 1999, which amounts to an 85 percent decline in transshipped volumes over just two years. The overall activity in the port has increased solely because of increases in importation.

Future Developments

Strategic Plans

In 1994, the Inter-American Development Bank financed a study of the Dominican port system. Two basic problems were identified: "1) Investments are needed to rehabilitate and improve port infrastructure, and to buy new equipment. A better use of the existent infrastructure is also recommendable, in terms of operations, administration and maintenance. 2) Reform of legal framework, to allow for more private participation at ports. The government does not have enough resources to finance all required work to rehabilitate port facilities. However, many private investors, who could be potentially attracted to the sector are probably not willing to risk entering into the business in the present conditions because the environment is not completely adequate to offer guarantees for their investments."[149] The legal structure for granting concessions must become more transparent, allowing for open bidding among private firms for long-term contracts, if the capital to upgrade infrastructure is to be raised.

There are periodic strategic long-range plans formulated for the port system of the Dominican Republic. Aside from the previously mentioned study conducted by the Inter-American Development Bank, Curaçao Port Developers, N.V., also did a study on the port. The study was completed during the last administration, and a copy was unavailable during a visit to the port in January 2001. The implementation of the plan seems unlikely under the new administration.

The Outlook for the Port of Haina

The outlook for and challenges to the Port of Haina require a wider view to understand. The strong growth experienced at the port in the 1990s coincided with a period of rapid growth in the GDP for the country as a whole. However, the port has experienced a recent decline in transshipment due to foreign competition. Additionally, Rio Haina has significant draft problems that do not allow large fully laden ships to enter the port. This problem is due to silting caused by deforestation in the mountains above the port. Therefore, dredging is often necessary. Also, there are possible challenges to the port from within the country. For several years there has been talk of a large greenfield private port development, spearheaded by CSX, to serve a free-trade zone on the other side of Santo Domingo. If this port is ever constructed, Rio Haina would experience an immediate decrease in volume. Rio Haina is in need of capital expenditures if it is to approach efficiency levels seen in other Latin ports. To reach this goal, the current system of ad hoc negotiations directly between private firms and the national port authority and ultimately the president of the Dominican Republic must be changed. A transparent and stable method of offering competitive bidding for long-term concessions must be sought.

Lessons Learned

There has been little change in the management structure of Dominican ports in the last 30 years. There has been no systemic reform of port laws. The ports have been managed since 1970 as tool ports with highly centralized organizational structures, which have limited the funding sources for port expenditures and have also led to a lack of modern infrastructure. As a result, the efficiency of Dominican ports is low.

The Port of Haina is in need of both capital investments and organizational changes. The defects in infrastructure at the port reflect the government's inability to either fund the needed changes without private inputs or create the necessary legal framework to encourage private involvement. The one site with significant private control, Rio Haina Occidental, was an ad hoc contract without firm legal grounding negotiated at the highest levels of the Dominican government.

Though these problems do exist in the Port of Hiana, there have been positive signs. The port has seen an incredible growth over the past ten years, with an annual growth rate of nearly 6 percent.[150] There is also tremendous competition as nearly 20 firms fight for container movements. The presence of competition has kept the port's related prices below average for the region.[151] So, though there are many changes that could be made to improve the port's efficiency, the port compares favorably in prices and continues to see increases in volume handled.

San Antonio, Chile

Background

The Port of San Antonio is located in the Central Valley region of Chile, approximately 100 kilometers from the capital and largest city, Santiago, and 60 kilometers south of Valparaiso, Chile's third-largest city and historically its most important port.

The main characteristics of Chilean maritime commerce are the concentration of the bulk of the nation's traffic located in the Central Valley region, with the majority of the exports being seasonal agricultural goods. Chile's trade needs are for exports of the hinterland products, as well as for satisfying domestic demands of imported manufactured goods. Cabotage traffic is minimal but has potential for expansion because of Chile's long coast. Therefore, growth in the maritime sector has traditionally been focused in the Central Valley area, where the majority of the national export production and import consumption are concentrated. San Antonio has developed because of its advantageous position in the Central Valley area and because of congestion and restriction on landside capacity for expansion in the Port of Valparaiso.[152]

In the last decade, Chile has liberalized trade barriers, producing an overall expansion in its export sector.[153] These exports have been mainly concentrated in agricultural goods, which, coupled with a weak production of industrial goods, has meant imports of most manufactured goods from abroad.

Infrastructure

The Port of San Antonio consists of five terminals. Two of these terminals are equipped to handle container traffic: the multioperator terminal (known as the "Espigón") and the

San Antonio International Terminal (STI), operated by a joint venture between Stevedoring Services of America (SSA) and Sudamericana Agencias Aéreas y Maritimas S.A. (SAAM), which received the concession to operate the Molo Sur area of the Port of San Antonio.

The Espigón consists of four berths, two on each side of its dock area. Berths 4 and 5 have 341 meters of docking space, while Berths 6 and 7 together have 370 meters. The range of draft in the Espigón is between 6.1 meters and 9.4 meters.[154]

STI consists of three adjacent berths that total 565 meters in berth space. It has a draft of 10.8 meters. STI also has the only four gantry cranes in Chile, supported by four RTGs that work a cargo yard of 4.4 hectares.[155]

Operations

The Port of San Antonio has experienced tremendous growth in container traffic since 1990. Since the concession of STI was awarded in 1999, the total container growth has continued its incline. The total amount of TEUs moved at San Antonio has increased from 415,001 in 1998 to 455,604 in 2000.[156] It is not prudent to attribute any growth in TEU traffic to the port concession process at this time, however, because the upward trend began before the private operation began in 1999.

The efficiency at the port has improved. The additional gantry cranes installed at STI have made TEU movements of 25-30/hour possible, an improvement from 8-10 moves/hour before privatization.[157]

Organization

Currently, the two largest ports in Chile—Valparaiso and San Antonio—have been operating under the new "hybrid"[158] system since 1997. The Port of San Antonio made a concession of its main container terminal, the Molo Sur, to a joint venture between SSA and SAAM,[159] known as STI. The concession contract for the Molo Sur Terminal is for a 20-year term, with an option to renew for another 10 years. In return, the SSA/SAAM consortium paid $121.3 million up front, plus an additional surcharge on all cargo of $7.50/ton for the duration of the contract. With the investment made by STI, the Port of San Antonio has become the premier container port in Chile, overtaking Valparaiso—which had traditionally been the primary port of the country.

The Port of San Antonio is under the administration of the Empresa Portuaria de San Antonio, a decentralized entity that administers the common areas of the port, as well as coordinating cargo handling in the multioperator port (the Espigón). The existence of the multioperator Espigón conforms to the "tool" model; the state provides both the infrastructure and the port equipment, while private operators provide the cargo-handling services. The existence of the STI concession, conforms to the "landlord" model: the state provides the infrastructure, and the concessionaire invests in superstructure equipment to conduct operations.

Reform Process

The 1981 Reform

The port privatization process in Chile has undergone several stages of development that have slowly devolved control of port operations from the state-owned port authority, Empresa Portuaria Chilena (EMPORCHI) under a "service port" model, to private producers under a "landlord port" scheme.[160] Under the EMPORCHI system, the port infrastructure belonged to state enterprise, and all land-side cargo handling was performed by EMPORCHI employees.[161] All on-deck cargo handling was the realm of cargo-handling crews that were certified by the Dirección del Territorio Marítimo y Marina Mercante, which issued a limited number of certifications—resulting in a fixed number of workers who were allowed to work in the port. This system resulted in abuses by laborers who were de facto owners of the right to work in the port as a direct result of the closed nature of port employment.[162] At the same time, the state operated a monopoly in port operations throughout the nation, via the centralized structure of the EMPORCHI system. Chilean ports were characterized by their inefficiency in cargo handling, strong labor control over port operations, and high costs for port users.[163]

The initial reform was undertaken in 1981 with the enactment of two port laws, Nos. 18.042 and 18.032, which restructured the national port system by permitting private operators in the ports for the first time and eliminating the licensing system for stevedores, removing this labor market from union control.[164] In order to reduce the social impact of the port reform of 1981, the government offered severance packages that indemnified the 2,700 who were displaced by the restructuring of the port system.

The 1981 reform produced the multioperator arrangement that persisted until the reforms of 1997. Under the 1981 scheme, private operators were allowed to handle the cargo in each of the EMPORCHI-owned ports, which is essentially a "tool port" arrangement.[165] The resulting port arrangement was known as the "Espigón," in which each private operator in the port was granted the right to operate in the port but was obligated to share the use of the infrastructure of the port. Scheduling use of port equipment, as well as the lack of investment in infrastructure, began to cause delays in the larger ports as calls increased during Chile's economic boom of the 1980s and 1990s.[166] Additionally, the labor arrangement promoted additional inefficiency because the laborers in the port were required to be licensed by the Maritime Authority, which also reserved the authority to assign labor to the port operators. This arrangement meant that laborers were not allowed to contract directly with the port operators, leaving the majority of port laborers as part-time workers,[167] with little sense of commitment to any one employer, who in turn could not offer additional incentives to employees for improved performance.[168]

The 1995 Reform

With the realization that the reforms undertaken in 1981 were incomplete and insufficient to satisfy the needs of a national economy fully integrated into the global marketplace, the government sought additional measures.[169] What was needed was a way to attract major investment into the ports so that governmental resources were freed for more needy projects,[170] while increasing efficiency and decreasing total costs for port customers.[171] There were two options: to promote development of new private ports to be built from the ground up, or to revamp the existing infrastructure at public ports.[172] It was decided that the latter course would be preferable, because of space limitations for feasible port sites on the coast and the favorable geography of the established public port sites, which would mean a smaller overall necessary investment. The reform plan was proposed in 1995 and spent two years in the Congress before being enacted as Port Law No. 19.542 in 1997.[173]

The reform process had two main features: the concession of entire terminals at the major ports (San Antonio, San Vicente, and Valparaiso) to one private operator over a long term and the decentralization of the port administration to regional port authorities. The first prong of this plan was implemented in order to attract the large-scale private investment necessary for modernizing the port infrastructure. The second part of the plan was undertaken in order to promote competition between national ports and purge the last vestiges of central control over port operations from EMPORCHI. The plan was to privatize cautiously, as had been done in the past, by concessioning only one terminal at each port in the beginning, in order to dampen the social and economic impact of the elimination of the small operators and the downsizing of stevedoring gangs that the concession process implied.[174] The end goal of the 1997 port reform law has been to evolve eventually to a mono-operator system for the terminals at the port.[175]

The other main concern with private concessions was to prevent the trading of a public monopoly for a private one, which is the other justification for maintaining a competitive environment in the port.[176] The preservation of the Espigón at both Valparaiso and San Antonio has been seen as an effort to counterbalance any potential monopoly abuses by the concessionaires in those ports.[177] The resulting arrangement in theory is a sort of public-private partnership in the operation of the port. Each port is managed by the state, in the form of the autonomous port authority, which acts on behalf of all the port operators.[178]

A continued state presence at the ports in the multioperator terminals is not the only mechanism for regulating competition. The 1997 port reform law also establishes several minimum performance standards for port concessionaires, with penalties for non-compliance.[179] The law guarantees performance by establishing maximum port tariff, a maximum berth time for a ship, and other contractual "incentives" designed to punish the concessionaire for not achieving a minimum level of performance. Failure to comply with the minimum performance levels results in contractually determined fines assessed by the port authority that include termination of the concession in the most-extreme cases.

The 1997 reform law also had built-in safeguards limiting the level for horizontal and vertical integration of the terminal concessionaires. The concession group could not hold more than 40 percent of an interest in another maritime transport link, such as shipping; nor could it hold more than 15 percent interest in one port concession if 25 percent was held in another concession in Chile. These are antimonopoly measures, designed to prevent consolidation of vital port concessions in the hands of an entity that could potentially abuse its favorable market position because of allegiance to other interests.[180]

Because Chilean ports do not have enough traffic to justify granting concessions to multiple concessionaires in port, the concession policy has implemented a series of requirements that allow a concession to one terminal operator, without fear of monopoly abuses. This model is an interesting solution to this common problem. Whether the Chilean model will be successful will depend on whether the objectives established to justify promulgation of a mono-operator system are fulfilled.

Labor

Organized labor at San Antonio has lost a significant part of the power that it exercised before commencement of the reform process in 1981. Since the 1997 reform, organized labor has lost control over determining the assignment of labor to the mono-operator ports, which had been empowered to enter into negotiations with their own employees without intervention by industry unions.[181]

One of the primary goals of the reform process was to reform the uncompetitive situation in the ports because of the structure of EMPORCHI and labor relations, especially the initial 1981 reform.[182] Opening the port labor market as well as the devolution of port operations severely undermined union control over port operations and is regarded as the catalyst for improvement of port performance during the 1980s and 1990s.[183]

During the interregnum between 1981 and 1997, the operator/labor relations were characterized by the creation of a national list of registered port workers that were assigned to the individual operators at the Espigón, resulting in a large labor pool of mostly part-time workers with no permanent contracts. Structurally, this system was acceptable because of the cyclical nature of port employment, which peaked during the months of the fruit harvest but tailed off outside this season.[184] Nevertheless, while this system may have provided employment for a wider base of the employment pool in the port community, that employment was not full time and often did not offer private operators any incentive to invest in training for their employees.[185] Coupled with the lack of cooperative operator/labor relations was the worldwide trend toward containerization that changed the nature of port operations from being labor intensive to requiring capital investment to stay competitive in terms of performance. There was an excess of labor in the port; yet at the same time a negotiation had to be made with labor leaders in order to dampen the social impact of the concession process.[186] Because the 1997 reform would transform the status of port workers from employees of the state to becoming ordinary workers in the private sector, guaranteed rights awarded government workers would be lost.

The 1997 reform implemented a plan of voluntary retirement with indemnification for those who met certain requirements of seniority in port employment.[187] Port workers were allowed to enter into negotiations with the private concessionaires, and by the end of 2000, 1,000 workers had signed contracts for full-time work at the private terminals.[188] Generally, these employees are better paid than their counterparts were during the multioperator scheme, and they are employed full time. Labor unions are allowed within the port per the Chilean labor code, but industrywide collective bargaining is no longer allowed.[189] Rodolfo García of the Maritime Chamber of Commerce of Chile, points out that because 80 percent of the cargo in Chile is moved by the large cargo-handling companies, which hire 90 percent of the labor, and because the strict terms of the concession contracts punish any sort of delay or shutdown at the concessionaire terminal, industrywide collective bargaining would prove to be too much of a disadvantage for terminal operators who would be disproportionately injured by a strike.[190] Labor leaders are concerned about the weakening of their position by the fragmentation of their movement. They see the fragmentation as undermining the only tool that they have ever been able to effectively use in protecting their rights, collective action.[191] Miguel Oses Lorca of the International Federation of Labor points out that the weakening of labor unions coincides with a strengthening of multinational corporations such as SSA, a Seattle-based corporation that received the concession for San Antonio. Oses Lorca observes that while Chilean workers at STI are not allowed to organize collectively with their counterparts in other ports, no one prevents SSA consolidation in operation ventures in several key ports along the north/south trade corridor. Why isn't the international monopoly power of SSA of equal concern to the Chilean government?

The weight of labor concerns with the 1997 reforms is the limited indemnification of port workers. Because the post-1981 system placed most cargo-handling workers under part-time employment status, most do not fulfill the requirements for employment that would qualify them for indemnification. Additionally, the union is concerned with the high incidents of accidents and work-related deaths among port workers, which they attribute to a lack of safety training.[192] The private industry views increased safety certification as another attempt by unions to control the certification of who will be allowed to work in the port, much as the *matriculación* was used in the past.[193]

The area of labor relations will prove to be the biggest challenge for the Chilean government to resolve during the port reform process. The social impacts in terms of unemployment and erosion of labor rights deserve attention because of their long- and short-term implications for Chilean society. The government should direct more of the significant revenue that it is receiving from the port concessionaires toward programs that diffuse the social tension or offset any negative impact resulting from the reform process. Job retraining programs that minimize the missing income for port worker families and their communities need to be expanded so that these workers gain the skills necessary to find work at or greater than the level they earned during their workdays at the port.

Performance

STI has fulfilled two of the goals expected of the concession process: there has been tremendous investment in port infrastructure, and the efficiency of port operations has doubled. As mentioned above, STI is the only terminal in Chile that is equipped with gantry cranes and RTGs. Total investment in the terminal will top $65 million over the next five years.[194]

Port operations have improved significantly as well. STI can perform 35 box moves per hour, compared to 10-18 per hour before privatization. The average dwell time for a ship in the berth is about an hour, and turnaround time is less than one day.[195] Although gang sizes remain somewhat high (20-22), productivity per worker has risen significantly.

Economic Impact

The increase in container traffic has proved to be positive overall for the export-driven Chilean economy. At the same time, however, the leveling off of container traffic as well as commentary by port operators indicates that the maximum capacity for the Chilean container traffic has been reached. Any further growth in container traffic will come from captured market share from other container ports.

The loss of labor has been offset somewhat by indemnity payments made to displaced workers. Nevertheless, if the wage level of the high-skilled laborers that operate in the capital-intensive terminal of the future does not increase to a level that corresponds to the productivity gains that they provide, then the additional profit will accrue to the operators as rents. The existence of these rents will have a detrimental effect on the local economy, because they represent sources of income leaking to the port operator that would have been spent as consumption in the community by port workers in the past.

Only a long-term analysis that compares the gains presented in export competitiveness with the lost income generated from displaced workers will give an accurate conclusion of the economic effects of port reform.

Competition

Officially, the Port of San Antonio operates in the context of national and international markets as a single entity. Its decentralized and autonomous nature places it in competition for cargo against other Chilean ports in the Central Valley region (especially Valparaiso), as well as in the regional cargo market, where it claims to compete with Buenos Aires for Southern Cone cargo.[196] Recently, however, there has been a controversy and discontent about the level of competition within the ports that have adopted the mono-operator concession scheme.

Claims have surfaced of the existence of unfair competition between the multioperator terminals with the concessioned terminals within the individual ports themselves, stemming from a slow growth of cargo moved nationally and a tendency of transfer of cargo to the multioperator port in the year since the concessions were made.[197] The concessionaires contend that the port authority has been favoring the development of multioperator ports under the new hybrid scheme—investing in infrastructure in the multiuser terminal, hindering performance at the concessioned ports with excessive regulatory oversight and promoting the competitive position of the multioperator terminals vis-à-vis the private, mono-operator terminals.[198] These actions by the port authority are a violation of the concession contract, say the concessionaires, because they violate the spirit of the agreement, are an abuse of the port authority's dual role of port administrator and competitor, and run contrary to the port authority's role as promoter of the well-being of all operators in the port.[199]

The allegations of a violation of the concession contract will probably never be resolved in favor of the concessionaires in court. The concession agreements are silent as to restrictions on state action with regard to investment in the port infrastructure it maintains control over. Because the operators at the multioperator port are the service providers, they are the competition for the concessionaires rather than the port authority. Therefore, because these operators are private, there is no direct evidence of unfair competition by the state.[200] As far as claims of unfair competition by excessive oversight of port operation regulations, because all the operators are subject to the same regulations, abuses of regulatory enforcement are difficult to prove and ultimately become questions of whose story one chooses to believe. However, the existence of such complaints is alarming for the implications that it has for public-private relations and the concession process as a whole.

Although there may be no violation of the contract in the strict sense, the basis of this argument is that further investment in port infrastructure by the state is in contradiction with its stated objective of diverting port spending toward investment in areas of greater societal concern. If, indeed, concessionaires were attracted by the promise of a public-private partnership whose result would benefit society as a whole, then governmental investment at the multioperator ports shows bad faith on the part of the government. This issue is of particular concern because it may ultimately cause a failure of the concession process due to disillusionment of the concessionaires whose experience would discourage any future investors.

If, indeed, the state is abusing its regulatory powers by disproportionately focusing compliance oversight on its concessionaires while ignoring similar violations in its own port, it is a troubling indication of the failure of the state to properly adapt to its new role as partner and regulator of all port operators. The manager of Development and Concessions at the Port of Valparaiso, explained that the port authority's role in the new operational scheme was to be partner, competitor, and regulator.[201] In order to preserve a balance between these different roles, the port authority divided these duties into three separate departments that will each have an equal standing within the department. In this way, personnel at the department will be specialized in each interest area and will lobby for each of their constituencies at any decision-making point. Above all, this manager stressed that the port authority was concerned with the well-being of the entire port, so any growth at either of the terminals benefits the port as a whole.[202]

It is doubtful, however, that the port authority can manage having to balance such inherent conflicts of interest. At the same time, it has been argued convincingly that the current competitive situation between the multioperator ports and concessionaires is temporary and will fade over time as the superior efficiency of the mono-operators eliminates the viability of cargo handling in the multioperator terminal.[203] Time may reveal the prudence of buoying the small operators at the Espigón in order to avoid the dramatic economic consequences associated with the sudden elimination of several small businesses and their corresponding employees.

Future Developments

The Port of San Antonio is in a state of transition. When the multioperator terminal is phased out, then the process will be complete. The termination of the multioperator terminal will have to be gradual, however, in order to avoid a sudden negative economic shock to the local economy. All displaced port laborers need to receive some sort of compensation in order to ensure that the port reform process has the appropriate level of political support from all affected sectors. Future growth will require that another container terminal may need to be developed at San Antonio. Relaxation of the port concession framework will be necessary at that time in order to ensure fair competition between operators.

Lessons Learned

San Antonio has engaged in a comprehensive port reform process. Although many of the changes have been developed over a period of 20 years, governmental intervention and regulation have been necessary in order to make the process politically feasible. The cautionary approach of the Chilean process is tailor-made to the small market that the Chilean ports serve. Provisions that ensure competition were designed to prevent trading a public monopoly for a private one, yet must offer enough flexibility for a private firm to justify capital investment in the concessioned terminals. Future export growth must justify the restrictions placed on port operators per the concession agreement, or the contractual obligations will prove to be an undue restriction on private port industry.

Santos, Brazil

Background

The Port of Santos is located in the southeast region of Brazil, approximately 345 kilometers south of Rio de Janeiro and 60 kilometers from the most industrialized region in South America—Greater São Paulo, a region inhabited by approximately 20 million people. The state of São Paulo is responsible for 38 percent of total Brazilian GDP and is also the largest consumer market on the continent.

The harbor of Santos extends along an estuary bounded by the island of Santo Amaro in the east and the island of São Vicente in the west. Santos is a multipurpose port, equipped with modern facilities to handle general cargo, dry and liquid bulk cargo, containers, and Ro-Ro cargo. The main export is coffee; other exports are soybeans, orange juice, bananas, fuel oil, sugar, raw cotton, cotton products, machinery, and vehicles. The principal imports are crude oil, wheat, salt, fertilizers, and petrol.[204]

Infrastructure

The port's total area is 7,765,100 square meters. The quay is 13 kilometers long, and its depth ranges from 5.0 to 14.5 meters. It has 499,701 square meters of warehouse space, 981,603 square meters of yard, 585,111 cubic meters of tanks, 55.6 kilometers of pipelines, and 201 kilometers of railroad.[205]

Operations

Santos is the largest port in South America by volume and handles the continent's second-largest container volume. The TEU movements in Santos for the past four years are as follows: Santos moved 829,486 TEUs in 1997, 799,476 TEUs in 1998, 774,959 TEUs in 1999, and 987,708 TEUs in 2000.[206] Cargo-handling costs have been notoriously high in Brazilian ports. Before privatization, the average cost ranged up to $500 per container. Privatization has improved terminal operation, management, and productivity and has attracted the capital investment for equipment, which has reduced the port cost to approximately $250 per container. This cost compares unfavorably, however, with costs at most other Brazilian ports where the average is $120-200 per container.[207]

Organization

The Brazilian Ports' Modernization Law No. 8630/93 of 1993 paved the way for privatization of port terminals. The law transferred the managing authority of the Port of Santos to the São Paulo Port Authority (Companhia das Docas do Estado de São Paulo, or CODESP). The state of São Paulo and the municipalities that compose the port's hinterland hold the majority of the capital stock. Still, the federal government maintains control of the port. CODESP provides channel- and berth-dredging services, maintains access routes and infrastructure, and handles the administration for the Port of Santos. The sources of CODESP's revenue are a portion of the port tariff, as well as an additional tax on private terminals based on the size of the area leased.[208]

Fundamentally important changes to port operations at Santos have commenced with CODESP's implementation of Project Santos 2000. In October 1997, the most profound transformation in labor relations at Santos was undertaken with the consolidation of all manpower management into the Labor Management Organization (Orgão Gestor de Mão de Obra, or OGMO) of the Port of Santos. Changes in tariff structure and the operation agreements in September 1996 reduced prices for equipment rental and warehousing. These changes revitalized lagging operations for transporting vehicles, sugar, paper, and cellulose and contributed to the revival of cabotage in the MERCOSUR area. Through zoning, the Port of Santos is establishing goals in different areas and developing investment plans. The port is also making an effort to resume rail cargo by rehabilitating and reorganizing existing railway lines.[209]

The Santos Port Leasing and Partnership Program (SPLPP) was organized to transform the Port of Santos into a modern, responsive, well-equipped, and competitive port, while lowering tariffs. The SPLPP is administered by CODESP. The program works to attract private enterprise and undertake port operations by creating lease agreements and joint partnerships. In order to stimulate competition, the program uses the concession process to create contractual compensations so that lessees make investments in port facilities. In so doing, CODESP uses its concessions strategically to achieve development objectives. Companies that seek to win bids for specific areas or terminals are subject to inspection and investigation by CODESP, undergoing a process of public hearings before the lease is granted.[210]

Implementation of the SPLPP began in 1997. By 2000, 79 percent of the port areas dedicated to specific functions were leased or at some stage of the lease process. The port anticipates a total of $721 million in superstructure and modernization investments, $409 million of which has already been guaranteed. Through the SPLPP, 24 areas in the Port of Santos have been leased and another 27 are under examination, including the Grains Terminal (Tegran), Santos Container Terminal 2 (Tecon 2), and the Fertilizers Terminal (Tefer). Among the substructure works planned is the construction of a 2,700-meter tunnel under the estuary of Santos linking the port's left and right banks. The open bidding process for the construction of the tunnel was already underway in early 2001. The tunnel is estimated to cost $55 million for construction, taking two and a half years to complete.[211]

The Port of Santos suffers from a sizable debt. Current leasing and tariff revenues, originally intended for reinvestment in the port, are being used to service CODESP's $175 million debt. Of this debt, 45 percent is part of the indemnity settlement owed to the 2,000 laborers who took early retirement when the port was privatized. The settlement fund is part of an ongoing dispute between the State of São Paulo and the Brazilian federal government.[212] The diversion of these revenues has paralyzed much-needed improvements to port infrastructure.[213] In March 2001, CODESP was visited by the president of Brazil because of recurrent financial problems despite a recent 30 percent increase in port charges.[214] The president and Santos City Council requested an investigation into the activities of CODESP. The city council has been under pressure to provide transparency and accountability for CODESP and has demanded the removal of its board and president. In an effort to alleviate its current financial shortfall, CODESP imposed a special tax on shipping lines to finance a $5 million emergency dredging fund. This tax provoked a reaction from shipping lines, which deemed the fund illegal and sued CODESP.[215]

Reform Process

The goal of privatization was to free the government from onerous expenditures, while attracting investment in the port that the government could not provide. However, soon after the law was passed, difficulties with implementation of the law and privatization occurred. The main problem with the Brazilian port reform has been planning. A successful port privatization regime is aided by inter- and intraport competition. In the case of Santos, because the port had previously run under a noncompetitive regime, no plan was enacted to ensure competition. Additionally, the authority and functions of the new port authority that the port law created were not clear. Finally, deciding on the appropriate division of labor in the face of pressure from all the different unions presented major challenges for CODESP.[216]

As described above, the reform process privatized large areas of the port under concession agreements, which created opportunities for the private sector's action in port operations, port works, leasing of areas, port equipment, container storage, and industrial centers.[217] Another important step in the reform modernization process was the introduction of a 24-hour operating schedule at the port. The new port hours of operation consist of four daily six-hour shifts, 362 days per year (Christmas, New Year's Day, and May Day are the only holidays observed). As a result, there are shorter vessel stays, and efficiency in cargo movement has been increased.

The way in which Santos terminals were privatized has not necessarily been beneficial to the operators of the concessioned terminals. Because port container operators in Santos borrowed heavily in order to win their concessions, they are highly leveraged financially. While the auction process used to award concessions may have benefited the Brazilian authorities in the short term, it may not necessarily reduce port costs in the long term. This auction process has pressured management to bring down costs, especially labor cost.[218] CODESP officials recently indicated that high initial concession payments will inevitably lead to higher tariffs.[219]

Labor

Labor composes 35-50 percent of container cost.[220] The 1993 modernization law set up a new organization in every port to oversee the deployment of casual labor pools. In order to coordinate this process, the Santos Labor Management Organization (Orgão Gestor de Mão de Obra, or OGMO Santos) was established and assumed its new responsibilities on November 27, 2000. OGMO Santos comprises representatives from private port operators, the government, and the port unions.[221] Although the power to appoint casual workers was transferred to OGMOs throughout the nation in the 1993 law, trade unions have fiercely resisted conceding this power. The court in Santos, in an affirmation of the 1993 law, ruled that this power should reside with OGMO Santos, a decision that effectively broke the monopoly enjoyed by the stevedores' union for the past 70 years.

Santos has a history of strikes and demonstrations, which have closed down port operations in extreme cases. Some previous demonstrations have degenerated in acts of violence when nonstriking workers attempted to cross the picket lines.[222]

There are 11 unions in Santos. Binding the unions together is a collective bargaining contract, which sets labor rates, hours, and duties. Among the unions are the port operators union (management) and the stevedores' union (labor), which is the largest and most established. Union privileges include setting the gang sizes and their compensation, plus obtaining regular salary increases. Under union contracts, workers are entitled to additional pay per container if their workloads surpass the minimum set by the union. As an example of union abuse of these privileges, Santos currently employs a gang size of 10 to 12 stevedores per container vessel when a gang size of 4 is all that is required. It has been a long-standing practice that some stevedores sell off their shifts to unqualified persons, while carrying on side jobs, such as taxi driver.[223] Politically, unions have strong support in the community of Santos, which makes it very difficult for terminal operators to win support from the government.[224] The stevedores' union is so strong that they managed to still control jobs after OGMO Santos was in place. In December 2000, fighting broke out at the port when OGMO Santos tried to control casual labor allocation. People were hospitalized and the life of the president of OGMO Santos was threatened. As a result, OGMO Santos and the stevedores' union reached a political agreement to limit gang size to eight-ten laborers to perform OGMO services.[225]

Currently, Santos operates with 15,000 port workers, despite OGMO Santos estimates that port operations require only 7,000 workers. Under the port modernization law of 1993, terminal operators have the right to hire permanent laborers at a salary, while hiring casual workers as needed. The peak season for operations at the Port of Santos is seven to eight months long. However, the same number of laborers are employed year round, though they work fewer days. Stevedores will not accept permanent jobs because of concern that they will run afoul of the powerful stevedores' union. They are also concerned that when the protection that the union provides is eliminated, terminal operators will bring in labor from outside Santos to the detriment of local laborers.[226]

Santos Brasil S.A. and Santos Container Terminal (Tecon)

The Concession Agreement

A shareholder consortium led by Santos Brasil won the Santos Container Terminal (Tecon) concession in a privatization auction at the São Paulo Stock Exchange in 1997. The consortium paid $250 million for a 25-year lease concession with an option for a 25-year renewal. Local investors currently control Santos Brasil.[227] But the company is suffering from the high price it paid at auction and is believed to be looking for a foreign partner in order to maintain a competitive position in relation to competitors within the port.

Performance

In 2000, Tecon handled 305,000 TEUs, an increase of 4 percent over the previous year, and boosted its handling rate from 30 to 37 containers per hour. Tecon projects a 15 percent increase in its operations during 2001.[228]

Terminal Facilities

Santos Brasil offers the following terminal facilities to its customers at Tecon:

- 350,000 square meters of total area;

- 11,000-TEU storage capacity;

- 210 reefer plugs;

- 13-meter quays;

- two container berths, 510-meter-length berth;

- five container gantries, two RTGs, two rail-mounted yard gantries, 25 front-end handlers, and 40 yard tractors; and

- computer systems for inventory control, load and discharge lists, and container and stripping lists.

Ancillary Services

Tecon is the only terminal at the Port of Santos with a direct six-track rail link that integrates Santos with the national railway network. The Tecon information system that manages port operations is integrated with the bonded operations system and allows for complete management of the cargo operations through all phases. Customers are able to track the status of their containers, as well as using other advanced EDI applications via the Internet.[229]

Modern security installations comprising closed-circuit TV-surveillance systems are located throughout the terminal in addition to infrared sensors along the boundary fences, which provide security to the terminal. A comprehensive, triple-A insurance policy fully covers the terminal's operations. At the terminal, clients, brokers, and forwarders may interface directly with the Santos Customs Authority, the Ministry of Agriculture, and the Ministry of Health, all of which have fully equipped offices.

Future Developments

Santos Brasil has embarked on a progressive $150 million investment program. In addition to rehabilitating existing infrastructure and acquiring modern equipment, the investment program plans construction of a third berth and expansion of storage area. The overall investment plan should result in an annual operating capacity of 1 million TEUs.[230]

Tecon is planning an expansion despite heavy financial losses during the past three years, aimed at increasing container-handling capacity to 807,800 TEUs by 2002.[231] The superstructure expansion at Tecon will require investments of $150 million over five years. The company has approved the initial phase of the project, a $30 million expansion project that will add a berth to the existing two and increase the berthing area from 510 meters to 760 meters and the overall terminal area from 366,000 square meters to 484,000 square meters. The expansion plan also includes new cranes that will significantly raise TEU throughput.[232]

Libra Terminals (Libra Terminais S.A.) and Terminal 37 (T-37)

Terminal 37 (T-37) was the first container terminal privatized during the 1995 tender. The concession to operate T-37 was awarded to a wholly Brazilian-owned company, Libra Terminals. After privatization, Libra Terminals began operations at a terminal that lacked any fixed shore cranes. Nevertheless, T-37 began by using ship cranes at the rate of 12 TEUs moves per hour. After a $55 million investment in improvements to terminal superstructure, power supply for reefers, pier reinforcement, a technology upgrade, and personnel retraining, T-37 now offers its clients modern port facilities. In 2000, T-37 moved 190,000 TEUs and increased productivity to 42 TEU moves per hour. Libra Terminals projects a 20 percent increase in container traffic for 2002.

Libra Terminals' T-37 maintains a tariff of $200-220 per TEU for loading or unloading, including container storage. Labor accounts for 30 percent of TEU charges. The São Paulo hinterland accounts for 35 percent of the container traffic at T-37, 30 percent is spread among surrounding states and municipalities, and the remaining 35 percent is transshipment. Imports and exports are closely distributed.[233]

Terminal Facilities

T-37 contains the following facilities:

- total area of 155,000 square meters;

- 1,110 meters of dock length;

- bonded warehouse of 16,000 square meters;

- container-handling capacity of 440,000 TEUs per year;

- 130,000-square-meter container yard with storage capacity of 8,500 TEUs;

- five berths (three equipped with dock-side cranes), five dock-side cranes, five RTGs, 14 reachstackers, 450 reefer plugs; and

- Comos computerized ship-and-yard management system.

Ancillary Services

Libra Terminals also offers the following services to its customers: fumigation, bonded transfers, integral insurance, and dedicated offices to customs and other regulatory agencies.

Future Developments

Ultimately, Libra Terminals intends to operate a total of ten gantry cranes at T-37 in order to provide the capacity to serve as the transshipment hub for South America. The long-term expansion plans for T-37 include the removal of old warehouses and the installation of five gantry cranes and the addition of five RTGs and five berths. In the short term, one gantry crane is planned for installation next year.

Competition

Intraport competition exists between Tecon and T-37, the two largest terminal operators in the port. In 2001, CODESP will auction Tecon 2, an independent area adjacent to the land occupied by Santos Brasil and its Tecon. In the spring of 2001, a new terminal, Tecondi, is scheduled to begin operations on the right bank of the harbor at Santos. With a total area of 170,000 square meters, Tecondi will begin operations at one berth, expanding to three berths and a 420,000-TEU capacity within 25 months.[234]

Intraport competition exists among the large and small terminal operators at Santos, making pricing very competitive. Inside the Port of Santos, competition is ensured by the existence of more than one container terminal operator.

Interport competition between Brazilian ports depends on two factors: the type of services provided at the port and its proximity to the industrial areas and consumer markets. Santos is clearly Brazil's largest container port because of the large capacity of the port, the diversity of the services provided by port operators, and its proximity to the most concentrated industry and consumer market in South America. However, Santos faces a major obstacle in the limited draft of the channel that it must deepen if it is to fulfill the expectations that port administrators have. New deepwater container terminals, like those in the northeast at Suape or southeast at Sepetiba, do not suffer the limitations of depth that constrain Santos. Both Suape and Sepetiba are promoting themselves as more-attractive options for a hub port for the region.[235] Currently, it is difficult to determine the prospects of each port because neither Suape nor Sepetiba approach Santos in TEUs moved.[236] Ultimately, if Santos continues to experience internal problems, it may be relegated to a second-class port as other Latin American ports capture its market share.

Economic Impact

As indicated above, TEU volume has varied since privatization. Although Santos lost its position as the top-ranking container port in South America to Buenos Aires, it experienced a large increase in volume in 2000 to 987,708 TEUs. Most of this increase, however, is due primarily to an increase in imports. The recession of the late 1990s has caused a decline in real wage earnings and disposable income. This decline has caused an increase in demand for inexpensive manufactured imports from Asia. The local economy has suffered because of the decrease in manufacturing and loss of revenue. As a result, many conclude that the increase in container volume has had little benefit to the economy.[237]

Lessons Learned

The Port of Santos is facing the growing pains involved in the privatization process. Concomitant with the efforts to privatize ports, the Brazilian federal and state governments sought to divest from other transportation infrastructure, such as railways and highways. As an attempt to overcome the country's fiscal crisis, Brazil embarked on port privatization in the context of reducing public expenditure and attracting private investment. However, in order to make ports palatable to the private sector, the federal government was forced to prepare the ports for sale through concession by financing a voluntary retirement program, which began the reductions of the labor pool at ports. In Santos, the legacy of the early retirement program continues with the staggering debt held by CODESP. This debt has severely curbed CODESP's ability to invest and modernize as current revenues pay debt service. As a result, CODESP has turned to the concession process through zoning and concession agreements as the instrument for development. However, as has been stated, the prices paid for Tecon and T-37 have also limited the private sector's capacity to invest. These problems are compounded by recent price hikes in the port tariff and terminal handling charges.

While the government of Brazil has taken action by passing laws in order to privatize the state-owned ports, the lack of agency organization, planning, and policy implementation has caused difficulties for the new port administration. It is important to note that unlike the oil and gas, electrical energy, and telecommunications sectors, the privatization of transportation infrastructure has not been overseen by a national, centralized agency. While there exist a National Petroleum Agency, a National Electrical Energy Agency, and a National Telecommunications Agency, which oversee the privatization process, there is no equivalently chartered transportation agency. Notwithstanding the experience of Tecon and T-37, the likelihood is high for more irregularities and growing pains.

To the detriment of efforts to make ports more efficient, powerful labor unions have stifled implementation of port modernization, which they see as a threat to their membership. Despite the creation of OGMO Santos and the Santos Port Authority to manage and oversee port operations, the deployment of casual workers in the labor pool is still influenced greatly by the stevedores. Gang-size deployment, though attributed to OGMO, is still far from being efficient, causing Santos labor to remain expensive. In Brazil, ports remain tied to their stevedores' unions where the predominant focus is on maintaining employment privileges rather than increasing economic development through competitiveness. This focus on labor may negatively affect Santos as newer ports without a strong labor past, such as Sepetiba and Suape, may attract cargo at a greater rate or even divert some trade from calling Santos. However, the proximity of Santos to Greater São Paulo makes calling the port unavoidable. Without proven alternatives, shippers are more or less forced to tolerate Santos, its high cost, and labor unrest if they want to do business in Brazil.

Six key political and organizational strategies for successful privatization implementation have been identified: (1) the need for a political champion, (2) a need to adopt a comprehensive approach, (3) comprehensive studies, (4) creation of a high-level central unit to manage competition, (5) uncoupling the "purchaser" and the "provider," and (6) designing an employee adjustment strategy.[238] Privatization is a proven cost-effective technique for delivering public services, especially in the port sector. Nevertheless, because of the political resistance from public employees and their unions, many governments experience resistance in pursuing privatization opportunities. Proper planning can overcome bureaucratic inaction and the resistance of interest groups and successfully implement competitive governmental strategies. But the major obstacle for Santos to overcome in order to continue with a successful privatization involves winning political will from historical adversaries, patronal port operators' union, and the stevedores' union. For a port-dependent city to radically alter its labor relations in a democracy, job training and early retirement programs may be the only ways to entice the stevedores into reducing their numbers. The issue in Santos is culture. Unless significant cargo shifts from Santos to other ports, the motivation may not come from competition. Risk and instability appear likely to continue as CODESP and port operators embark on their investment and concession programs.

Veracruz, Mexico

Background

The Port of Veracruz services most of the states in Mexico. It is the main port for handling containers, agricultural products, general cargo, and liquid products from the states of Sinaloa, Durango, Cohahuila, Nuevo León, San Luis Potosí, Veracruz, Campeche, Yucatán, Chiapas, Oaxaca, Puebla, Tlaxcala, Morelos, Hidalgo, Querétaro, Guanajuato, Jalisco, and Michoacán. It is estimated that the influence zone of the Port of Veracruz encompasses an economic region that includes 80 percent of the Mexican population and 75 percent of the nation's GDP. The port's external influence zone consists of the countries with which Mexico has trade relationships. Specifically, the shipping lines that serve Veracruz also make port calls in the United States, Canada, Venezuela, Argentina, Spain, Belgium, England, Netherlands, and Russia, as well as in other Western Hemispheric and European countries.[239]

Infrastructure

To date, the Port of Veracruz has nine specialized terminals, which are those for containerized cargo, naval vessels, agricultural bulk, fluids and mineral bulk, sugar, ship repair and construction, general cargo, automobiles, and petroleum and derivatives. The Integral Port Administration (Administración Porturias Integrale, or API), which is discussed under "Organization," administers concession contracts with five of these terminals. They are Corporación Integral de Comercio Exterior (CICE), Compania Terminal de Veracruz (CTV), Operadora Portuaria del Golfo, S.A. de C.V. (OPG), Internacional de Contenedores Asociados de Veracruz (ICAVE), and Terminales de Cargas Especializadas (TCE). ICAVE is the Port of Veracruz's major container terminal, moving about 358,000 TEUs.[240] The privatization of facilities in 1996 and competition for market share among Mexico's main port operators have given rise to improvements in the Port of Veracruz's handling capacity and services. From 1996 to the end of 2000, port administrators spent about $200 million to triple berthing capacity from 7 million to 22 million tons and increase warehouse capacity on nearby cleared land. This spending plan included the construction of a 1.9-mile breakwater on the north end of the harbor and an enlargement of various port areas. A new pier for a multipurpose terminal, warehouse demolition, and upgrading of a grain terminal were constructed. Several liquid-bulk terminals came online, bringing the total to the five terminals that currently exist. Three of the four existing warehouses were torn down and reconstructed, including a refrigerated warehouse, which was expanded to be suitable for ships of up to 328 feet in length.[241]

The port administration (API), since decentralization, has cleared approximately 247 acres for land-side construction that will provide value-added services. Likewise, new docks for bulk agriculture and general cargo, as well as additional internal roads and a new access to the port are presently being built. Since 1999, for example, ICAVE and TCE, two of the Port of Veracruz's main concession holders, have operated berths with a minimum depth of 35 feet, compared to the former government berth, which had a depth of only 31 feet. In addition, TCE's storage capacity rose from 36,000 tons to 72,000 tons with the building of six new silos in addition to the original warehouse.[242]

The port is directly connected to all of Mexico's central and southern states with extensive rail and road networks. The port has double-stack container rail service in operation with dry bulk and fluids being transported to and from the port through two railway trunk lines and is a key link in the southeast portion of Mexico's railway network. Among other services available to the port, the rail line provides vehicle transport, multilevel closed cars, container transport between Veracruz and Mexico City, which is the principal source and destination for the port's cargo. Federal Highway 150, a double-lane superhighway, connects the port to Mexico City. Highway 180 extends along the Gulf of Mexico west to connect Veracruz to Altamira/Tampico and the Texas border.[243]

Operations

In 1993, the port handled 43 containers per hour of operation. As of 1999, it handled an average of 84 containers per hour, and, for certain other vessels, it surpassed 100 containers per hour of operation. In the monthly port traffic report for August 1999, the Port of Veracruz recorded 1,104,862 tons in total operated vessel load. Of that, 893,728 tons consisted of imports and 211,133 tons consisted of exports. The total container TEUs for that month was 40,897.[244] Since privatization of the port administration, Veracruz has experienced relatively steady growth in traffic. In 2000, the total tonnage moved was 1,222,086, a 15 percent increase from the previous year. Of that, 1,014,189 tons consisted of imports and 207,897 tons consisted of exports.[245] There was a 14.7 percent increase in TEUs from August 1999 to September 2000, as the total container TEUs for the month of September 2000 was 50,069.[246]

International Container Terminal Services, Inc., based in Manila, Philippines, teamed up with Mexican engineering giant Grupo ICA to win a 20-year concession contract to operate the Veracruz box terminal. The terminal is being operated by a joint venture known as Internacional de Contenedores Asociados de Veracruz, or ICAVE. In 1991, port traffic was at 741 vessels; by 1994, the number rose to 1,245. The port handled 121,682 TEUs in 1991; it handled 256,055 TEUs, or 47 percent, of Mexico's container traffic in 1999 and 398,987 between January and September of 2000. The port handled 1.2 million tons of general cargo in 1994 operating at 118 percent capacity. Agricultural and liquid- and mineral-bulk products also moved at more than 100 percent of capacity, creating the need for expansion of port infrastructure. ICAVE's modernization program will expand the terminal handling capacity at its facilities from 360,000 TEUs to 520,000 TEUs. Stacking capacity will increase to 540,000 TEUs or more. ICAVE is also in the process of building a second berth, which will bring the total length for the company's two berths to 507 meters, compared to the 360-meter-long original berth left behind by the government.[247]

Organization

The Port of Veracruz is a landlord port. Since 1993, management of Mexico's ports has resided with autonomous port operators known as Integral Port Administration (Administraciónes Porturias Integrale, or APIs). These APIs are responsible for day-to-day operation of ports, which was intended to result in increased flexibility with port operations and policies that would attract more carrier calls.[248] By law, the port's assets (water zones, infrastructure, terminals, facilities, and land area) must remain under federal ownership; only the employment, use, and exploitation of port assets are granted to the independent APIs.[249] The general administration, port master plans, as well as the supervising of services that are offered by the private ports operators, are still the responsibility of the federal government through the APIs.[250] Every API at each Mexican port is granted the right to acquire 49 percent foreign private investment capital to develop services, terminals, and other port infrastructure and development activities.[251] The private sector is allowed to take charge of the port development, maintenance, dredging, and basic infrastructure construction. In reality, the private firms manage almost all the services offered by the terminals in the main commercial ports. More than 630 firms manage terminals and render services at the ports.[252]

The API is unique because, even though it is a government-based entity, it still has to obtain concession from the state to administer the port. This right is established in a 50-year concession contract given to the API to administer the port. The API also has a right to operate a terminal or port if it chooses to do so. This right is found in the revision of the 1993 Law of Ports of Mexico. The API in Veracruz has chosen not to operate any terminals and merely serves as administrators. Rather, it has granted concession contracts to private investors for the operation of terminals.[253]

Reform Process

In the early 1990s, Mexico realized that something had to be done to upgrade the nation's port system. Ports were experiencing a low quality of service. Ships could not be sure how long they would be held up at a port or at what cost. There was a lack of uniformity in tariffs and a mishandling of cargo. Service quality and productivity were not internationally competitive. Equipment was obsolete and facilities were insufficient. The ports were very centralized with uneven investment distribution.[254]

The government decided that actions had to be taken to overhaul this system and allow for private operators to improve port efficiency. Private companies would be able to provide investment and security by developing projects and following through with them.[255]

The Objectives of Reform

Port reform had four main objectives. Mexico wanted to enlarge and modernize its port infrastructure to satisfy the growing needs of maritime transportation. It also wanted to increase the port efficiency. Furthermore, it wanted to promote commercial, industrial, fishing, and tourist development, to provide more job opportunities. Finally, Mexico wanted more private investment so as to reduce the need for public funding.[256]

Investments

After the Law of Ports was enacted in 1993, both public and private investments took place in the Port of Veracruz. The government (API in this case) used investment to improve the port's facilities as a way to attract more private firms. Private firms provided more than 60 percent of the investments put into the port.[257]

API's investment included a road at the perimeter of the port and an adoption of 73 hectares for the widening of the yard north of the port. Furthermore, the API initiated the extension of breakwaters in the north zone, the construction of a multiuser terminal, an extension of a 660-trailer capacity parking lot in the north zone, and reparations to various terminals, including Terminals 2 and 4. Private investors invested in things such as a refrigerated storage for containers, renovation of a crane in the container terminal, and the addition of several terminals.[258]

The Law of Ports allows for 49 percent foreign investment, but most of the private operators and investors are Mexican companies.[259] The private sector has made important investments in machinery, equipment, and storage facilities, as well as in the reconstruction of installations, yards, specialized terminals, berths, and dredging.

Terms of Concession Contracts

Concession tariffs for operators are established through public bidding or soliciting for better operations. It is a system based on performance as well as money. The concessionaire must pay a 7-12 percent tax to the government (the API must also pay this tax). Any change to the contract must be written up in a formal letter to the Secretariat of Communications and Transportation (SCT), which usually accepts the modification.[260] The SCT must also do cost analysis to check the efficiency of the concessionaires, who must maintain certain productivity levels.[261]

Labor

Labor unions were a big part of Mexican port history. They were a powerful group that caused much unrest and inefficiency in the Port of Veracruz. The labor unions essentially controlled the port's operations.

Privatization had a significant impact on the employees of the Port of Veracruz. The labor unions had to agree to forgo the contract they were then under, which had established wages according to the relation of the employee with the union and was not in accordance with the characteristics of the work done and which contained biased clauses.[262] The contract eliminations were accomplished through letters and word of mouth. No formal contract was ever established. Thus, the majority of employers were absorbed into the new system. It was difficult at first but later accepted by the workers.[263]

Today, there are no port labor unions, and each firm has its own union. The new labor system establishes wages based on labor productivity, which creates a positive impact on the port itself.[264] The contract is now based on an eight-hour workday, although the eight hours are not always met if there is insufficient work. Each firm establishes its own labor contract annually, and the collective contract is reviewed. The state has little involvement in labor issues.[265]

Laborers were generally positively affected because they received increased benefit packages from the private firms. Workers can now also freely negotiate with their firms, allowing for increased flexibility in wages and positions.[266]

Performance

Before privatization, tariffs fluctuated because of syndicates. The government or these syndicates would operate the port, often not very efficiently, because revenue could not be properly invested in the port. Even if a port was successfully managing cargo and making profit, the profit belonged to the government. The government would then take the revenue from all ports collectively and distribute it as the government wished, often causing an uneven distribution scheme because ports that were doing better than others would not see the added benefits they deserved. The change to private operators allows for revenue to remain at the ports and can be invested in improvement projects that increase the port's efficiency level.[267]

Veracruz increased its productivity from 43 to 84 containers per hour of ship operation. It, furthermore, increased agricultural bulk from 2,500 to 20,000 tons per day. There has been an improvement in towing operations for the port as well.[268]

Privatization also reduced tariffs because it produced competition among the operators, which created a self-regulating mechanism for tariffs and gave investors and clients security. Monopolies no longer existed. The costs to clients went down significantly. There are lower fees for handling/stevedoring bulk, agriculture, minerals, and containers. There was a decrease of about 10.2 percent in container fees, which dropped from

1,891.82 pesos in January 1995 to 1,698.55 in June 2000. This decrease was a benefit to the port because there is now a growing number of shipping lines that frequent the Port of Veracruz. Before reform, there were about 21 regular shipping lines; there are now 37 shipping lines that frequent the port.[269]

Economic Impact

The local economy has improved since privatization. The private concessionaires have created services that have employed many people. These employees are generally better paid with better benefits than those in the public sector. Even when some workers are laid off from one terminal, they can find jobs in another. Before the reform, there were close to 4,500 direct employees; now there are around 10,000 direct employees in the Port of Veracruz. As a result, many new operators and services are available.[270] Employment has been augmented because of the growth in cargo volume and the free entrance of operators and private service suppliers. For example, more work is available because of the increase in TEUs moved by terminals such as CICE and ICAVE.[271]

The port has also expanded Veracruz's hotel industry because of the stream of business people that pass through the port. This activity strengthens the economy since Veracruz is not a very touristy place and provides a new field of employment for citizens.[272]

Competition

The Port of Veracruz, in terms of cargo traffic, surpasses all other Mexican ports. Veracruz faces no serious competition from other Mexican ports on the Gulf of Mexico coast. However, the Port of Tuxpan has been touted as a potential alternative to the Port of Veracruz, which some shippers and carriers acknowledge is becoming extremely congested and where fees are high at the terminals. Nevertheless, Veracruz continues to be the leader in containerized cargo in that region and is regularly included in the trade lanes of most major shipping lines.[273]

The port does face U.S. competition for cargo specifically from the ports in Houston and New Orleans. In 1998, all Mexican ports moved approximately 1 million TEUs across their docks, doubling the number of containers moved in 1993. In contrast, the port in Houston alone moved nearly 1 million TEUs through its terminals in 1999.[274]

Future Developments

The Port of Veracruz plans to continue development. One of its strategic plans is a program called "Programmo Desarollo (2000-2010)," which is not yet available. This program includes the development of technology to facilitate documentation through the EDI system for accessing cargo information.[275]

Growth is another main objective. The port reached its 50 percent of grain throughput goal in 2000 and wants to continue to expand. An increase in container storage capacity is a goal for the future.[276]

Lessons Learned

Privatization was clearly a wise choice for the Port of Veracruz. The most interesting facet of its reform was the way it managed to restructure the system so as to also benefit Veracruz's local economies. This local investment created a feeling of trust among the people because they were given job security. The port also benefited from increases in productivity and efficiency.

Labor unions pose an obstacle for privatization in many developing ports. Veracruz managed to overcome the strong labor union opposition to privatization and created a new labor system. Port authorities included the laborers in the planning and restructuring process to give them an increased sense of security. Private firms had the funds to increase the benefits packages of their employees (health insurance, etc.). The capital-intensive environment that the private companies created established a labor system based on productivity. Workers now had incentives to be more productive, which is a benefit of private industry.

A striking observation is the way privatization helped alleviate corruption in the Mexican port system. The new stability in tariffs and stevedore costs proves that the port systems became less decentralized and corrupt. The users and shipping agents can now count on stability and fixed prices, which in itself lead to new investors. Privatization actually decreases corruption and benefits the user and provider.

Willemstad, Curaçao

Background

The Port of Willemstad lies on the southern coast of Curaçao, part of the five-island country state of the Netherlands Antilles, which is part of the Dutch realm. Curaçao sits 35 miles north of Venezuela in the southern Caribbean and has a population of 150,000 people. The port is located on Schottegat Bay, a large inland body of water, which is accessed by the three-quarter-mile-long, fingerlike St. Anna's Bay. Cruise ships bring tourists to Curaçao in great numbers, where they disembark on the banks of St. Anna's Bay in the old section of Willemstad. Further inland in Schottegat Bay, oil tankers bring crude from Venezuela for processing in one of Curaçao's numerous refineries. All the island's containerized trade enters through the modern container terminal on the north side of Schottegat Bay. Koningsplein, a free-trade zone, is located adjacent to the container terminal.

Infrastructure

The Curaçao Port Authority (CPA) owns and manages the entire port infrastructure and superstructure, while Curaçao Port Services (CPS), a privately held company, holds concessions to manage the container movements. Both the CPA and CPS have recently achieved ISO 9002 certification.[277] The Port of Willemstad has nearly 20 wharves and berths, most of which are dedicated to tourists or petroleum products, the island's two most important industries. There are more than 500 meters of berth length dedicated to general cargo, bulk cargo, and Ro-Ro activities for other types of trade. The container terminal has 500 meters of berth length with an alongside draft of 12.2 meters. Two large gantry cranes of 50 tons of lifting capacity each and a 50-ton mobile container-handling crane serve it. The activities at the container terminal are computerized at each stage. The EDI Container Cargo System plans and directs the crane operations, while the Multi-Use Container Control System administers container movements on the ground. The total container terminal area is more than 30,000 square meters with some room for possible future expansion. There is storage space for some 3,280 TEUs when three to four boxes are stacked vertically. The port currently handles 76,000 TEUs each year. However, a study has shown that without any infrastructural changes, the potential handling capacity may be as high as 195,000 TEUs per year.[278]

Operations

In the early 1980s, the annual TEU movements for the Port of Willemstad averaged 40,000. By 1990, TEU movements had increased to 60,000 and over the past ten years have increased to 75,000 per year. In 1999, the total TEUs were 75,471; 67,873 TEUs (about 50 percent of these were unloaded) consisted of local traffic, and 7,598 TEUs (of which more than 70 percent were unloaded) consisted of transshipped traffic. Thus, more than 10 percent of the port's traffic was transshipment.

CPS has actively encouraged transshipment in the port with a two-tiered pricing system, in which the rate for local traffic far exceeds that of transshipped traffic. Karel Aster, the managing director of CPS, believes that capital investment for a port may be determined by long-range forecasts of local transport needs. However, in the short term this type of planning may leave a port with excess capacity. The opportunity costs for additional movements in the excess capacity range of activity are taken to have a far lower value than the operating costs of the local capacity.[279]

Organization

In 1981, CPS signed a three-year concession agreement with the CPA to manage the stevedoring operations for the port. The CPA remained the sole owner of all infrastructure and superstructure managing the port as a tool port. CPS is a privately held company that was originally made up of an association of several of the private companies that had owned the docks previously. The CPA is barred from holding any equity stake in CPS to avoid any conflict of interest. The concession agreement between the CPA and CPS has been renewed several times. In 1991, a ten-year contract was signed and another was to be signed in the summer of 2001, once again for a ten-year term. These concession contracts are negotiated directly by CPA and CPS, and neither the negotiations nor the contracts are made public. Agustin Diaz, current director and former chairman of the board of the CPA, states that the negotiation process is generally smooth as both parties recognize that they have common goals and that "what is good for one is good for the other."[280] In this year's negotiation, CPS sought more control over the superstructure of the port and possible ownership of the three cranes; it is not known if CPS was successful in its attempts. If this change was accomplished and CPS gained ownership of the port cranes, Willemstad will be run as a landlord port. The CPA will be responsible for the port infrastructure and nautical operations, and CPS will be responsible for all aspects of container movements.

Reform Process

Until the early 1980s, six private companies owned docks in Schottegat Bay. Each managed their own area and worked in direct competition with the others, but each was generally associated with a particular shipping agent. The operations in the port were very labor intensive, relatively inefficient, when compared to containerized ports of the day, and in need of modernization. There was a growing recognition between both the island and national government that for the port to be competitive in the international market, it needed to increase its ability to handle containerized trade. Yet, it was generally perceived that none of the six private companies was sufficiently large to attract the necessary capital for these improvements. The Dutch government encouraged a governmental body that owned and managed the entire port as one entity, through requirements for development loans. Thus, in 1981, the six existing private firms were bought out and the CPA was formed in an act of "deprivatization." The money to create the CPA came from a 30-year development loan from the national government set at 2.5 percent annual interest. The loan was granted on the agreement that the port would remain publicly held with concession agreements for labor activities. An act of the Curaçao municipal, or island, government created the CPA, which is a limited liability company with 95 percent being held by the local Curaçao government and 5 percent by Dutch Bank. A 21-member municipal board elects the director of the CPA, in an effort to steer the position away from political pressures. Additionally, efforts are made to run the CPA as a private company with investment decisions being based on profit concerns.

To have port reform that effectively consists of the deprivatization of a port is rare. All involved in the process in Curaçao, from the CPA and CPS to the representatives of the labor unions, agree that the island's trade has been and remains too small to maintain fierce competition among many companies. Rather, the model that they have employed is one of cooperation, each recognizing that because their interests sufficiently overlap, agreements are reached. Whether this creates the most efficient port costs is unknown, but it certainly has created harmonious port operations that receive very high marks from users. Given the recent signing of a ten-year contract, any type of port reform or further privatization is unlikely in the port.

Labor

Before 1980, the Port of Willemstad was split into six different owner/operators in harsh competition. The activities were not modernized and very labor intensive. At that time, there were 1,300 laborers working the dock for the six companies. Hence, there were many contracts between different unions and the private firms. Also, many casual workers were employed during busy times. During the restructuring and buying process that the CPA was partaking in, the future of these workers was an important consideration of the project and was included as part of the project's financing. The goal of the restructuring was to modernize the port's facilities by purchasing a container crane, which inevitably meant a reduction in labor if the port was to run efficiently. However, to offset this, efforts were made to develop and internationally market Koningsplein, a free-trade zone adjacent to the port, and create replacement jobs in this new area. Intermodal connections were improved between the port and local industry. The vision of the port redevelopment was seen within the larger community. In the years following 1981, the size of the port workforce was steadily decreased to about 80 workers, where it remains today. This reduction was accomplished through retirements, early buyouts, and retraining of workers leaving the docks for other types of work. During this same time employment was increasing at Koningsplein, and today the free-trade zone employs more than 1,500 people. Workers who remained at the docks were given training on the new equipment and now are skilled port workers.

When CPS received the first concession agreement in 1981, it signed a contract with a newly united union, Sindicato de Trabajadores Cristianos del Puerto (Union of Christian Port Workers). Giby Marchena, current president of the union, states that it was a difficult time for the workers, but all realized that the changes were necessary. Mr. Marchena believes that the contracts, and all subsequent contracts, have been signed without strikes because the two sides have common interests and bargain in good faith.[281]

Performance

The cost of nearly all activities associated with container movements in the Port of Willemstad are explained in the public document "Harbour Tariff #5." This booklet has prices calculated by CPS and approved by the CPA for all costs charged by CPS for the actual movements. The CPA charges additional harbor and wharfage fees, and a different private firm owns and operates the tugboats required to enter the port.

The average total cost for importing or exporting a local container through the Port of Willemstad has been stable for several years at $420.[282] The price for a transshipped container is significantly less than this amount; the average total cost is less than $100.

Economic Impact

The impact of the Port of Willemstad on the overall economy of Curaçao does not come from the number of workers employed, as that number is quite small. Rather, the port must be viewed as a component of the island's economy. The free-trade zone of Koningsplein is adjacent to the port, and the two are dependent on each other for continued economic well-being. The CPA and local government include the port's economic impact on the general economy when creating the long-range plan for the port. This was most recently completed in 1998 with the publication of the two volumes *Economic Impact Study (EIS) for the Maritime Sector of the Netherlands Antilles* by the Dutch firm Policy Research Corporation.

Competition

Intraport

Competition does not exist within the Port of Willemstad, as CPS has the sole rights to conduct stevedoring services. The check on this monopolistic practice comes from the CPA, which is responsible for safeguarding the public good in its concession contract negotiations with CPS. Additionally, the CPA has the authority to examine and approve proposed changes to the tariffs by CPS. There have been local controversies over the higher charges for local movements in the port, but the port fees continue to be below average for Caribbean ports.

Interport

CPS sees the Port of Willemstad in competition primarily with Venezuelan ports and other smaller ports in the south Caribbean basin.[283] The port currently moves about 8,000 TEUs per year in transshipment, or about 10 percent of the total port moves. A large part of these moves are connected with Venezuelan trade, and any liberalization of cabotage laws in Venezuela would likely reduce the transshipment number for the port.

Future Developments

The deprivitization and subsequent restructuring into a tool port at the Port of Willemstad has worked for Curaçao. The port has below-average prices for both local and transshipment movements and has been recognized as a well-run port by the ISO. Conversations with representatives of the interested parties at the port had similar themes of cooperation. The small number of yearly TEU movements on the island makes both harsh competition and continued capital investment for technologically modern equipment incompatible. The interested parties of the local government, dock workers' union, and private companies have worked together to create a solution that has worked for 20 years and will continue into the foreseeable future.

Lessons Learned

The Port of Willemstad is notable for two reasons. First, there is no competition within the port, as CPS owns the sole rights to conduct all stevedoring activities. Tough competition is generally thought of as all-important for fair pricing. The port's prices are below average for the Caribbean basin,[284] indicating that the requirement that the CPA approve the price structure implemented by CPS has been effective in controlling this monopoly. The second notable item is the planning process employed at the port. Long-range plans for the port are crafted with the consideration of economic goals. The island and national governments began the reform process of the port more than 20 years ago with the purpose of creating an efficient modern port. The recent gaining of the ISO 9002 seal for both CPS and CPA acknowledges that the process has been successful.

Panama

Background

Panama possesses some unique characteristics in addition to its advantageous location at the intersection of major shipping trade lanes. The country is located on the southern edge of Central America, bordering Colombia to the south and Costa Rica to the north. It is also the narrowest point between the Atlantic Ocean and Pacific Ocean in the Western Hemisphere. Since its completion in 1914, the Panama Canal has linked the Port of Balboa on the Pacific Ocean and the Port of Colón on the Atlantic Ocean.

In 1903, Panama and the United States entered into a treaty by which the United States undertook to construct an interoceanic ship canal across the Isthmus of Panama. The following year, the United States purchased the rights and equipment of the French "Canal Inteoceanique" for $40 million and took over the construction of the canal. Following its completion in 1914, the canal was operated as a noncorporate agency of the U.S. government, administered by the Panama Canal Commission. Today, the Panama Canal Authority (PCA) operates the canal with the oversight of the Panama Maritime Authority (PMA). However, the PCA is a governmental corporation that is independent of the PMA.[285]

Built in 1855, the "Land-Bridge Railroad of the Americas" is Panama's transcontinental rail link between Balboa and Colón.[286] Kansas City Southern Railways and Mi-Jack Products have formed a joint venture, the Panama Canal Railway Company (PCRC), to operate the railway. The railway offers an alternative to the canal for moving containers between ports.

Organization

Seventeen ports make up the Panamanian port system, five of which are private, while the government manages the remaining twelve. This case study examines the private container terminals and their operators. The Port of Balboa Terminal operates as a transshipment container terminal and serves Panama City and the hinterland. The Port of Colón operates as a transshipment container terminal and serves the Colón Free Zone and the hinterland of Panama. There are three private container terminal operators within the Port of Colón: Colón Container Terminal, Port of Cristóbal Terminal, and Manzanillo International Terminal.

National Maritime Authority

Established by Law No. 7 of 1998, the PMA assumed control over every aspect of Panama's maritime sector. Before the enactment of the law, the maritime sector had been the responsibility of several governmental agencies. The PMA is an entity that assembles all the former national port authority institutions. The PMA's objective is to administer, promote, regulate, plan, and execute the policies, strategies, plans, and projects that are related to the functioning and development of the maritime sector. The PMA also promotes the socioeconomic development of the country.[287] Within its role, the PMA is responsible for the execution of the national maritime strategy, the administration of the maritime strategy, and the administration of the marine and coastal resources, as well as the fulfillment of the provisions of the United Nations Convention of the Law of the Sea. The PMA operates within four directorates: Directorate of Merchant Marine (6,212 ships registered in Panama), Directorate of Ports and Maritime Auxiliary Industries, Directorate of Marine and Coastal Resources, and Directorate of Seafarers.

Performance

The National Port Authority (NPA) of Panama was responsible for port operations before privatization. During that time, Panamanian ports experienced little transshipment, low port activity, no investment, and poor installations for container cargo and received a limited number of superliner calls. In 1994, Panama's ports boasted just two ship-to-shore container gantry cranes, each of which was more than 25 years old. Box volumes totaled just 142,791 TEUs, and handling rates averaged only 12 moves an hour. Under the old NPA system, the official discharge rate per container move was $235. However, additional charges were routinely assessed causing the real rate per container move to range between $500 and $750.[288]

The Panamanian government implemented a policy of port privatization in 1994, as part of its countrywide modernization plan. This plan had the twin aim of increasing the competitiveness of Panamanian ports in seeking regional transshipment traffic and of lowering the costs of handling Panama's international trade. Privatization allowed free market competition in the port and in the region with limited governmental intervention. Privatization has increased port efficiency and reduced port operations costs by more than 50 percent.[289]

Increased productivity and lower costs have granted Panamanian ports the opportunity to fully exploit its geographical position as a world trade center. Today, Panama boasts three world-class container terminals, supported by 19 quay cranes, of which 11 are post-Panamax in design. Panama has invested more than $700 million in port infrastructure. In addition, annual traffic volumes have risen sharply and surpassed 1,300,000 TEUs in 2000. Competition is the main reason behind the success of privatization in Panama.[290]

Customs

Customs is viewed as the bottleneck in the cargo transport systems in Panama and needs to be modernized and streamlined. Because customs is a governmental agency, there is no market pressure to perform well and the documentation process is slow and bureaucratic, resulting in poor customer service. Because of the bottlenecks, customs has an adverse impact on port efficiency, cost, and competitiveness. Many firms in the shipping industry suggest using paperless terminals to improve the facilitation of customs. In the fast-paced world of maritime shipping, decisions need to be made quickly; time is money, and delays can add substantial cost to shipping.

150

Labor

After privatization, the governmental union was eliminated. Union members were compensated before the transfer of port operations to the private sector.[291] Labor contracts are now negotiated between private terminal operators and in-house unions. After concessions were granted, terminal operators continued to hire labor from the same labor pool that the government had used, and, as such, minimal training was needed.[292]

Economic Impact

Major round-the-world shipping lanes pass through Panama. Approximately 40 ships a day wait before transiting the canal, that is, more than 14,000 vessels per year. Of the 14,000 vessels transiting the canal, only 39 percent, or 5,500 vessels, call on Panama's ports every year. It takes 24-36 rotation-waiting hours in Panama to enter the canal, mainly because of the locks system of the canal. Of that waiting time, 8-10 hours are spent actually transiting the canal, leaving 14-26 hours for ships to call on the ports to load or unload cargo or have other services performed on the vessel or containers.[293]

The waiting period presents companies an opportunity to set up facilities for the provision of services to the ships and passengers transiting the canal. Investment opportunities within the ports and local areas include processing zones, ship suppliers and maintenance, crane and container maintenance and repairs, maritime training, crew rotation, insurance services, and logistics centers.

Among the projects that have been developed are two export processing zones (EPZs), a transshipment park, and a seafood-processing center.

1. The Davis EPZ is a joint venture funded by the Panamanian and Taiwanese governments, which has created a 112-hectare EPZ at a former U.S. military base near Colón Free Zone. Several Taiwanese companies are now operating in the zone, producing glassware, jeans, umbrellas, small refrigerators, and car parts. The Panamanian company Zona Procesadora de Exportaciones de Albrook is creating a light industrial park on a 5-hectare site to the immediate north of the new Marcos A. Gelabert Airport in Albrook. A number of companies have already expressed interest in setting up factories or offices in the park.

2. A major logistics, transport, and cargo transshipment park is to be developed near these EPZs by the U.S. company ICF Kaiser. It is to invest nearly $30 million over the next four years in developing the 14-hectare site, and the project will create more than 1,000 jobs.

3. Marpesca SA, the leading Panamanian seafood-processing company, was granted the concession to develop the Corozal cold store facilities of the Strategic Food Export Center. It aims to develop these facilities into the most modern food-processing plant in Central America and is to make an initial investment of $43 million in five new factories and in the upgrading of plant and technology.[294]

4. Industrial development within the Panama Canal zone is a primary goal of the government. New financial and legal incentives have been introduced to stimulate investment in industry and increase productivity. Privatization programs, market liberalization, job-training schemes, and decentralization of state enterprises are also taking place with a view to making Panama the ideal location for companies seeking to expand into the whole of Latin America and beyond.[295]

Of the jobs in Panama, 30 percent are transportation related and 70 percent are service related.[296] There is general optimism among ocean carriers and freight forwarders about trading prospects between the United States and Panama. U.S. investors are still very active in the country. The United States and Panama are keen on establishing closer ties between North and South America. Panama sees itself as an important staging post in the growing trade that is likely to take place between North and South America. Panama is developing the necessary system processes and additional infrastructure that will be needed for Panama to play the role of an international logistics and distribution center for the Americas.[297]

Colón Free Zone

Background

The Colón Free Zone (CFZ) was created in 1948. The CFZ administration is a semiautonomous department of the government of Panama, which administers the CFZ. It is located at the Port of Colón and is the largest free zone in the Western Hemisphere, second in the world only to Hong Kong, China. The CFZ has developed into a major world logistics center and generates approximately 9 percent of the country's GNP. A total of 1,780 domestic and international companies are now based in the CFZ's 400-hectare site, generating more than 14,000 jobs directly and another 6,000 indirectly. Historically, the CFZ has staked its ground on importing goods duty-free from around the world and selling them throughout Latin America. The reduction of tariff barriers throughout Latin America has eroded the business base, and the CFZ has had to reshape and expand its business. The CFZ aims to be the main commercial distribution center for the hemisphere.

Special Tax Treatment

The CFZ offers incentives by eliminating sales tax, production tax, import/export taxes, capital investment tax, and municipal and other local taxes. In addition, income tax for the companies established in the CFZ is lower than it is at the national level. There is no capital gains tax on the sale of CFZ assets that have been held for a minimum of two years. Non-Panamanian executives pay the same personal income taxes and other levies as any other resident of Panama.

Additionally, a series of discounts from taxable income are provided in proportion to the number of Panamanian nationals employed by the company on a permanent basis. These discounts on income tax are based on the following rates: 0.5 percent of net taxable income if 30-100 Panamanian workers have been employed permanently, 1.0 percent of net taxable income if 101-200 Panamanian permanent workers have been employed, and 1.5 percent of net taxable income if more than 200 Panamanian permanent workers have been employed.

The Users Association; The Only Business Organization of the Colón Free Zone

The Colón Free Zone Users Association, one of the most important business organizations in the country, was established on November 5, 1979. Its purpose was to unite and represent the users of the CFZ in a nonpolitical organization and to defend the rights and interests of associates. The association has also sought to maintain CFZ's level of competition, attracting foreign investment and new companies in an era of great challenges, a globalized economy, and open markets. In addition, the association has kept a strong relationship with the CFZ's administrative board in order to promote the CFZ as a logistics center of international commerce. The association has 17 working commissions, which participate in an active manner in studies concerning all modes of transportation, security, customs, and commercial exchange.

Railroad

Panama Canal Railway Company (PCRC) was awarded a 50-year investment and operating concession for the Panama railroad. The 47-mile rail link between the Atlantic port (Colón) and the Pacific port (Balboa) opened for business in July 2001. Initially, PCRC will offer six trips a day in both directions and plans to increase to ten in the near term. PCRC has the capacity to offer 16 trips a day. Each train will have a maximum loading capacity for about 80 containers. The update rail link is expected to carry about 500,000 containers a year. PCRC expects a full discharge and load operation to take a maximum of two hours, with a full ship-to-ship cycle being accomplished in approximately four hours. This schedule compares with a vessel transit time for the canal of eight hours. PCRC believes ocean carriers, freight forwarders, third-party logistics providers, and shippers will look more favorably on Panama as the hemisphere's distribution hub if Panama can offer a good range of cost-competitive and efficient transport options.

Competition

Intraport Competition

Today, intraport competition exists between terminal operators within the Port of Colón. In 2000, the Port of Colón had a combined TEU volume of 1,353,727, which is a 7.2 percent rise from 1999's 1.27 million. More than two-thirds of Panama's business is transshipped cargo.[298]

The percentages of TEU volume in individual private terminals were as follows:

- Manzanillo International Terminal, 67 percent
- Colón Container Terminal (Evergreen), 24 percent
- Port of Cristóbal, 9 percent[299]

There is no direct competition with the Port of Balboa Terminal.

Interport Competition

Interport competition exists between the following ports in the Caribbean region: Kingston, Freeport, Miami, Puerto Cabello, Rio Haina, and Cartagena. There is a growing tendency to transship cargo at all aforementioned ports. Panama's ports as transshipment centers will keep gaining in importance because of the great advantage of having the canal combined with advancements in port operations due to privatization.[300] Panama's geographical location provides it with a natural competitive advantage.

The Panama Canal

Background

The Republic of Panama assumed full responsibility for the administration, management, operation, maintenance, and modernization of the Panama Canal on December 31, 1999. This event marked the culmination of a 20-year transition process that started in October 1979, two years after the signing of the Panama Canal Treaty on September 7, 1977, by the United States and Panama.

Panama Canal Authority

Panama carries out its responsibilities through the Panama Canal Authority (PCA), an autonomous Panamanian government corporation created by Panama's Constitution and organized through Law No. 19 of June 11, 1997. An 11-member board of directors heads the PCA, which enjoys financial autonomy and the right to manage the canal. In addition, it has exclusive charge of operation, administration, management, preservation, maintenance, improvements, and modernization of the canal and its related activities and services, pursuant to legal and constitutional regulations in force. Under Panamanian administration, the canal is managed as a business, adapting to customer needs and market conditions to remain competitive. The Panama Canal constitutes an inalienable patrimony of the Panamanian nation; therefore, it may not be sold, assigned, mortgaged, or otherwise encumbered or transferred.[301]

Canal Operations

Eighty countries operating along 160 trade routes use the canal to gain access from the East Coast of the United States to Asia, from the East Coast of the United States to the West Coast of South America, and from Europe to the West Coast of the United States and Canada. The Panama Canal is 40 miles long from shore to shore. Three double locks raise vessels, on average, 85 feet above sea level. The locks' chambers are 110 feet wide and 1,000 feet long. The maximum vessel dimensions allowed to traverse the canal is limited to a draft of 39.5 feet (12.04 meters), beam of 106 feet (32.31 meters), and length of 965 feet (294.13 meters). The principal commodities that transit the canal are grains, petroleum and derivatives, and containerized cargo. Nearly 200 million tons of cargo passed through the canal in 1999, representing about 4 percent of the world trade.[302]

Canal Toll Rates

Toll rates to transit the canal are determined per ton using the Panama Canal Universal Measurement System (PCUMS). PCUMS applies a mathematical formula to a vessel's total volume measurement to determine the PCUMS net tonnage. The total volume measurement is the same as used in the vessel's International Tonnage Certificate, a document that vessels are required to obtain as part of the governmental registration process. Canal toll rates as of January 30, 2001, are as follows: laden, $2.57 per PCUMS; ballast, $2.04 per PCUMS; and displacement, $1.43 per PCUMS. [303]

Canal Transit Volume

In October 2000, the PCA reported that oceangoing transits averaged 34.2 per day. Panamax vessels accounted for 39.6 percent of all oceangoing traffic, well above the PCA forecast of 35.2 percent. In October 2000, Panamax transits reached approximately 420, a growth of 9.7 percent compared to 382 Panamax transits registered in October 1999. Total Panama Canal transits for 2000 were 13,653 vessels. A recent long-term traffic demand forecast indicated that, over the next 50 years, the number of vessel transits could grow to almost double the current average number of approximately 14,000 transits per year and that the tonnage passed would increase even further.[304]

Future Developments

In February 2001, the Panama Canal Commission (PCC) endorsed a $4 billion canal expansion plan for a third set of larger locks. Currently, the canal is limited to vessels of approximately 4,000 TEUs.[305] As a result, some ships lose 20 percent of their capacity since they are unable to traverse the canal fully loaded. [306] The PCA has future plans to expand its infrastructure to accommodate ships between 4,800 TEUs and 6,000 TEUs. [307]

In regards to canal expansion, the PCC is requesting the PCA to broaden its feasibility and impact studies to examine, in detail, issues involving engineering, sociological, environmental, and financial matters first. The final decision to expand the canal is dependent on the completion of these studies.[308] One of the issues in expanding the canal is the existence of the technology necessary to build the 200-foot gates required for post-Panamax locks. Moreover, the PCA has not determined how to finance the expansion of the canal and is examining alternative capital resources that include private and public investment.[309]

The PCA is undertaking two projects to increase canal capacity that are prerequisites for a third set of locks. These are to deepen the artificial Lake Gatun by 3 feet, providing water for six more lock movements per day, and to excavate the canal's Pacific entrance to 46 feet, allowing Panamax-sized bulk carriers to enter fully laden. These projects would also boost the newly refurbished Port of Balboa. The cost would be $300-400 million, and work would begin in early 2002 after the end of the widening of Gaillard Cut, the canal's narrowest point, to allow two Panamax ships to pass each other there.[310]

The PCA is accelerating the completion of a $1 billion capital investment program to modernize and improve the canal and ensure the waterway is prepared to meet traffic demands and provide quality transit services. The major parts of the modernization and improvement program include widening of Gaillard Cut, increase in the towboat fleet, purchase of new and more-powerful locks locomotives, modernization of the marine traffic management and locks control systems, and replacement of 50,000 feet of locks tow track. Completion of the modernization and improvement program will increase canal transit capacity by about 20 percent. This program will guarantee a modern waterway and sufficient capacity for the canal to safely and efficiently meet projected traffic demand well into the 21st century.[311] Regarding the Gaillard Cut widening program, the PCA advised that the dry excavation is currently 97.5 percent complete while the underwater excavation is 85 percent complete. Likewise, 89.4 percent of the dry drilling and blasting has been completed, and underwater drilling and blasting are currently 94.2 percent completed.[312]

Colón Container Terminal S. A.

Background

The Panamanian government and Evergreen Marine Corporation (EMC) signed a 20-year development and management concession contact for the construction of Colón Container Terminal (CCT) in Coco Solo in January 1996, with the option to renew for another 20 years. CCT is centrally managed from the EMC home office in Taiwan and is the group's first terminal operation. The terminal is designed to operate on a common-user basis, open to all shipping lines calling on Panama; it also acts as a major transshipment hub for EMC. CCT is served by a number of transportation links: immediate water links with Pacific trades, Atlantic trades, and North-South American trades.

Operations

Total throughput at the terminal in 2000 was approximately 300,000 TEUs, of which about 70 percent was transshipment traffic. Of the remainder, more than 90 percent is earmarked for the CFZ. CCT is now averaging 30 crane movements per hour when handling the EMC mother ships and 27 moves an hour for the feeder services.[313] A rate for loading or discharging a domestic laden container is $260 a move, an empty container is $170 a move, and a laden or empty transshipment container is $120 a move.

The following services are covered by the container rates:

- operation of loading or discharging ISO standard containers to or from the vessels, including transportation between container yard and shipside;

- opening and closing of all hatch covers, booming of cranes up and down, and lashing and unlashing of the containers;

- tallying fee of the containers, gate inspection charges, issuing Equipment Interchange Receipt (EIR), and weighting charges for export loaded containers;

- visual inspection of containers and reporting of damages;

- straight time and overtime (except stand-by time) pay;

- controlling and reporting of containers and equipment at the terminal;

- wharfage for import/export loaded and empty containers;

- one security guard on board while vessel berthed; and

- receiving and delivering of information to and from shippers and receivers concerning container lifts and movement in and out of the terminal gates.[314]

Infrastructure

Covering 25 hectares, the first phase of CCT's $100 million project became operational in October 1997. The first development phase consisted of the construction of a 612-meter-long quay with 14 meters of water depth capable of handling two Panamax vessels or three regional feeder ships simultaneously. Five Mitsubishi 50-ton capacity Panamax gantry cranes serve vessels, and CCT has an annual capacity of 500,000 TEUs.[315]

CCT provides the following facilities to its customers; 25 hectares of total area, 612 meters of container berth, 14 meters of draft, 400,000-TEU storage capacity, 180 reefer plugs, five gantry cranes, 10 (3+1) Mi-Jack Travelifts, two top loaders, three side loaders, one forklift of 10 tons, three forklifts of 2.5 tons, 30 tractors and 30 chassis, two electronic weighbridges, agricultural quarantine, container maintenance and repair shop, fumigation services, and administration building with office space for shipping lines' agents.[316]

Security

Checkpoints and 24-hour patrols are manned throughout CCT. They are backed up by a closed-cable-TV system with 28 cameras that monitor the entire facility and a K-9 unit trained in narcotics detection. Additionally, CCT has a bike patrol unit trained under the regulation of International Mountain Bike Police Association and boat patrol system to guard the surroundings during operation. CCT's security system has been designed to comply with Super Carrier Initiative standards on security guard training, terminal access, cargo security, vehicle control, and lighting.

Computer System

CCT has an advanced computerized system to control and monitor shipside and yard operations with the following functions: Top-X real-time terminal operation system, yard planning and control, vessel preplanning and control, crane scheduling and berth planning, gate/shipside activities, and bay plan information available via EDI express.

Competition

CCT's main competition is with Manzanillo International Terminal (MIT); both terminals are located in the Port of Colón. CCT contracts with small independent liner shipping companies that do not require the connectivity and capacity of larger carriers. These liner shipping companies seek out the lowest rates to maintain their competitiveness.

Future Developments

CCT has 47 hectares of available land for expansion in Phases II and III. In 2001, CCT will start to develop Phase II, which will consist of 320 meters of berth, two post-Panamax gantry cranes, and container yard area. According to CCT's schedule, Phase II will be finished at the end of October 2002. Upon completion of Phase III, CCT will have nine gantry cranes, 72 hectares of container yard, 360 plugs for reefer containers, and a capacity of 1 million TEUs. An area of 20,000 square meters is planned for stacking more than 7,000 TEUs of empty containers with five tiers, and also a parking area of 4,570 square meters is reserved to park around 75 trailers.[317]

Manzanillo International Terminal S.A.

Background

The first terminal concession was awarded to the joint-venture partnership between SSA Panama, Inc., and the Motta and Heilbron families of Panama, for the construction and operation of Manzanillo International Terminal (MIT). SSA Panama, Inc., is the Panamanian affiliate of Stevedoring Services of America (SSA), a privately owned company headquartered in Seattle, Washington, that operates 152 terminals around the world. The Motta and Heilbron families introduced SSA to the MIT investment and development opportunity in the Republic of Panama. MIT is located in the Port of Colón adjacent to the CFZ. MIT began operations in April 1995, when it obtained a 20-year concession from the PCA with the option to renew for an additional 20 years.[318]

Operations

After privatization, MIT dominated the container traffic in Panama and is the largest container terminal in Panama. MIT operates as a transshipment terminal with 75 percent of its cargo moving through the port to other destinations. Transshipment container cargo moves through the terminal in approximately 3-5 days, real-time rotation. Of the remaining local container cargo, approximately 20 percent is moved to the CFZ. The balance is moved to the hinterland. Local container cargo moves through the terminal in 12-15 days. These time delays are mainly due to the limited warehousing in the CFZ and the hinterland. Cargo operations are carried out 24 hours a day, 7 days a week. In 2000, MIT handled more than 1.1 million TEUs. On average, the gantry cranes make 30 container moves per hour. MIT accommodates approximately 40 mainline shipping companies a month and 90 feeder calls. MIT offered liner shipping companies contracts for three to five years. The maximum vessel size that MIT can accommodate is 9,800 TEUs.[319] Over the past five years, rates for container moves are $265 per local container move and $175 per transshipment move, full or empty all-inclusive. Today, there is added competition in the Port of Colón from CCT and PCT.

Infrastructure

MIT has invested $300 million in superstructure capital improvements over the past five years. MIT provides the following facilities to its customers: 1,239 meters of contiguous container berth; 200 meters of berth for Ro-Ro; 25 meters of Ro-Ro ramp; 14 meters of draft in the access channel; 13 meters of draft alongside the berths; a 600-meter turning basin; 37 paved hectares of adjoining stacking and container yard area; two super post-Panamax rail-mounted gantry cranes; six post-Panamax rail-mounted gantry cranes; two Panamax rail-mounted gantry cranes; 500 reefer connections (220/440); 59 hectares of land available for automobile and container storage; terminal handling equipment for grounded operation (RTGs, top picks, side picks, yard tractors, and yard chassis); automated computer system for terminal, vessel, and gate activities with free customer access; and on-site office space for steamship lines and their agents.[320]

Security

MIT has terminal and vessel security provided in compliance with the Super Carrier Initiative Agreement. Other security features include an intelligent closed-circuit video system; high, broad-spectrum illumination for night operations; an elevated terminal surface and completed fenced facility; and an electronic cargo release system.

Quarantine Zone

MIT offers an on-dock container freight station (MIT-CFS) for the loading and unloading of consolidated freight. MIT-CFS also provides secure inspection services, cargo warehousing, container transloading, and inland transport services.

Direct Access to Colón Free Zone

Because of its physical proximity to the CFZ, MIT is the only terminal in Panama that has direct access link to the largest free zone in the Western Hemisphere.

Container Equipment Maintenance

The Container Equipment Maintenance Department (CEM) performs equipment inspections, preventive maintenance, corrective maintenance, and damage repair to container equipment, including dry boxes, over-the-road trailers, refrigerated containers, clip-ons, generator sets, reefer units, and container chassis. The CEM is also responsible for all live reefer monitoring, control, and maintenance. Steam cleaning and pretripping services are also available through the CEM. The MIT-CEM is a licensed Carrier/Transicold service center and parts distribution center with five certified Carrier/Transicold technicians. CEM personnel are available 24 hours a day and follow ISO guidelines.

Competition

Port capacity is a key consideration for liner shipping alliances. In order for a major shipping alliance to operate out of a terminal, the terminal has to have the capacity to service transshipment as well as regional feeder services business. A number of liner shipping companies have set up offices at MIT and are connected to their EDI computer systems.

Future Developments

In 2001, MIT plans to install an additional post-Panamax container crane at the cost of $6.1 million. The approximate time for installation and operation of the crane is 18 months. MIT is now drawing up plans to convert its Ro-Ro berth into an additional container-handling facility, move terminal administration to a new location across the street, and demolish the old building to add more hectares for container storage. In addition, MIT has 24 hectares of container yard currently under development and plans for a rear-dock intermodal rail facility scheduled for the year 2000-01   In the long term, 59 additional hectares and 250 meters of container berth with gantry cranes are scheduled future developments. MIT management is also examining the possibility of opening a second container terminal on the Pacific Coast to compete with Balboa as a transshipment port.[321]

Panama Ports Company

Background

Panama Ports Company (PPC) is a subsidiary of Hutchison Port Holdings (HPH), an independent port investor, developer, and operator with global interests in Asia, Europe, and the Americas. HPH, a subsidiary of Hutchison Whampoa Ltd. (HWL), is one of the listed companies under the Cheung Kong Group. PPC was awarded a 25-year concession from PMC, with an option to renew for an additional 25 years, to modernize, expand, and operate the Port of Balboa located on the Pacific Ocean and the Port of Cristóbal located on the Atlantic Ocean. PPC assumed control of the ports in March 1997; however, the official opening of Balboa Container Terminal was on November 14, 2000. Both ports handle containerized cargo, general cargo, bulk cargo, and vehicles. PPC is the only terminal operator in Panama with terminals on each side of the Panama Canal.

Operations

PPC strives to develop a dedicated transshipment hub managing and operating the Port of Balboa and the Port of Cristóbal as a coordinated facility. Port of Balboa Terminal (PBT) and Port of Cristóbal Terminal (PCT) customers can take advantage of their waiting times before transiting the canal by carrying out loading/discharging operations at either port. Thus, shipping lines may add Panama as a destination for local cargo or as a hub port for transshipment cargo while maintaining their original vessels' schedules.

Cargo operations are carried out 24 hours a day, 7 days a week. Working shift start and finish times are adjustable in order to suit the vessel and the customer's requirements. Both ports use computer systems for park and vessel planning and provide cargo information to their customers through EDI links. Container rates are the same for both ports: full local containers, $260 per move; empty local containers, $170 per move; and full or empty transshipment containers, $130 per move. If a PPC gantry crane is not available, the containership will be allowed to perform loading and discharging operations with the ship's own gear, in which case each container handled will be subject to a $20 discount per move.

Port of Balboa Terminal

Background

PBT is the only terminal on the Pacific Coast of Panama and is positioned with potential to be the transshipment hub for the West Coast of Latin America, servicing the world's major carriers operating on transpacific routes and the hinterland of Panama City. PBT has a key advantage in the depth of water alongside the quays. At 16 meters, the facility can handle the largest containerships, both afloat and on order. In terms of operations, such deepwater can allow existing operators transiting the canal to load up to 400 more containers on their vessels before commencing their passage. PPC has invested $120 million in the new container-handling facilities at PBT, for an annual handling capacity of 600,000 TEUs. Brand new RTGs with higher stacking capacity will increase terminal capacity, and additional off-dock container yards will be quickly developed to cope with extra volumes.

Infrastructure

PBT provides the following facilities to its customers: 181 acres of total area, 350 meters of container berth, 1,466 meters of general-cargo berth, three super post-Panamax quay cranes, nine RTGs, two reachstackers, four container toplifters, five empty handlers, 6,800-TEU stacking capacity, and 468 reefer plugs.[322]

Competition

PBT has no direct competition on the Pacific Ocean side of Panama. The closest, fully equipped container terminal to PBT in South America is located in San Antonio, Chile, approximately 2,700 miles away. Manzanillo, Mexico, is the closest container terminal in North America, approximately 1,750 miles away.

It is PPC vision that PBT will quickly become one of the major transshipment hubs for the world's container shipping lines. PPC's goal is to provide world-class service to all major carriers to further enhance their options to transport cargo to and from Asia, Europe, and the Americas.[323] However, PBT is still in the process of improving infrastructure and training labor in order to catch up with volume demands.

PBT has room to grow and will continue to dominate the Panamanian Pacific Coast and, very possibly, the entire Pacific Coast of Latin America. Nevertheless, there are a number of investors interested in developing a second terminal on the western side of the canal on the Pacific Coast of Panama. A second terminal will be very costly to build, requiring an investment of approximately $300 million.[324]

Future Developments

A modernization program is planned for PBT. After completing all phases of the modernization program, Balboa will have 1,500 meters of deepwater quay, 50 hectares of container storage area equipped with 12 post-Panamax container-handling cranes, and 28 RTGs. The annual capacity will be in excess of 1.5 million TEUs.[325]

Port of Cristóbal Terminal

Background

Port operations in Cristóbal started in 1851, when a wooden pier was built to handle the import of passengers and materials required for the construction on the Panama Railway. The state owned and operated the port until privatization in 1997. PCT extends out into the Port of Colón and is located at the gateway to the Atlantic side of the canal. PCT is a regional transshipment hub, using a well-established network in domestic and international markets. Reflecting the importance of the Port of Cristóbal, a modernization program of the existing facilities has begun. PCT work is focused on improving facilities at the existing, but small, container terminal. In 1999, PCT handled 69,510 containers. A cold freight storage (CFS) of 6,110 square meters is available for the storage of cargo and the stuffing and stripping of containers. PPC has acquired a new mobile harbor crane from Liebherr-Werk Nenzing GMBH, equipped with lift facilities to handle containers in the range of 20, 40 and 45 feet. This crane is state of the art and the largest in the Republic of Panama, capable of loading and discharging in excess of 30 containers per hour, which will allow PPC to offer shipping lines highly efficient container handling on all vessels up to Panamax size. The two gantry cranes are being refurbished while a heavy-duty mobile crane has been purchased to enhance cargo-handling activities.[326]

Terminal Facilities

PCT provides the following facilities to its customers: 143 acres of total area, 450 meters of container berth, 314 meters of Ro-Ro berth, 1,750 meters of general-cargo berth, two Panamax quay cranes, four RTGs, three reachstackers, seven container toplifters, two side lifters, four empty handlers, 5,400-TEU stacking capacity, 6,110 square meters of CFS area, and 27,809 square meters of warehousing.[327]

Competition

PCT's market is regional transshipment and the domestic market. Its overall market niche is breakbulk. Major infrastructure investment is needed in order for PCT to remain competitive.

Future Developments

An additional 450 meters of quay are planned for development, and the container storage area will be extended to 18 hectares, increasing the port's annual capacity to more than 300,000 TEUs. The terminal will also offer 2,855 meters of quay for self-sustained operations of containerized cargo, general cargo, bulk cargo, vehicles, and passengers.

When the modernization programs of both terminals are complete, PPC will have a combined annual handling capacity of 900,000 TEUs.[328]

Lessons Learned

In recent years, the liner shipping industry has undergone major changes in the way cargo is transported. The industry is seeking efficiency, standardization, and economies of scale to maintain competitiveness and lower unit cost. These goals have led to containerization and the building of larger vessels that can carry an increasing number of containers. There is also a growing tendency toward transshipment, which is one of the principal reasons that ports need to modify infrastructure. Privatization of port operations has provided the necessary capital to meet infrastructure requirement that governments simply cannot afford to do.

Private terminal operators are making the required investments to work toward being a major transshipment hub. However, infrastructure restrictions within Panama and governmental complacency could slow the development process. There is still no decent first-class road link between the ports at each end of the canal. Additionally, the dimension of the canal is limiting the size of vessels that can use the canal. The reopening of the rail link will provide carriers needed alternatives to the canal and allow increased container movement from coast to coast. The planned construction of a third set of locks will definitely provide increased capacity to move containers from coast to coast but will take time and major investment.

Panama has a very competitive inter- and intraport market. In order to compete, terminal operators must define and develop niche markets. There is a growing tendency for terminal operators to provide in one place as many services as they can. Terminals are using advanced computer-operating systems, improving logistics, and providing in-house employee training. It is crucial that terminals match capacity with demand and build capacity without overinvesting.

Notes

[1] Antonio Estache Ginés de Rus, ed., *Privatization and Regulation of Transport Infrastructure*, WBI Development Studies (Washington, D.C.: The World Bank Institute, 2000), p. 120.

[2] Ibid.

[3] Ibid.

[4] Port of Buenos Aires, *Welcome*. Online. Available: http://www.bairesport.gov.ar/welcome.htm. Accessed: March 18, 2001.

[5] Comisión Económica para America Latina y el Caribe, *Port Moves, Latin American and the Caribbean, Top 20 moves*. Online. Available: http://www.eclac.cl/transporte/perfil/index.html. Accessed: March 18, 2001.

[6] For the purposes of this case study, we will include all container terminals in the province of Buenos Aires, rather than just those located in the Puerto Nuevo area.

[7] Port of Buenos Aires, *Movimiento de Contenedores en el Puerto de Buenos Aires*, Buenos Aires, Argentina, 1999 (pamphlet).

[8] Port of Buenos Aires, *Terminales—Terminales Rio de la Plata*. Online. Available: http://www.bairesport.gov.ar/english/e-ingenier/e-infraest/t1t2-e.htm. Accessed: March 18, 2001.

[9] Ibid.

[10] Ibid.

[11] Port of Buenos Aires, *Terminales—Terminales Portuarias Argentinas*. Online. Available: http://www.bairesport.gov.ar/english/e-ingenier/e-infraest/t3-e.htm. Accessed: March 18, 2001.

[12] Ibid.

[13] Terminales Portuarias Argentina, *Container Operation*. Online. Available: http://www.tpa.com.ar/. Accessed: March 19, 2001.

[14] Port of Buenos Aires, *Terminales—BACTSSA*. Online. Available: http://www.bairesport.gov.ar/english/e-ingenier/e-infraest/t5-e.htm. Accessed: March 18, 2001.

[15] Buenos Aries Container Terminal Services, *Informational Brochure*, Buenos Aires, Argentina, 2000 (pamphlet).

[16] Ibid.

[17] Ibid.

[18] Exolgan, *Shareholders*. Online. Available: http://www.exolgan.com/institucional/tecnologia/ing-frame.htm. Accessed: March 19, 2001.

[19] Exolgan, *Infrastructure and Technologies*. Online. Available: http://www.exolgan.com/institucional/tecnologia/ing-frame.htm. Accessed: March 19, 2001.

[20] Ibid.

[21] Administración General de Puertos Sociedad del Estado, *Estadistica Del Movimiento Portuario Ano 1999* (Buenos Aires, 2000), Grafico No. 3.

[22] Ibid., Cuadro No. 9.

[23] Interview by Celestino Gallegos with Capt. Aldo Moroz, Superintendent, BACTSSA, Buenos Aires, Argentina, January 15, 2001.

[24] Ibid.

[25] Ibid.

[26] Martin Sgut, *Estudio sobre reestructuración portuaria—Impacto Social*. Online. Available: http://www.ilo.org/public/spanish/dialogue/sector/papers/port-ba/bsas3.htm. Accessed March 20, 2001.

[27] Ibid.

[28] Ibid.

[29] Ibid.

[30] Moroz interview; Mario de Pedro, ed. *Argentine Ports*, Manrique Zago ediciones (Buenos Aires, 1998), p. 34; and interview by Celestino Gallegos with Ing. Ricardo H. Del Valle, Interventor, Administración General de Puertos S.E. Puerto Buenos Aires, Buenos Aires, Argentina, January 17, 2001.

[31] Sgut, *Estudio sobre reestructuración portuaria* (online).

[32] Ibid.

[33] Interview by Celestino Gallegos with Antonio Zuidwijk, Director, Murchison S.A., Buenos Aires, Argentina, January 16, 2001.

[34] Sgut, *Estudio sobre reestructuración portuaria* (online).

[35] Ibid.

[36] Ibid.

[37] Ibid.

[38] Ibid.

[39] Ibid.

[40] Ibid.

[41] Ibid.

[42] de Pedro, ed., *Argentine Ports*, pp. 38, 42.

[43] Ibid.; see also Del Valle interview.

[44] Sgut, *Estudio sobre reestructuración portuaria* (online).

[45] Port of Buenos Aires, *Nuevo Comisión para el Consejo Portuario Argentino*. Online. Available: http://www.buenosairesport.com.ar. Accessed: April 23, 2001.

[46] Zuidwijk interview.

[47] Sgut, *Estudio sobre reestructuración portuaria* (online).

[48] Ibid.

[49] Moroz interview.

[50] Sgut, *Estudio sobre reestructuración portuaria* (online).

[51] Gerencia Comercial de la Administración General de Puertos, *Posicionamiento del Puerto de Buenos Aires en el Mercado* (Buenos Aires, 2000), p.1.

[52] Zuidwijk interview.

[53] Ibid.

[54] Del Valle interview.

[55] Ibid.

[56] Gerencia Comercial de la Administración General de Puertos, *Posicionamiento del Puerto de Buenos Aires en el Mercado*, p.1.

[57] Ibid.

[58] Zuidwijk interview.

[59] Del Valle interview.

[60] Zuidwijk interview.

[61] Interview by Celestino Gallegos with Lic. Alberto Ramirez, General Manager, Camara de Puertos Privados Comerciales, Buenos Aires, Argentina, January 17, 2001.

[62] Ibid.

[63] Zuidwijk interview.

[64] Ibid.

[65] *Puerto Cabello Port Handbook*, 1st ed. (Essex, U.K.: Land and Marine Publications Ltd., 1999), p. 7.

[66] Instituto Puerto Autonomo de Puerto Cabello, *Port Statistics Handbook 1999* (Puerto Cabello, Venezuela, 1999), pp. 139-41.

[67] Unpublished data obtained from O. Guerreiro, Marketing Director, Instituto Puerto Autonomo de Puerto Cabello, Puerto Cabello, Venezuela, December 22, 2000.

[68] Interview by Ravi Subramanian with Tomas Palacios, Operations Supervisor, H. L. Boulton and Company/Terminal Port Services, Puerto Cabello, Venezuela, December 20, 2000.

[69] Interview by Ravi Subramanian with L. Blanco, General Manager, P&O Nedlloyd Maritime of Venezuela, Puerto Cabello, Venezuela, December 21, 2000.

[70] Instituto Puerto Autonomo de Puerto Cabello, *Compilacion Legal,* 3rd ed. (Puerto Cabello, Venezuela, n.d.).

[71] Interview by Ravi Subramanian with G. Vierma, President, EMESCA Stevedoring Terminal Operators, Puerto Cabello, Venezuela, December 21, 2000.

[72] Interview by Ravi Subramanian with O. Guerreiro, Marketing Director, Instituto Puerto Autonomo de Puerto Cabello, Puerto Cabello, Venezuela, December 22, 2000.

[73] *Puerto Cabello Port Handbook*, p. 54.

[74] Instituto Puerto Autonomo de Puerto Cabello, *Port Statistics Handbook 1999,* p. 104.

[75] Interview by Ravi Subramanian with J. Pizzolante, Sabatino Pizzolante Maritime and Commercial Attorneys, Puerto Cabello, Venezuela, December 20, 2000.

[76] Port Authority of Jamaica (PAJ), *The Jamaica Ports Handbook 2001-2002* (Essex, U.K.: Land and Marine Publications Ltd., 2000), p. 22.

[77] Ibid., p. 16.

[78] Interview by Anna Okola and Daniel Stein with Bryon G. Lewis, Senior Vice President, Special Projects, Port Authority of Jamaica, Kingston, Jamaica, January 11, 2001.

[79] PAJ, *Jamaica Ports Handbook*, p. 7.

[80] Lewis interview.

[81] Ibid.

[82] Ibid.

[83] Interview by Anna Okola and Daniel Stein with Roger Hinds, CEO Transocean Shipping Limited, and separate interview with Robert Kinlocke, Managing Director, Kingston Terminal Operators Limited, Kingston, Jamaica, January 12, 2001.

[84] Kinlocke interview.

[85] Ibid.

[86] Interview by Anna Okola and Daniel Stein with Condell G. Stephenson, General Manager—Operations, Kingston Terminal Operators, Kingston, Jamaica, January 12, 2001.

[87] Interview by Anna Okola and Daniel Stein with Nicholas Baylis, Security Safety Manager, Kingston Terminal Operators, and with Marguerite Cooke, Public Relations and Community Relations Manager, Port Authority of Jamaica, Kingston, Jamaica, January 11, 2001.

[88] Kinlocke and Condell G. Stephenson interviews.

[89] Ibid.

[90] PAJ, *Jamaica Ports Handbook*, p. 23.

[91] Lewis interview; and separate interviews by Anna Okola and Daniel Stein with Grantley Stephenson, President, and Alvin C. Henry, General Manager, The Shipping Association of Jamaica, Kingston, Jamaica, January 11, 2001

[92] Lewis interview.

[93] Ibid.

[94] Ibid.

[95] Grantley Stephenson and Henry interviews.

[96] Ibid.

[97] Ibid.

[98] PAJ, "Transshipment & Domestic TEUs at the Port of Kingston (1975-1999)," Kingston, Jamaica, January 2001 (computer printout).

[99] Ibid.

[100] Interview by Anna Okola and Daniel Stein with Joseph Lowe, Managing Director, Hamburg Süd/Columbus, Jamaica Limited, Shipping Agents, Kingston, Jamaica, January 12, 2001.

[101] PAJ, "Port Costs for Sample Container," Kingston, Jamaica, March 2001 (response to Lyndon B. Johnson School of Public Affairs student survey).

[102] Lewis interview.

[103] Ibid.

[104] Ibid.

[105] PAJ, *Annual Report 2000* (Kingston, Jamaica: March 31, 2000), p. 1.

[106] Ibid., p. 7.

[107] Interview by Cindy Rosales Bush with Uwe Brietling, Port, Transport and Training Consultant, TRAINMAR, San José, Costa Rica, January 10, 2001.

[108] Secretaría de Integración Económica de Centro America (SEICA), "Central American Transport Study," Guatemala, November 2000 (draft), n.p.

[109] Junta de Administración Portuaria y de Desarollo Económico de la Vertiente Atlantico (JAPDEVA), Administración de Desarollo, *Plan de Desarollo Regional Provincia de Limón 1999-2004/2009+*, Document I (Limón, Costa Rica, 2000), p. 138.

[110] Ibid.

[111] Ibid.

[112] Interview by Cindy Rosales Bush with Karl McQueen, Superintendent, Port of Limón, JAPDEVA, Limón, Costa Rica, January 12, 2001.

[113] JAPDEVA, *Plan de Desarollo Regional Provincia de Limón,* pp. 136-37.

[114] Ibid., p. 140.

[115] Carlos Lucas, "Actualidad Portuaria De Costa Rica" (paper presented at the [First] Ecícuentro Iberoamericano Sobre Intercambio Tecnológico Portuario, Cancún, Mexico, April 2000), p. 8.

[116] The English translation is the Board of Directors for Port Administration and Economical Development of the Atlantic Coast.

[117] Lucas, "Actualidad Portuaria De Costa Rica," p. 8.

[118] SEICA, "Central American Transport Study," n.p.

[119] Interview by Cindy Rosales Bush with Marlon Clarke Spencer, Port Consultant, JAPDEVA, Limón, Costa Rica, January 11, 2001.

[120] Breitling interview.

[121] United Nations Economic Commission for Latin America and the Caribbean (ECLAC), *Maritime Profile of Latin America and the Caribbean: Container Traffic*. Online. Available: http://www.cepal.cl/transporte/perfil/indexe.html. Accessed: February 18, 2001.

[122] Lucas, "Actualidad Portuaria De Costa Rica," p. 14.

[123] JAPDEVA, *Plan de Desarollo Regional Provincia de Limón,* p. 138.

[124] Brietling interview.

[125] Interview by Cindy Rosales Bush with Carlos Thomas, Director of Port Operations, Chiquita Brands, Limón, Costa Rica, January 12, 2001. Thomas maintains that even though tariffs dropped, the clients did not realize the savings because they were forced to compensate those workers who lost their jobs as a result of the reform.

[126] Chiquita Brands is not completely satisfied with the services received from the stevedoring company. However, because of an oral agreement with the same company for more than 20 years, this is an obligation. Thomas interview.

[127] Interview by Cindy Rosales Bush with Gilberto Wilson, Department of Planning, JAPDEVA, Limón, Costa Rica, January 11, 2001.

[128] Lucas, "Actualidad Portuaria De Costa Rica," p .8.

[129] SEICA, "Central American Transport Study," n.p.

[130] Ibid.

[131] Some argue that moneys were appropriated from the Taiwanese loan, acquired to construct the Taiwanese dock in the Port of Moín, for the purpose of the crane but that national bureaucratic practices and corruption prevent the release of funds necessary for the purchase of the crane.

[132] Both Karl McQueen and Carlos Thomas accentuate that privatization will take place because it is the only feasible solution to the overcrowding and inefficient problems that the port complex currently faces. McQueen and Thomas interviews.

[133] Gerardo Martinez of Crowley Liner Services said that JAPDEVA has been cooperative and strives to accommodate the needs of his company. He referred to a new "Ro-Ro" ramp put in place for its ships and JAPDEVA's dedication to the strategic plan it published and subsequent request for infrastructure equipment (reference is made to the short-term strategic plan mentioned under subtopic "Future Plans"). He also praised JAPDEVA for deregulating the stevedore oligopoly. Interview by Cindy Rosales Bush with Gerardo Martinez, Port Agent, Crowley Liner Services, Limón, Costa Rica, January 12, 2001.

[134] Last year the Costa Rican government attempted privatization of the national electric and telecommunications company ICED. The people revolted with strikes and protests. It proved to be a failure. Brietling interview.

[135] JAPDEVA currently invests 10% of its earnings in the social and educational development of the province of Limón. Interview by Cindy Rosales Bush with Gilberto Brown Fairclough, Coordinator, Regional Development Plan, JAPDEVA, Limón, Costa Rica, January 11, 2001.

[136] Karl McQueen stated that job loss is something to expect; in the end, a more efficient port will benefit everyone. McQueen interview.

[137] In August 2000, a new administration came into office in the country; the new president was from a different political party than the exiting president. As is the tradition in the country, the change in president signaled the removal of the civil workforce including those in the port authority.

[138] *Containerisation International*, "Ports" database. Online. Available: http://www.ci-online.co.uk/. Accessed: March 11, 2001.

[139] Gustaaf de Monie et al., Policy Research Corporation N.V., *Strategies for Global and Regional Port— The Case of Caribbean Container and Cruise Ports* (Boston: Kluwer Academic Publishers, 1998), p. 67.

[140] ECLAC, *Maritime Profile* (online). Accessed: March 11, 2000.

[141] Interviews by David Wortman with Silvio Ureña Mendoza, Secretary General, Federation of Dominican Port Workers (Federación Dominicana de los Trabajabores Portuarios), Santo Domingo, Dominican Republic, December 2000 and January 2001.

[142] Ureña Mendoza interview, January 2001.

[143] ECLAC, *Maritime Profile* (online).

[144] de Monie et al., *Strategies*, pp. 46-47.

[145] Chris Peters et al., Policy Research Corporation N.V., *Economic Impact Study (EIS) for the Maritime Sector of the Netherlands Antilles—Conclusion and Recommendations* (Delft, The Netherlands: Delft University Press, 1998), p. 13.

[146] Interview by David Wortman with Federico Schad, Vice President, F. Schad Shipping Agents, and former President, Dominican Shippers Association (Asociación de Naverios de la Republica Dominicana), Santo Domingo, Dominican Republic, December 15, 2000.

[147] Antonio Estache, Gustavo Nombela, and Lourdes Trujillo, "Towards Increased Port Competition in the Dominican Republic," May 2000 (draft report).

[148] de Monie et al., *Strategies*, p. 67.

[149] Estache, "Towards Increased Port Competition," p. 1.

[150] Ibid.

[151] de Monie et al., *Strategies*, pp. 46-47; and Estache et al. "Towards Increased Port Competition."

[151] Estache, et al., "Towards Increased Port Competition." p. 1.

[151] de Monie et al., *Strategies*, pp. 46-47.

[152] Interview by Celestino Gallegos with Alberto Borquez and Peter McGivern at San Antonio International Terminal, San Antonio, Chile, January 12, 2001.

[153] Ministerio de Transportes y Telecomunicaciones del Gobierno del Presidente Eduardo Frei Ruiz-Tagle, *Modernizacion Portuaria en Chile 1994-2000* (Santiago, Chile, 1999), p. 12.

[154] Puerto de San Antonio, *Index*. Online. Available: http://www.puertosanantonio.cl/puerto/index2001.htm. Accessed: February 26, 2001.

[155] Ibid.

[156] ECLAC, *Perfil Maritimo—Port Moves*. Online. Available: http://www.eclac.cl/transporte/perfil/index.html. Accessed: April 23, 2001.

[157] Borquez and McGivern interview.

[158] The system cannot be called be called a true mono-operator system yet because of the continued presence of the "Espigón" terminal at each port. Despite the long-term goal of phasing out this system, there has not been any effort to make concession agreements for its operation in the near future. The belief is that the increased efficiency of the concessioned terminals will capture the lion's share of the container traffic and eventually render the multioperator terminals obsolete. The lack of a proactive stance by the government has generated criticism from the private concessionaires in the port as well as from officials from the Maritime Chamber of Commerce.

[159] SAAM is a subsidiary of the Chilean Shipping Line Compania Sudamericana de Vapores S.A. (CSAV).

[160] Cámara Marítima y Portuaria de Chile A.G., *Memoria Annual No. 56: 1999*, p. 10 (private report).

[161] Ibid.

[162] Ibid.

[163] Ibid.

[164] Ministerio de Transportes y Telecomunicaciones del Gobierno del Presidente Eduardo Frei Ruiz-Tagle, *Modernizacion Portuaria en Chile 1994-2000*, p. 10.

[165] The multioperator system is a "tool port" scheme, where the state maintains ownership of all the port infrastructure but allows private operators to offer cargo-handling services at the port. This arrangement was solidified by the enactment of Port Law No. 18.966, which assigned all port handling to private operators and relegated Emporchi to an administrative role in the ports—its primary responsibility became maintaining port infrastructure and offering storage services.

[166] Ministerio de Transportes y Telecomunicaciones del Gobierno del Presidente Eduardo Frei Ruiz-Tagle, *Modernizacion Portuaria en Chile 1994-2000*, p. 22.

[167] Interview by Celestino Gallegos with Jose Luis Mardones, Santiago, Chile, January 11, 2001.

[168] Interview by Celestino Gallegos with Enrique Morales, Development and Concessions Manager, Port of Valparaiso, Valparaiso, Chile, January 12, 2001.

[169] Ministerio de Transportes y Telecomunicaciones del Gobierno del Presidente Eduardo Frei Ruiz-Tagle, *Modernizacion Portuaria en Chile 1994-2000*, p. 22.

[170] Ibid., p. 14.

[171] Ibid., p. 22.

[172] José Luis Mardones Santander, *Concesiones Portuarias en Chile: Una Reforma Para Crear Valor* (Santiago, Chile, November 2000), p. 6.

[173] Ibid., p. 7.

[174] Mardones Santander interview.

[175] Ministerio de Transportes y Telecomunicaciones del Gobierno del Presidente Eduardo Frei Ruiz-Tagle, *Modernizacion Portuaria en Chile 1994-2000*, p. 14.

[176] Morales interview.

[177] Mardones Santander interview.

[178] Morales interview.

[179] Mardones Santander interview.

[180] Mardones Santander, *Concesiones Portuarias en Chile*, p. 20.

[181] Ibid., p. 29.

[182] Ministerio de Transportes y Telecomunicaciones del Gobierno del Presidente Eduardo Frei Ruiz-Tagle, *Modernizacion Portuaria en Chile 1994-2000*, p. 10; Mardones Santander, *Concesiones Portuarias en Chile*, p. 6; and Cámara Marítima y Portuaria de Chile A.G., *Memoria Annual No. 56: 1999*, p. 10

[183] Ibid.

[184] Morales interview.

[185] Cámara Marítima y Portuaria de Chile A.G., *Memoria Annual No. 56*, p. 15.

[186] Ministerio de Transportes y Telecomunicaciones del Gobierno del Presidente Eduardo Frei Ruiz-Tagle, *Modernizacion Portuaria en Chile 1994-2000*, p. 34.

[187] Mardones Santander, *Concesiones Portuarias en Chile*, p. 29.

[188] Ibid., p. 30.

[189] Interview by Celestino Gallegos with Rodolfo García, Executive Vice President, Maritime Chamber of Commerce of Chile, Valparaiso, Chile, January 11, 2001; and interview by Celestino Gallegos with Miguel Oses Lorca, Coordinator, International Federation of Labor, Valparaiso, Chile, January 12, 2001.

[190] García interview. Mr. Garcia offered as an example the concession clause that terminates the contract if six days pass without operations. A strike that blocked access for six days would effectively cause the concessionaire to lose its concession and forfeit all investment made in that terminal.

[191] Oses Lorca interview.

[192] Ibid.

[193] Cámara Marítima y Portuaria de Chile A.G., *Memoria Annual No. 56*, p. 1.

[194] Puerto de San Antonio, *Index* (online). Accessed: March 1, 2001.

[195] Borquez and McGivern interview.

[196] Ibid.

[197] José Luis Mardones Santander, *Concesiones Portuarias: Hay Competencia Desleal?* (Santiago, Chile, January 10, 2001), p. 1.

[198] Ibid., p. 3.

[199] Ibid.

[200] Ibid.

[201] Morales interview.

[202] Ibid. Mr. Morales offered the existence of a common marketing delegation to maritime trade shows as evidence of the port authority's concern for the performance of the port as a whole. Still, complaints have been made that such marketing efforts are superficial, because there is little area for participation by the concessionaires allowed in the development of marketing materials as well as during marketing presentations.

[203] Mardones, *Concesiones Portuarias*, p. 1.

[204] Companhia Docas do Estado de São Paulo, *Porto de Santos*. Online. Available: http://www.portodesantos.com.br. Accessed: March 22, 2001.

[205] Companhia Docas do Estado de São Paulo Porto de Santos, *Port of Santos-profile*, Santos, Brazil (pamphlet).

[206] ECLAC, *Maritime Profile of Latin America and the Caribbean* (online). Accessed: March 21, 2001.

[207] Robert Ward, "The Battle of Santos," *Containerisation International* (February 2001), p. 62.

[208] Companhia Docas do Estado de São Paulo Porto de Santos, *Port of Santos-profile*.

[209] Interview by Richard Rodarte with Fabio Ferraro Oliari, Administrator, Companhia Docas do Estado de São Paulo Porto de Santos, Santos, Brazil, January 24, 2001.

[210] Companhia Docas do Estado de São Paulo, *Porto de Santos* (online).

[211] Ibid.

[212] Interview by Richard Rodarte with Henry James Robinson, Technical Director, Libra Terminals, Santos, Brazil, January 25, 2001.

[213] Ibid.

[214] Fairplay Daily News, "Santos Comes under the Spotlight," *Fairplay Publications Ltd.* (February 21, 2001). Online. Available: http://fairplay.co.uk/magazine/. Accessed: March 25, 2001.

[215] Ibid.

[216] Robinson interview.

[217] Oliari interview.

[218] Ward, "The Battle of Santos," p. 62.

[219] Fairplay Daily News, "Santos Seeks Foreign Partner," *Fairplay International Shipping Weekly* (March 8, 2001). Online. Available: http://fairplay.co.uk/magazine/. Accessed: March 25, 2001.

[220] Interview by Richard Rodarte with Ubiratan Vargas Xavier, Supervisor, Operations, Orgao de Gestao de Mao-de-Obra do Trabalho Portuario do Porto Organizado de Santos, Santos, Brazil, January 25, 2001.

[221] Ibid.

[222] Fairplay Daily News, "Santos Paralysis Averted," *Fairplay Publications Ltd.* (February 5, 2001). Online. Available: http://fairplay.co.uk/magazine/. Accessed: March 9, 2001.

[223] Ward, "The Battle of Santos," p. 62.

[224] Xavier interview. The current governor of São Paulo is from Santos, and his father was a stevedore.

[225] Xavier interview.

[226] Ibid.

[227] Fairplay Daily News, "Santos Seeks Foreign Partner" (online).

[228] Ibid.

[229] Tecon: Terminal de Conteineres, *Investiments*. Online. Available: http://www.santosbrasil.com.br. Accessed: March 22, 2001.

[230] Ibid.

[231] Terminal Updates, "New Cranes for Santos as Traffic Rises," *Containerisation International* (June 1999), p. 3. The TCT recorded losses of $8 million in 2000, making a total of $42 million lost since taking on the terminal in September 1997.

[232] Fairplay Daily News, "$30m Expansion at Tecon One," *Fairplay Daily News* (February 2, 2001). Online. Available: http://fairplay.co.uk/magazine/. Accessed: March 25, 2001.

[233] Robinson interview.

[234] Fairplay Daily News, "Ports Vie for Mercosur Hub," *Fairplay International Shipping Weekly* (October 26, 2000). Online. Available: http://fairplay.co.uk/magazine/. Accessed: March 21, 2001.

[235] Ibid.

[236] Sepetiba began operations in December 1999 and reached approximately 50,000 TEUs in 2000. Sepetiba is located near the industrial heartland of the country and is well located to receive cargo to and from São Paulo and Rio de Janeiro. It has developed an entrance channel with a depth of 19 meters, making it a sufficient deepwater option to Santos. Currently, only two liner shipping companies use

Sepetiba's terminal: Maersk and Docenave. Suape is located on the extreme coastal point of Brazil. If a vessel intends to come from Europe and the United States to drop their cargo in just one port, Suape has good conditions to be this port, because of its geographical location. However, geography has not made it a rich or industrial area as of yet. Suape handled 62,500 TEUs in 2000; with the right investment, it could be handling more than 500,000 TEUs within the next ten years. As of March 12, 2001, the Philippine port operator International Container Terminal Services, Inc. (ICTSI) had won a $180 million 30-year concession contract to operate a private terminal at the Port of Suape. Suape will be used as a hub for ICTSI in Latin America. According to CODESP, ICTSI will have to pay $4 per full box moved through the port.

[237] Oliari interview.

[238] Privatization.org, *Political and Organizational Strategies for Streamlining*. Online. Available: http://www.privatization.org. Accessed: March 30, 2001.

[239] Lyndon B. Johnson (LBJ) School of Public Affairs, *Transportation in the Americas: Its Role in International Trade, Economic Integration, and Sustainable Development,* Policy Research Project Report Series, no. 135 (Austin, Tex., 2000), p. 97.

[240] Administración Portuaria Integral de Veracruz, S.A. de C.V., *Puerto de Veracruz Movimiento de Carga y Buques Septiembre del 2000 y Acumulado Enero-Septiembre del 2000* (Veracruz, Mexico, September 2000), p. 43.

[241] LBJ School of Public Affairs, *Transportation in the Americas,* pp. 97-98.

[242] Ibid.

[243] Ibid., p. 98.

[244] Ibid.

[245] Administración Portuaria Integral de Veracruz, S.A. de C.V., *Puerto de Veracruz Movimiento de Carga y Buques Septiembre del 2000 y Acumulado Enero-Septiembre del 2000,* p. 3.

[246] Ibid., p. 14.

[247] LBJ School of Public Affairs, *Transportation in the Americas,* p. 99.

[248] Alicia Herrera, "Mexico: Port Administrations," International Marketing Insight, U.S. & Foreign Commercial Service and U.S. Department of State. Online. Available: http://www.tradeport.org/countries/mexico/mrr/mark0236.html. Accessed: December 1, 1999.

[249] Ibid.

[250] Ibid.

[251] Ibid.

[252] Ibid.

[253] Interview by Angelica Cervantes with Serafin Vasquez, Director, Planning and Development for Administración Porturia Integral de Veracruz, Veracruz, Mexico, January 16, 2001.

[254] Ibid.

[255] Interview by Angelica Cervantes with Wenceslao Tejeda Delgado, Director, Operations of Terminales de Cargas Especializadas, Veracruz, Veracruz, Mexico, January 16, 2001.

[256] Mexican Ministry of Communications and Transport, *Transformation of the Mexican Ports System Strategies and Achievements to Increase Private Investment* (Mexico City, September 2000).

[257] Secretariat of Communications and Transportation, "Estrategia Para la Transformacion Portuaria," *La Transformacion Portuaria y Avances 1994-1999,* n.d., p. 109.

[258] Ibid., pp. 110-11.

[259] Interview by Angelica Cervantes with Gustavo Jimenez Vasquez, Manager, Commercialization for Corporacion Integral de Comercio Exterior, Veracruz, Mexico, January 15, 2001.

[260] Serafin Vasquez interview.

[261] Gustavo Jimenez Vasquez interview.

[262] Mexican Ministry of Communications and Transport, *Transformation of the Mexican Ports System Strategies and Achievements.*

[263] Interview by Angelica Cervantes with Arturo Cruz Aguilera, Instructor, Trainmar in Veracruz, Veracruz, Mexico, January 15, 2001.

[264] Mexican Ministry of Communications and Transport, *Transformation of the Mexican Ports System Strategies and Achievements.*

[265] Serafin Vasquez interview.

[266] Mexican Ministry of Communications and Transport, *Transformation of the Mexican Ports System Strategies and Achievements.*

[267] Serafin Vasquez interview.

[268] Mexican Ministry of Communications and Transport, *Transformation of the Mexican Ports System Strategies and Achievements.*

[269] Serafin Vasquez interview.

[270] Ibid.

[271] Gustavo Jimenez Vasquez interview.

[272] Cruz Aguilera interview.

[273] LBJ School of Public Affairs, *Transportation in the Americas,* p. 100.

[274] Ibid.

[275] Ibid.

[276] Tejeda Delgado interview.

[277] International Organization of Standardization in Geneva issued certification to Curaçao, which is the only port in its region to receive the ISO 9002.

[278] Peters et al., *Economic Impact Study*, p. 116.

[279] Interview by David Wortman with Karel Aster, Managing Director, Curaçao Port Services, Willemstad, Curaçao, January 5, 2001.

[280] Interview by David Wortman with Agustin Diaz, current Director and former Chairman, Board of Curaçao Port Authority, Willemstad, Curaçao, January 6, 2001.

[281] Interview by David Wortman with Giby Marchena, President, Union of Christian Port Workers (Sindicato de Trabajadores Cristianos del Puerto), Willemstad, Curaçao, January 5, 2001.

[282] de Monie et al., *Strategies,* p. 35.

[283] Aster interview.

[284] de Monie et al., *Strategies,* p. 35.

[285] Paul Couch, *Panama Maritime Yearbook 2000* (Norfolk: Compass Publications Limited, 1999), p. 9.

[286] Panama Canal Railway Company, *Land-Bridge Railroad of the Americas*, Balboa, Panama (pamphlet).

[287] Panama Maritime Authority, *Maritime Index*. Online. Available: http://www.intersite-pma.com/maritime/indexing. Accessed: February 20, 2001.

[288] Interview by with Thomas Kenna, Marketing Director, Panama Canal Railway Company, Balboa, Panama, January 16, 2001.

[289] Ibid.

[290] John Fossey, "Top Class," *Containerisation International* (July 2000), p. 71.

[291] Interview by Richard Rodarte with Rommel Troetsch, Customer Service and Public Relations Manager, Panama Ports Company S. A., Balboa, Panama, January 17, 2001.

[292] Interview by Richard Rodarte with Carlos Urriola Tam, Vice President, Marketing, Manzanillo International Terminal, Colón, Panama, January 15, 2001.

[293] Urriola Tam interview.

[294] Couch, *Panama Maritime Yearbook 2000*, p. 57.

[295] Ibid.

[296] Interview by Richard Rodarte with Ruben Reyna, President, International MarConsult, Panama City, Panama, January 16, 2001.

[297] John Fossey, "Panamanian Pulse," *Containerisation International* (October 2000), p. 61.

[298] ECLAC, *Profile of Latin America and the Caribbean ECLAC 2000*. Online. Available: http://www.eclac.org. Accessed: February 21, 2001.

[299] Couch, *Panama Maritime Yearbook 2000*, p. 35.

[300] Interview with Jan Hoffmann, Economist, Transport Unit, Economic Commission for Latin American and the Caribbean, Santiago, Chile, January 19, 2001.

[301] Panama Canal Authority (PCA), *General Information*. Online. Available: http://www.pancanal.com. Accessed: February 25, 2001.

[302] PCA, Corporate Communications Division, *The Panama Canal*, Balboa, Panama (pamphlet).

[303] Interview by Richard Rodarte with Lilibeth Langoni, Customer Relations, Department of Corporate Planning and Marketing, Panama Canal Authority, Balboa, Panama, January 16, 2001.

[304] PCA, *Maritime Operations*. Online. Available: http://www.pancanal.com. Accessed: January 29, 2001.

[305] Langoni interview.

[306] Reyna interview.

[307] Langoni interview.

[308] "Panama Canal Panel OKs Wider Locks, Seeks Further Study," *Journal of Commerce Online*. Online. Available: http://www.job.com/. Accessed: February 16, 2001.

[309] Interview by Richard Rodarte with Onesimo V. Sanchez, Department of Corporate Planning and Marketing, Panama Canal Authority, Balboa, Panama, January 16, 2001.

[310] "Panama Canal Panel OKs Wider Locks," *Journal of Commerce Online* (online).

[311] PCA, *Programs and Projects*. Online. Available: http://www.pancanal.com. Accessed: January 29, 2001.

[312] PCA, *Maritime Operations* (online).

[313] Couch, *Panama Maritime Yearbook 2000*, p. 38.

[314] Email from Ragbir Singh, Sales and Marketing Representative, Colón Container Terminal S.A., "Schedule A, Basic Rates and Charges," to Bryant Renato, Senior Operations Supervisor, February 25, 2001.

[315] Couch, *Panama Maritime Yearbook 2000*, p. 38.

[316] Singh email.

[317] Ibid.

[318] Couch, *Panama Maritime Yearbook 2000,* p. 31.

[319] Urriola Tam interview.

[320] Ibid.

[321] Ibid.

[322] Hutchison Port Holdings Group, *Panama Ports Company,* Balboa, Panama (pamphlet).

[323] Troetsch interview.

[324] Reyna interview.

[325] Hutchison Port Holdings Group, *Panama Ports Company.*

[326] Fossey, "Top Class," p. 72.

[327] Hutchison Port Holdings Group, *Panama Ports Company.*

[328] Troetsch interview.

Chapter 4. Hub Ports

Introduction

This chapter focuses on existing and emerging transshipment hub ports. Transshipment is the transfer of cargo from one ship to another in a hub-and-spoke style of operation between ports, similar to air service provided by commercial airlines. It is a service-oriented operation, designed to assist large carriers seeking to minimize transportation costs in the form of fuel use and travel time. For the purposes of this report, a hub port is defined specifically as a transshipment center that handles containerized cargo. In this layered hub-and-spoke system, local ports feed regional ports, which in turn feed global ports.

As there is no one way to classify these ports, for the purposes of this chapter, we will have three categories: hub ports may be global, serving as the major stopover point of international trade throughout the world; they may be regional, which are used primarily for shipments to the ports' hinterland while operating transshipment facilities; and they may serve as feeders to or from local ports. Examples of global hub ports are Kingston, Jamaica, and Manzanillo International Terminal (MIT) in Panama, both of which will be discussed in this chapter. The chapter will also analyze the development and transshipment activity of regional hubs and feeder hub ports.

While all ports differ in terms of their size, capacity, operations, ownership, and so forth, it is possible to identify a number of criteria common to successful hub ports. These variables will be used to predict which ports in the region have the potential to become the next hub port. Experts generally agree that a successful hub port must, at a minimum (a) be well located in relation to feeder ports and shipping lanes, (b) have adequate draft to handle large ships, (c) possess adequate facilities to handle containerized cargo, (d) maintain high efficiency and low costs, and (e) sustain an environment free from the threat of labor unrest. These and other criteria will be discussed later in the chapter.

This chapter will demonstrate the outcome of hub port development, provide a descriptive model of the current situation and a prescriptive model for the evaluation of hub ports, and present forecasts of future transshipment traffic in the region.

Regional Containerized Trade

Traditionally, Latin American and Caribbean countries have viewed their ports predominantly as sources of employment and national income and less as a means to improve and expand trade. As a result, while new equipment was purchased and older equipment was renovated, these items did little to expand the ports' capacity to handle more cargo and efficiently move this cargo. As recently as 1996, there were only 17 ship-to-shore gantry cranes in the entire region. Unfortunately, the region is still paying for this lack of development.

Table 4.1
Latin American Containerized Trade Forecast by Region
(1,000 TEUs)

Region						Average Annual Percent Change	
	1997	2000	2001	2005	2010	1997-2000	1997-2010
Inbound							
C. America & Caribbean	1,143	1,413	1,524	2,028	2,672	7.3	6.8
East Coast South America	1,157	1,447	1,581	2,195	3,000	7.7	7.6
West Coast South America	556	629	671	903	1,261	4.2	6.5
Total Inbound	2,859	3,490	3,776	5,124	6,934	6.9	7.1
Outbound							
C. America & Caribbean	1,041	1,222	1,285	1,592	2,112	5.5	5.6
East Coast South America	1,165	1,312	1,378	1,744	2,330	4.0	5.5
West Coast South America	638	725	771	1,019	1,464	4.4	6.6
Total Outbound	2,843	3,258	3,434	4,356	5,908	4.6	5.8
Inbound and Outbound							
C. America & Caribbean	2,184	2,635	2,809	3,620	4,784	6.5	6.2
East Coast South America	2,322	2,759	2,959	3,939	5,330	5.9	6.6
West Coast South America	1,194	1,354	1,442	1,922	2,725	4.3	6.6
Grand Total	5,702	6,748	7,210	9,480	12,842	5.8	6.4

Source: Data from *Containerisation International* (November 1998), p. 75.

Although ports are expanding and transshipment is on the rise, the region handles relatively little containerized traffic as compared with other areas of the globe. Now, however, governments and private interests are recognizing the effects of neglected port development on regional economic productivity.[1] By 2010, containerized traffic in the region is expected to reach almost 6 million TEUs in outbound shipments and almost 7 million TEUs inbound.[2] Table 4.1 illustrates regional containerized trade forecast through 2010.

By and large, however, port development is increasing to meet the demands of this trend toward increased containerization. In continental South America, more than $2 billion has been invested to finance 16 large-scale port development projects, already underway. The Panama Canal Authority (PCA) has announced a $1 billion project to expand three locks and further update facilities in the hope of accommodating post-Panamax vessel traffic through the canal.[3] Transshipment has become a successful method of meeting these demands.

At this time, approximately 30 percent of worldwide container movement is transshipped.[4] Maritime shipping relies on transshipment as a means of reducing the number of ships in use at one time. The cost of transshipment will decrease with technological progress. Although overall transit time may be lengthened as a result of transshipping cargo, the system facilitates the use of larger vessels capable of traveling faster than their predecessors. Cargo will, therefore, move faster during the bulk of its journey. As containerization increases, transshipment will increase along with it.[5]

The need for hub ports stems from an increase in international maritime cargo. As trade increases, larger ships will be needed to carry greater amounts of containerized cargo. And as ship size increases, the need for hub ports rises. In addition, the process of global port and carrier consolidation contributes to the need for transshipment: ports will need to compete for business with greater intensity and shippers will rely on hub-and-spoke systems to a larger extent as the amount of port traffic by smaller vessels increases. In the case of Latin America, *Containerisation International* predicts that between 1997 and 2010, Latin American box traffic will grow at a rate of 7 percent per year and that the Asia route to Latin America will show the most growth (although the United States will remain Latin America's top trading partner).

The average vessel operating in Latin America currently carries approximately 1,500 TEUs. If vessels remained the same size, the number of weekly vessel services would need to double in order to accommodate such growth in trade. One logical response to this increased traffic is to build ships with a greater capacity for containerized cargo, and transshipment will become increasingly important.[6] *Containerisation International* suggests that the opposite is true as well. In other words, as more hubs are created, business should increase. Therefore, Latin American hub ports are expected to become actual catalysts of global and regional trade, eventually becoming an important component of the region's future economic growth.[7]

In addition to growth in international trade, the very increase of containerization has spurred a need for transshipment as a more viable option than direct shipping to a final destination. Transshipment services provide shippers with additional routing options and briefer transit periods. Owing to transshipment, carriers can better meet shippers' demands and simplify scheduling.[8] Maritime traffic between Latin America and Asia and between Europe and North America is the primary impetus behind transshipment-related investment in improving port facilities and expanding capacity.[9]

Deep-sea transshipment consists of the following two methods:

- Carriers transship to the region from their mainline vessels bound for the United States. Cargo is then relayed to smaller services, stopping in Latin America. The Port of Miami is a popular choice for transatlantic shipping to Latin America. Cosco, for example, ships Asian cargo bound for the West Coast of South America and back from the Port of Long Beach, California.[10]

- Carriers operate transshipment services, supported by existing global and "pendulum" services that pass through Latin America.[11] ZIM Container Service uses Kingston for transshipment services in the region, accounting for 42 percent of total container throughput in the port,[12] while Evergreen Marine Corporation opened a terminal in MIT to handle transshipment of its global cargo.[13]

Necessary Criteria

While debate persists over where the next hub port will develop, experts have pointed to a number of features that should exist at successful hub ports and should, therefore, be common to the hub ports of the future.

In their book *Strategies for Global and Regional Ports*, Gustaaf de Monie et al. identify necessary criteria for either global or regional hub ports:

1. <u>Location</u>: The port must be geographically located in a suitable position. It must have a central position with respect to the ports to be served as feeder ports.

2. <u>Minimum Deviation</u>: Potential hubs will be differentiated from the general pool of possible stops if they allow only a "minimum deviation" from main shipping lanes. This deviation should be measured in terms of time and not distance.

3. <u>Access</u>: The port should have adequate draft for the ships it intends to serve—for global and regional ports this would be the largest ship traversing that particular route and making calls to the selected port.

4. <u>Container Terminals</u>: As the use of transshipment increases globally, a hub port (global or regional) should have facilities to accommodate these needs, in terms of both equipment and storage space.

5. <u>24-Hour Operations</u>: The ability to offer year-round service on a 24-hour basis and availability of all support services, such as pilotage, towage, and mooring, are critical elements.

6. <u>Turnaround</u>: Ports hoping to serve as hubs within their regions of influence should minimize turnaround time; hub ports should offer a "central position" with respect to the feeder ports. This condition also assumes that the ports exhibit high levels of productivity and are operating efficiently.

7. <u>Costs</u>: The ability to offer competitively priced port and terminal services, which would ideally fall below industry/regional averages.

8. <u>Favorable Business Environment</u>: The selected port should be located in an environment that not only enjoys political stability but also can guarantee that there will be no interruptions to port operations because of labor unrest.

9. <u>Elimination of Bureaucratic Rules</u>: The elimination of bureaucratic rules, regulations, procedures, and practices would enhance port productivity.

10. <u>High-Frequency Feeder Network</u>: In order to satisfy the shipping industry's demands, ports should offer an array of high-frequency feeder services,

connecting the hub with its network of feeder ports. In addition, the availability of high-frequency intermodal links will benefit ports that handle a significant amount of domestic cargo.[14]

The authors claim that it is "imperative" that all these conditions be met for a hub to succeed but mention that most researchers and analysts have focused on only the physical requirements, that is, port infrastructure and equipment, and have failed to fully appreciate the importance of price competitiveness and efficient operations as a whole. As shippers and carriers owe no loyalty to individual ports, it is not particularly important where cargo is transhipped as long as transshipment is conducted in an efficient and effective manner. Shippers and carriers attempt to locate the most cost-effective means to conduct their business, and, as such, ports vying to become hub ports would benefit from assuring their clients and prospective customers high levels of productivity, while charging clients competitive costs.

Jan Hoffmann has also developed a list of criteria for transshipment centers:

1. Have a strategic location in relation to multiple trade routes and desired markets.

2. Charge market-determined dues and tariffs.

3. Be surrounded by a dynamic local economy that provides a balanced cargo base load (except in the case of off-shore megahubs).

4. Offer modern infrastructure encompassing berths of 900-1,100 feet in length.

5. Own at least three or four gantry cranes.

6. Provide 40-50 acres per berth of container storage space.

7. Possess dock or contiguous railway connections.

8. Maintain minimum water depth of 14-15 meters.

9. Require minimal transit time from sea to dock.

10. Be served by competitive ocean feeder and inland transport services.

11. Be known for harmonious labor relations and productive workers.[15]

Although both lists of criteria are similar, the second specifies minimum physical criteria. Neither list specifically identifies the need to accommodate Panamax or post-Panamax ships, although given the global trend toward larger ships, all hub ports should possess drafts capable of accommodating such vessels. The typical draft for a fully loaded Panamax vessel is 38 feet and for a fully loaded post-Panamax vessel is 42 feet.[16] Hoffmann's recommended water depth of 14-15 meters (approximately 46-49 feet) addresses this issue. Kingston, for its central location, and MIT, for its proximity to the

Panama Canal, render both ports ideal stopping points for transshipped cargo in Latin America.

Experts do note that serving a large, local economy would be advantageous to hub port development. For Caribbean ports, however, this is not always the case. There exist limited local markets, and, as such, it is improbable that balanced cargo loads will be observed throughout the region. However, the existence of "special advantages" may facilitate hub port development. Also worthy of mention is that in the case of Caribbean port's focusing on transshipment, railway connections may not be as important as investments in equipment and port facilities intended to boost port productivity. Computer software for yard planning and management, for instance, is an area in which many ports have already begun to invest. Still, railway connections are important, as are other intermodal links, for cases where local cargo merits inland transportation development. In the case of Brazil, where domestic cargo constitutes a significant portion of cargo handled, intermodal connections may play a role in the determination of a regional hub.

The above requirements do not constitute a prescription for success, however, as it is not preordained that adhering to the above criteria guarantees hub port development. No set of criteria can provide such a guarantee. There are other variables at stake, however, that could influence the decision to invest heavily in transshipment infrastructure. Once all the requirements are satisfied, the issue of a committed clientele becomes extremely important. Given that several ports meet all the requirements mentioned above, there is no guarantee that shipping lines will pick one port over the other, even if they have already established a relationship with a particular port. This uncertainty exemplifies the volatile nature of the shipping industry in general and especially for the ports that invest heavily in the hopes that the capacity generated will be used. Furthermore, hub port development is based, in part, on the expectation that ship sizes will continue to increase in the foreseeable future.

Cautionary Note about Hub Port Development

A worldwide trend toward large-scale hub ports capable of servicing trade throughout an entire region has been widely reported and justified in the media. This chapter has presented the views of experts who reinforce not only the criteria necessary for hub port development but also the importance and inevitability of the process. These same individuals also point to an overall demand for large ships stemming from an increase in containerization. However, Martin Stopford, managing director of Clarkson Research, disagrees that this trend is necessarily the market's correct path.

While acknowledging that an increase in the use of larger ships and containerized trade is certainly taking place, Stopford argues that the overall growth in container ships and hub ports will actually lead to slower transit times compared to direct shipping by smaller carriers. He also believes that this growth will not mean greater profitability. Ship-related costs are less than one-quarter of the total cost of service, and as ships grow and feeder services are used, economic benefits shrink. Figure 4.1 shows the cost per TEU on a 7,000-mile round-trip voyage. As ship sizes increase from 4,000 TEUs to 6,500 TEUs, mainline costs are reduced using larger vessels, but total distribution costs are not. Once feeder charges are factored in, any savings secured on the main voyage could be lost.[17]

Figure 4.1
TEU Costs

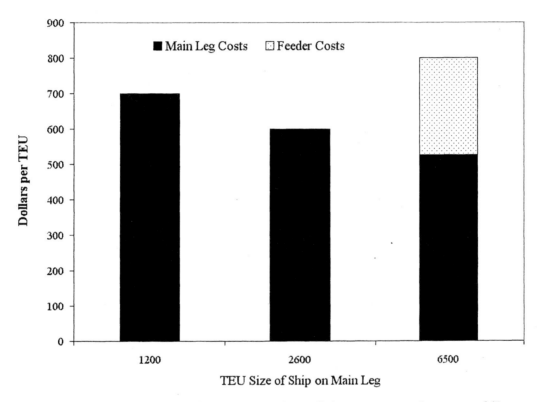

Source: Adapted from Mark Stopford, "A New Revolution," *Containerisation International* (January 2001), p. 47.

Stopford also suggests that while containerized shipping will be sufficient for transporting bulk commodities, such as steel and waste paper, premium cargo will require a higher level of service than that provided through containerization. He predicts that global liner companies, medium-sized operators, and freight forwarders/logistics operators will compete for these shipping contracts. While the global companies appear to be in the predominant position, medium-sized operators may provide competitively priced direct services plus a superior knowledge of their customers' needs. This type of service will likely lead to predatory pricing on the part of global operators in an attempt to freeze out smaller competition, but Stopford feels that new services will develop wherever a potential for moneymaking exists. In addition, the logistics providers will offer the global liner companies a good deal of competition, as they could potentially turn ship owners into little more than transport wholesalers, shuttling containers between ports and selling space to logistics providers, which is an extreme, but foreseeable, example.[18]

Finally, Stopford identifies three inducers of change in global shipping: (1) low-cost computer technology, which will reduce shippers' overhead costs; (2) the growth of containerization and the movement toward larger ships, which has led to a greater availability of ships that ship operators may charter and use for direct shipments; and (3) pressures from environmental lobbies to decrease the number of container-carrying trucks on the road, which will encourage direct services to local ports, leading to a waterborne as opposed to a land option.[19]

Port Principal Component Model: Descriptive Model of Current Situation

This section will employ principal component analysis or factor analysis of port statistics as introduced by Jose L. Tongzon.[20] The method attempts to efficiently summarize information on various ports. Ports grouped together function similarly and, therefore, provide more beneficial candidates for comparison. As a caveat, the groupings themselves do not explain functional similarities between ports; an analysis and discussion of the model are required in order to comprehend the ways in which ports relate to one another.

A brief explanation of principal component analysis will aid in the understanding of the model to follow. A principal component analysis model produces a set of uncorrelated equations describing individual indices, or principal components, of the data. Some of these equations will describe a greater portion of data than any single variable of the original data set and, therefore, provide more pertinent and compact information. The principal component equations that satisfy this criterion will be kept and used to compare the ports. These principal component equations (PRINs) consist of weighted constants for each variable in the model. To find the PRIN value for a particular port, the port's standardized variable indices are inserted into the PRIN equation. These PRIN values have no meaning outside the model but are instead used to compare the ports included in the model.

The purpose of this analysis is to ascertain whether the ports generally mentioned as global transshipment ports, namely Colón, Kingston, and Freeport, cluster together and, therefore, function similarly. The analysis will be completed without an input for transshipment volume, as this would immediately separate those ports. Rather, we wish to see if beyond the single statistic of transshipment TEU volume, these ports act differently than other ports of similar size. The model will include 17 of the largest ports from South America, the Caribbean, and the Gulf of Mexico. Each of the ports moved at least 250,000 TEUs for the year of 1999. The included ports are San Juan, Puerto Rico; Buenos Aires, Argentina; Colón, Panama (Manzanillo International Terminal, or MIT, and Coco Solo/Cristóbal taken separately); Santos, Brazil; Kingston, Jamaica; Puerto Limón, Costa Rica; Freeport, Bahamas; Veracruz, Mexico; Puerto Cabello, Venezuela; Rio Haina, Dominican Republic; Guayaquil, Ecuador; Callao, Peru; San Antonio, Chile;

Cartagena, Colombia; Manzanillo, Mexico; and Port of Spain, Trinidad and Tobago. Two American ports, Miami and Jacksonville, have also been included to see if the Caribbean transshipment ports function more similarly to the American ports or other Latin ports. (See Appendix A for calculations.)

The criteria chosen for the principal component analysis reflect the type of information sought. In this case, a grouping of ports is desired that not only compares the scale of the port but also gives an idea, or dimension, of how the port functions. The variables used in the model capture that mix. The scale of the port, or the amount of activity, is reflected in the TEU (1999) variable and the direct calls variable. The remaining four variables, berth length, total port area, TEU storage, and number of cranes, attempt to capture how the port functions relative to its scale of activity. The following is the list of variables in the order they will appear in the model (see Table 4.2):

TEU99	The number of total TEU movements in the port for 1999 as reported in *Containerisation International Yearbook 2001* (CI2001) or on the *Containerisation International* Webpage.
Berth Length	The meters of berthing dedicated to container movements. A multipurpose general-cargo berth that also handles containers was counted at 50 percent of its length. These values were taken from the CI2001.
Terminal Area	The area in square meters of the terminal. These values were taken from the CI2001.
TEU Storage	The number of TEUs that can be stored at the terminal. These values were taken from the CI2001.
Gantry Cranes	The number of ship-to-shore gantry cranes. These values were taken from the CI2001.
Direct Calls	The number of direct calls by liner shipping services as listed on the CI Webpage on May 23, 2001. This number would be highly correlated to the number of ship visits a port receives.

The complete results of the Latin American/Caribbean/North American East Coast ports model are presented in Table 4.3. PRIN1 accounts for nearly 58 percent of the variation in the model. The second principal component, PRIN2, accounts for 17 percent of the variation in the data. Therefore, the first two principal component equations together account for 75 percent of the variation in the model. The equations for PRIN1 and PRIN2 are as follows:

PRIN1 = 0.26 TEU99 + 0.45 Berth + 0.46 Area + 0.35 Storage + 0.49 Crane + 0.40 Calls
PRIN2 = 0.74 TEU99 + 0.17 Berth - 0.07 Area - 0.45 Storage + 0.18 Crane - 0.44 Calls

Table 4.2
Port Database

Port	TEU99	Berth Length	Terminal Area	TEU Storage	Gantry Cranes	Direct Calls*
San Juan	2,084,711	1,505	288,000	6,200	6	41
Buenos Aires	1,021,973	4,319	1,240,000	28,595	15	100
MIT (Panama)	878,206	1,340	370,000	20,000	10	69
Santos	871,779	1,600	505,000	19,500	10	116
CocoSolo/Cristóbal	771,306	1,220	110,000	9,150	5	54
Kingston	689,677	1,901	766,345	16,050	10	56
Puerto Limón	590,000*	358*	75,000*	560*	1*	39
Freeport	543,993*	519*	370,000*	10,000*	4*	17
Veracruz	532,472	510	420,000	35,000	4	47
Puerto Cabello	496,315	1,250	10,000*	25,570*	0	77
Rio Haina	415,629∞	451	42,000	2,800	2	35
Guayaquil	378,000	555	235,000	6,750	1	48
Callao	376,045	2,000	56,000	3,700	0	65
San Antonio	374,474	383	61,000	1,800	0	49
Cartagena	347,023	1,516	360,000	12,000	2	73
Manzanillo	321,893*	250	135,000	7,000	2	54
Port of Spain	252,482	480	120,000	3,500	2	40
Miami	777,821	3,167	2,630,700	20,000#	14	109
Jacksonville	771,882	3,661	628,000	5,100	10	29
Mean	657,667	1,420	443,266	12,278	5.16	58.8
Standard Deviation	410,556	1,177	611,860	9,984	4.87	26.7

Source: Data from Informa Group, *Containerisation International Yearbook 2001*, ed. Jane Degerlund (London: Black Bear Press Ltd., 2001).

* Data from *Containerisation International*, "Ports" database. Online. Available: http://www.ci-online.co.uk/. Accessed: May 27, 2001.

∞ Data from Economic Commission for Latin America and the Caribbean (ECLAC) Website. Online. Available: http://www.eclac.cl/transporte/perfil/indexe.html. Accessed: May 27, 2001.

Data from Port of Miami homepage. Online. Available: http://www.metro-dade.com/portofmiami/facil.htm. Accessed: May 23, 2001.

Table 4.3
**Results of Factor Analysis for Latin American/Caribbean/North
American East Coast Ports Model**

Correlation Matrix

	TEU99	Berth Length	Terminal Area	TEU Storage	Gantry Cranes	Direct Calls
TEU99	1.000	0.382	0.235	0.150	0.506	0.129
Berth Length	0.382	1.000	0.672	0.346	0.780	0.504
Terminal Area	0.235	0.672	1.000	0.424	0.779	0.563
TEU Storage	0.150	0.346	0.424	1.000	0.495	0.563
Gantry Cranes	0.506	0.780	0.779	0.495	1.000	0.522
Direct Calls	0.129	0.504	0.563	0.563	0.522	1.000

Eigenvalues of the Correlation Matrix

	Eigenvalue	Difference	Proportion	Cumulative
PRIN1	3.458	2.430	0.576	0.576
PRIN2	1.028	0.358	0.171	0.748
PRIN3	0.670	0.263	0.112	0.859
PRIN4	0.406	0.103	0.068	0.927
PRIN5	0.303	0.168	0.051	0.977
PRIN6	0.135	-	0.023	1.000

Eigenvectors

	PRIN1	PRIN2	PRIN3	PRIN4	PRIN5	PRIN6
TEU99	0.257	0.736	0.517	0.221	0.177	0.212
Berth Length	0.452	0.174	-0.356	0.033	-0.740	0.301
Terminal Area	0.456	-0.069	-0.414	-0.232	0.622	0.420
TEU Storage	0.348	-0.447	0.645	-0.459	-0.157	0.164
Gantry Cranes	0.495	0.185	-0.093	-0.241	0.051	-0.807
Direct Calls	0.395	-0.436	0.095	0.792	0.088	-0.099

The first principal component, PRIN1, has positive values, ranging between 0.35 and 0.5, for five of the six variables. The value for TEU movements is somewhat lower at 0.26. This value suggests that PRIN1 is measuring the overall scale of port, emphasizing port infrastructure. The second principal component, PRIN2, has fairly low values for three of the six variables; two variables, TEU storage and direct calls, have fairly strong negative values. The coefficient for TEU movements has a very strong positive value. PRIN2 is complicated, but valuable information can be derived from an analysis of it. The strong positive coefficient for TEU movements with the weaker positives for berth length and gantry cranes implies that a port designed specifically for containers (a port that has dedicated berth length and cranes available and that uses this infrastructure with large volumes of moves) will have a relatively high value. The negative coefficients for

TEU storage and direct calls would seem to pull in the opposite direction. Consider this example: if two ports have similar TEU activity but one has a higher PRIN2, the port with the higher PRIN2 tends to use less TEU storage space and have fewer direct calls. The lower number of direct calls would imply that larger ships are calling in the port. The lower value for TEU storage may show higher space efficiency or possibly poorer intermodal connectivity at the port with the lower PRIN2 value.

Figure 4.2
Graph of the Two Principal Components of Latin American/Caribbean/North American Ports Model

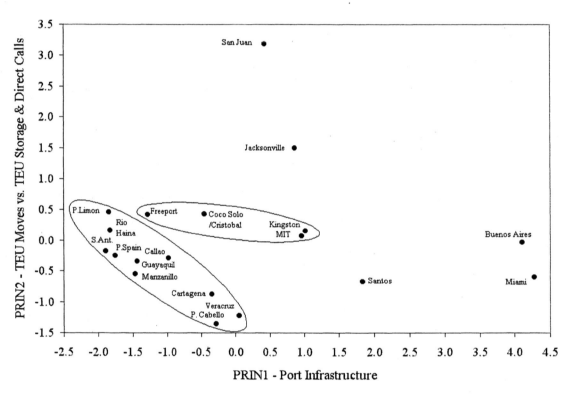

The PRIN1 is called the "Port Infrastructure" component as it gives weight to the size of the port; likewise, the PRIN2 is renamed the "TEU Moves vs. TEU Storage & Direct Calls" component. Figure 4.2 shows the Caribbean ports that are generally used as examples of large transshipment centers, the Panamanian ports of MIT and Coco Solo/Cristóbal, Kingston, and Freeport, group together on a line of slightly negative slope. A large group of other Latin American ports group together around a line of much greater negative slope.

As previously mentioned, for ports with similar annual TEU movements, lower scores on PRIN2 would indicate that for a similar scale of operation in a port, there was a greater requirement for TEU storage and a greater number of direct calls, meaning a smaller average ship size. It is dramatic to observe that Freeport and Veracruz both have around

535,000-TEU moves annually but are placed very differently on the graph. Freeport has a significantly lower PRIN1 value and a significantly higher PRIN2 value than Veracruz. An examination of the PRIN equations can explain these trends and shed light on the functioning of a hub port. Freeport's lower PRIN1 score is a reflection of its smaller amount of terminal area and TEU storage and lower number of direct calls. Freeport's higher PRIN2 score similarly indicates the coefficients with negative values, that is, berth length and direct calls, were lower than the score for Veracruz. Comparing the two Panamanian ports with Santos reveals the same relationship. The three ports have similar annual TEU movements, but the transshipment ports accomplish this with less infrastructure and fewer direct calls.

Therefore, the greater sloping line running through the large grouping of other Latin ports shows that these ports tend to require greater amounts of TEU storage, larger terminal areas, and a larger number of direct calls. The grouping of the transshipment centers, with their relatively lower PRIN2 values, indicates just the opposite. That these ports tend to have fewer direct calls and, therefore, larger ship size, with respect to their scale of activity, is hardly surprising. It is interesting to note, however, that these ports seem to require less TEU storage and terminal area than a similarly active traditional port. A conversation with Rick Couch, president of the Osprey Line, confirmed these trends. Mr. Couch states that transshipment centers are generally designed from the ground up for the specific purpose of transshipment. He also believes these ports tend to be more technologically advanced because they have had more recent capital input.[21] These two facts contribute to greater space efficiency, whereas a traditional intermodal port is more often a hodgepodge result of successive demands and not systematically designed.

The principal component analysis shows there exist functional differences between the Caribbean global hub ports and most other Latin ports, which suggests ports with similar amounts of container activity, such as Freeport and Veracruz, will not share many other statistics. Continuing with the idea that these global hub ports function differently than most ports in the region, the next section seeks to determine if there is also a difference in the importance of location for global hub ports.

Caribbean Transshipment: Location Linear Regression Model

It is common knowledge that one of the primary factors in determining a port's possibility of functioning as a transshipment center is location. At issue is what is meant by "location"; is this concept of location the same for a pure transshipment center—such as those found in the Caribbean Sea that have from 85 to nearly 100 percent of traffic being nonlocal—as it is for a port that has its own traffic and looks to transshipment traffic only as a supplement to its own movements?

Both global hub ports and regional hub ports were discussed earlier in this chapter. These two different concepts of transshipment ports and the varying ways in which location is important to each will now be discussed.

It should be noted that finding accurate statistics is problematic. The statistics for general container movements for ports in Latin America and the Caribbean can vary greatly, depending on the source. Accurate statistics for the number of transshipped containers are even more difficult to obtain. While most ports will report their annual TEU movements in their publications or on their Web homepage, only those ports that specialize in transshipment publish transshipment numbers. Traditional sources for trade movements, such as *Containerisation International* and the United Nations Commission for Latin America and the Caribbean (ECLAC), do not have similar numbers for transshipped trade. The percentage of transshipment numbers used in Table 4.4 come from several chapters in *Strategies for Global and Regional Ports*, by de Monie et al.[22] The Monie book was published in 1998, and, therefore, container volumes from that year were used whenever possible.

Trade lanes crisscross the Caribbean Sea. This section attempts to explain the volume of transshipment trade in ports throughout the Caribbean by their deviation distances from major trade lanes using regression analysis. A couple of cautions should be given. The 11 ports listed in Table 4.4 were the only ports included in the de Monie study, and though they do represent the majority of traffic in the area, the inclusion of other ports, such as Port-au-Prince, Haiti, or Havana, Cuba, could alter the regression results. Also, the deviation distances were taken from a large maritime trade map. Because sea-lanes are not fixed like highways, these values are not exact, but they are accurate enough to yield reasonable and valuable results.

The purpose of this analysis is to examine the effects that proximity to a major trade lane has on transshipment volumes. Three different models are presented: the Panama-North America East Coast trade lane model, the Panama-Europe trade lane model, and the Panama-South America East Coast trade lane model. Only ports that lie within 300 miles of each trade lane are included in the model for that lane.

Panama-North America East Coast Trade Lane Regression Model

The Panama-North America East Coast (P-NAEC) model includes the largest ports in the northern half of the Caribbean Sea: Colón (MIT, Coco Solo, and Cristóbal), Kingston, Rio Haina, and Freeport, along with Cartagena. The dependent variable is the number of transshipped TEUs at each port, with the independent variable being deviation distance from the largest trade lane in the northern Caribbean, the P-NAEC trade lane. The results of the P-NAEC regression model are given in Table 4.5 and graphed in Figure 4.3

The independent variable, deviation distance from the P-NAEC trade lane, is statistically significant at 10 percent as shown by the P-value of the t-statistic of 0.100. This model accounts for nearly two-thirds of the variance, given the R^2 of 0.649. This value implies that deviation distance from the P-NAEC trade lane is a significant variable in explaining the amount of transshipped activity in a port in the northern Caribbean. The regression equation obtained is as follows:

Trans. TEUs = 785,028 − 1,885 • (deviation distance from P-NAEC trade lane)

This equation states that with every mile farther away from the P-NAEC trade lane a port experiences a 1,885-TEU decrease in yearly transshipment volume. This result gives a numeric value to the accepted notion that distance from a major trade lane is an important factor in the quantity of transshipment taking place in a port.

Table 4.4
Caribbean Ports' Transshipment/Location Database

Port	1998 TEU Movements☺	Percent Tranship*	1998 TEU Tranship	Deviation Distance from		
				P/NAEC Lane+	P/E Lane+	P/SAEC Lane+
Colón	1,425,788	60	855,473	0	0	0
Kingston	671,130	90	604,017	80	300	425
Cartagena ∞	347,023	7	24,292	250	175	75
Rio Haina %, ∞	415,629	56	232,752	300	100	380
Freeport	470,047	97	455,946	300	900	1,000
San Juan	2,071,385	14	289,994	525	75	400
Willemstad	71,360	12	8,563	550	320	70
Puerto Cabello	529,299	28	148,204	670	470	175
Pointe-A-Pitre	103,473	4	4,139	850	350	300
Fort-de-France	135,700	2	2,714	950	500	225
Port of Spain	230,830	50	115,415	1,100	750	30

Sources: ☺ Data from Informa Group, *Containerisation International Yearbook 2001*, ed. Jane Degerlund (London: Black Bear Press, 2001), pp. 107-22.

* Data from Gustaff de Monie et al. *Strategies for Global and Regional Ports—The Case of Caribbean Container and Cruise Ports* (Boston: Kluwer Academic Publishing), 1998.

+ Data collected by author. Measured from a large wall map, the values are approximations.

∞ 1999 data, 1998 data unavailable.

% Data from Economic Commission for Latin America and the Caribbean (ECLAC) Website. Online. Available: http://www.eclac.cl/transporte/perfil/indexe.html. Accessed: May 27, 2001.

Table 4.5
Results of P-NAEC Trade Lane Regression Model

Multiple R	0.806	**Stnd Error**	220,413		
R Square	0.649	**Observations**	5		
Ad R Square	0.532				

	df	Sum of Squares	MS	F	Signif. F
Regression	1	2.70E+11	2.70E+11	5.550	0.100
Residual	3	1.46E+11	4.86E+10		
Total	4	4.15E+11			

	Coefficients	Standard Error	t-Stat	P-value	Lower 90.0%	Upper 90.0%
Intercept	785,028	178,479	4.40	0.022	365,003	1,205,054
P-NAEC Dist	-1,885	800	-2.36	0.100	-3,767	-2

Figure 4.3
Transshipped TEUs vs. Deviation Distance from P-NAEC Trade Lane

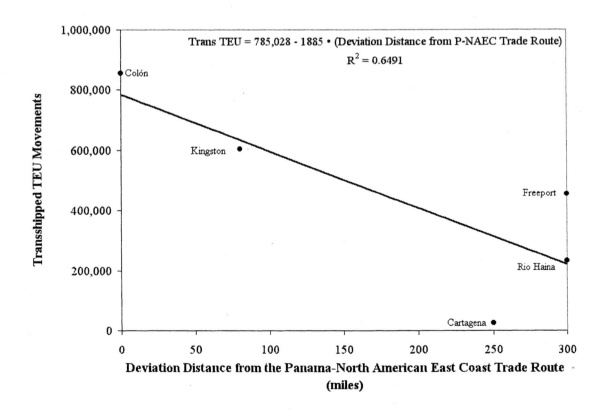

Trans TEU = 785,028 - 1885 • (Deviation Distance from P-NAEC Trade Route)

$R^2 = 0.6491$

Panama-Europe Trade Lane Regression Model

The Panama-Europe (P-E) model includes many of the same ports as the previous model. In this model, of course, the deviation distances are different as they are now taken from the P-E trade lane. The ports included are Colón (MIT, Coco Solo, and Cristóbal), Kingston, Rio Haina, San Juan, and Cartagena. The results of the P-E regression model are given in Table 4.6 and graphed in Figure 4.4.

The P-value of the t-statistic for the independent variable shows a 0.743 level of significance, a very low level of significance. This low level implies that the deviation distance from the P-E trade lane is not a good predictor of transshipment for Caribbean ports. This is not to say that the distance from the P-E trade lane has absolutely no effect, but these two models taken together do indicate that distance from the P-NAEC trade lane is far more important than distance from the P-E route in determining transshipment volumes in the northern half of the Caribbean.

Figure 4.4 graphs transshipped TEU volumes at all ports within a 300-mile deviation distance from the P-E trade lane. Comparing this graph to the previous graph, it is easy to see that there is a greater relationship in the P-NAEC model than in the P-E model.

Table 4.6
Results of P-E Trade Lane Regression Model

Multiple R	0.204	**Stnd Error**	370,801
R Square	0.041	**Observations**	5
Ad R Square	-0.278		

	df	Sum of Squares	MS	F	Signif. F
Regression	1	1.78E+10	1.78E+10	0.130	0.743
Residual	3	4.12 E+11	1.37E+11		
Total	4	4.30E+11			

	Coefficients	Standard Error	t-Stat	P-value	Lower 90.0%	Upper 90.0%
Intercept	477,591	269,072	1.77	0.174	-155,633	1,110,816
P-E Dist	-587	1,630	-0.36	0.743	-4,423	3,249

Figure 4.4
Transshipped TEUs vs. Deviation Distance from P-E Trade Lane

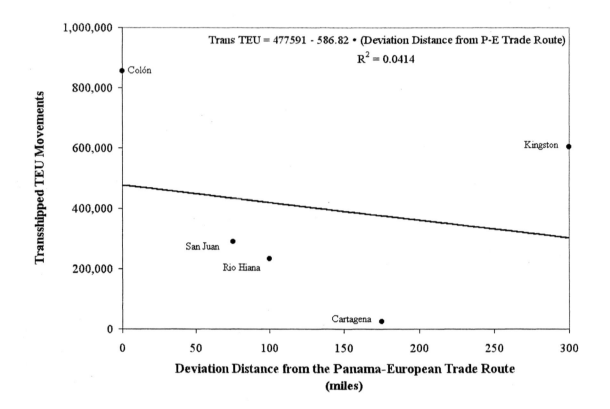

Panama-South America East Coast Trade Lane Regression Model

The Panama-South America East Coast (P-SAEC) model examines the large ports in the southern Caribbean, including the ports on the northern coast of South America. The ports within 300 miles of the P-SAEC trade lane are Colón (MIT, Coco Solo, and Cristóbal), Cartagena, Willemstad (Curaçao), Puerto Cabello, Pointe-A-Pitre (Guadeloupe), Fort-de-France (Martinique), and Port of Spain. The results of the P-SAEC regression model are given in Table 4.7 and graphed in Figure 4.5.

The independent variable, deviation distance from the P-SAEC trade lane, is not statistically significant at 10 percent as shown by the P-value of the t-statistic of 0.210. This result suggests that the distance from the P-SAEC trade lane is not an important factor in determining transshipment volumes for these South American and Caribbean ports.

Table 4.7
Results of P-SAEC Trade Lane Regression Model

Multiple R	0.541	**Stnd Error**	285,428		
R Square	0.293	**Observations**	7		
Ad R Square	0.151				

	df	Sum of Squares	MS	F	Signif. F
Regression	1	1.69E+11	1.69E+11	2.070	0.210
Residual	3	4.07E+11	8.15E+10		
Total	4	5.76E+11			

	Coefficients	Standard Error	t-Stat	P-value	Lower 90.0%	Upper 90.0%
Intercept	355,137	170,308	2.09	0.091	11,958	698,316
P-SAEC Dist	-1,517	1,054	-1.44	0.210	-3,641	608

It should be noted that Colón was included in all three models at its full value. An argument could be made that the amount contributed by Colón for a particular model should only reflect the movements at Colón coming from this trade lane. Including this data was not possible, however, because Colón's TEU transshipment volume broken down by incoming or outgoing trade lane was not available. An attempt was made to account for this lack of data. The P-SAEC model was run several times with Colón's transshipment volume varying from the current 885,473 TEUs down to 0 TEU. At no point did the model approach 10 percent statistical significance, which more strongly confirms the results of the P-SAEC model that the transshipment volumes in the southern Caribbean and the northern coast of South America are not explained by distance from the P-SAEC trade lane.

Figure 4.5
Transshipped TEUs vs. Deviation Distance from P-SAEC Trade Lane

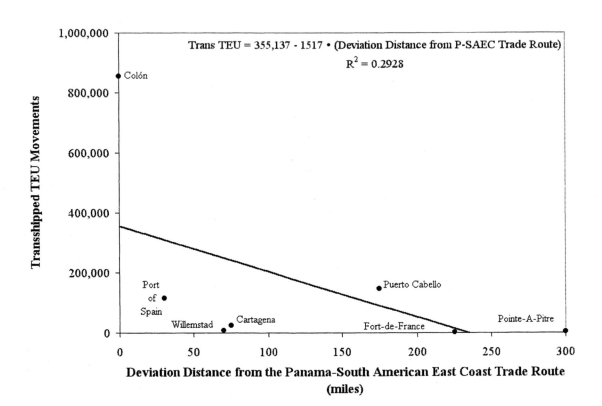

The conclusion that the deviation distance from the local trade lane does not explain the amount of transshipment volume at a port does not imply that location is not important in determining the volume of transshipment. Rather, these regression models, when taken together, show that different concepts of location are needed for different ports. The three global hub ports of Colón, Kingston, and Freeport are shown in the P-NAEC model to have distance from a trade lane as a significant indicator of transshipment trade. But the South American ports do not show the same relationship. The ports in the P-SAEC model, except for Colón, are all regional or local ports. A regional port that experiences transshipment is most often acting as a feeder port, concentrating trade from the immediate area. Therefore, a port acting as a regional port must be well placed with respect to surrounding trade and not necessarily the local trade lane. When considering regional ports from this perspective, the P-SAEC regression makes more sense. A port like Puerto Cabello is the largest port in its area; it likely receives transshipment activity for smaller neighbor ports.

Theo Notteboom et al. noted: "Hub ports are major nodes within the global transport system and act as international distribution centers for entire regions or continents. Feeder ports have a more local function and are connected to the main nodes by means of

202

small-scale shipping services."[23] By definition, the location of a hub port is directly connected to the global transport system (i.e., global trade lanes). This relationship is confirmed in the first Caribbean linear regression model (see Table 4.5) for the three large global hub ports, as their transshipment volumes are dependent on distance from the P-NAEC trade lane. Feeder ports, however, depend on local trade to a greater extent. They concentrate trade from the immediate area surrounding the port and feed cargo into the global transport system on smaller vessels traversing less-traveled trade lanes. As such, ports' locations with respect to local trade are more important than ports' locations with respect to international trade lanes.

Port Development

The obvious question, at this point, is which Latin American ports will next become hubs? Regrettably, there is no way to make an entirely accurate prediction as there is no one set of determining factors that lead to the creation of a hub port. Thus far, ports have developed into hubs as a result of geography, in that they were situated near a major shipping route and/or because the port was home to an important local market, to name two contributing factors. The linear regression models from above suggest that future transshipment activity on the North and East Coasts of South America may be more shaped by the local market than by the global trade lanes. Therefore, it is possible to list key elements that should be present in any hub port and develop a forecast.[24]

In order to develop into a hub, Latin American and Caribbean ports must possess the necessary physical variables, such as berthing length and sufficient draft to accommodate large ships, an adequate supply of labor, modern port facilities, and sufficient water space for the movement of ships in and around the port. In addition, the port will need to have the ability to ship cargo to at least one entire zone within the region, whether this is Central America, the Caribbean, or South America.[25]

Draft Requirements

The physical requirements for receiving large vessels eliminate many ports from acting as major transshipment centers. Table 4.8 lists the necessary draft and length for typical vessels of various TEU capacities when fully laden. This table contains important and interesting information when considering the future of South American ports. Currently, the port in the area with the greatest container activity is Buenos Aires, with over one million yearly TEU movements. Buenos Aires, however, has a draft of only 10 meters, meaning that fully laden ships of 2,000 TEUs or greater cannot enter the port.

Table 4.9 lists the drafts for all the major ports on the North and East Coasts of South America. Taking the required drafts from Table 4.8 and comparing them to the actual drafts of different ports found in Table 4.9 removes most South American ports from ever becoming major transshipment centers. Only two or three ports have sufficient depth to allow large-scale transshipment activities to take place at their docks. This reasoning relies on two assumptions: first, the importance of draft assumes that when transshipment activity increases in South America, the transshipment vessel size will be at least 3,000 TEUs; second, dredging to significantly increase draft is prohibitively expensive. Buenos

Aires, for example, will need to increase its current draft of 10 meters by at least 3 meters to receive loaded ships carrying 3,000 TEUs.

Table 4.8
Typical Draft Requirements for Various Ship Sizes

Capacity (TEUs)	Draft (m)	Length (m)
1,000	9.5	170
2,000	11.0	255
3,000	13.0	290
4,400	13.6	275
6,000	14.0	318
7,000	14.5	350

Source: Data from Gustaaf de Monie et al. Policy Research Corporation N.V., *Strategies for Global and Regional Ports—The Case of Caribbean Container and Cruise Ports* (Boston: Kluwer Academic Publishers, 1998), p. 72.

The only ports on the North and East Coasts of South America with drafts that allow ships of 3,000 TEUs or greater are Santos, Sepetiba, and Suape. The relative advantages of these three ports are compared below.

Location Loading Factor

This chapter has suggested that the future development of transshipment activity on South America's East Coast will be shaped more by a port's location relative to local container traffic than by global shipping lanes. Thus, an attempt has been made to capture the amount of container activity in the general vicinity of a port by constructing the location loading factor (LLF). The LLF compares the amount of activity taking place in and around different ports and is calculated by applying an exponential decay function, as seen below, to all container movements taking place around the port. This function applies a diminishing value to TEU activity taking place at a greater distance from a port. In the equation, Port xi, in turn, represents all the ports included in the database, including Port A, meaning a port's own activity is included in its LLF.

$$\text{LLF}_{\text{Port A}} = \sum (\text{TEU}_{\text{Port xi}}) \bullet (e^{-(\text{distance from Port A to Port xi} / 150)})$$

The value in the denominator of the exponential function can be changed to apply greater or lesser importance to trade taking place at different distances. The value of 150 miles was chosen so that TEU movements taking place 100 miles from a port would be added at 50 percent of their value, as demonstrated by raising e to the negative of 100 divided by 150. Table 4.9 contains the LLF values for all the major ports on the North and East Coasts of South America. (See Appendix B for distance matrix calculations.)

204

The LLF will be used to compare the three ports on the East Coast of South America that have been identified by the depth criterion as having the possibility of acting as major transshipment centers: Santos, Suape, and Sepetiba.

Table 4.9
Location Loading Factor and Draft
for South American Ports

Port	Annual TEUs (98 & 99 avg)	Location Loading Factor	Draft (m)
Suape	44,047	70,403	15.0
Sepetiba	-	583,676	14.5
Santos	787,219	964,605	13.0
Willemstad	74,870	434,340	12.2
Puerto Cabello	491,545	728,829	12.0
Rio Grande	243,253	428,065	12.0
Rio de Janeiro	201,243	481,639	12.0
Cartagena	336,560	374,688	11.0
São Francisco	133,909	578,324	11.0
Buenos Aires	1,107,916	1,237,735	10.0
Montevideo	258,060	767,953	10.0
Vitoria	93,516	198,892	10.0
Fortaleza	51,676	51,693	10.0
Recife	23,101	68,012	10.0
Port of Spain	254,937	332,487	9.7
Paranagua	178,254	647,760	9.5
Itajai	132,813	534,468	9.1
Belém	38,563	40,031	9.0
La Guaira	270,058	642,885	8.5
Salvador	65,246	82,343	8.0

Sources: Data from ECLAC Website. Online. Available: http://www.eclac.cl/transporte/perfil/indexe.html. Accessed: February 27, 2001; and *Containerisation International*, "Ports" database. Online. Available: http://www.ci-online.co.uk/. Accessed: March 11, 2001.

Future of Transshipment on the South America East Coast

Currently, most transshipment in the South America East Coast zone takes place in Santos, though it is not alone. Buenos Aires also handles transshipped cargo from Argentina, Bolivia, Paraguay, and Uruguay. The chapter has pointed out, however, that Buenos Aires has little potential for growth because its draft will not allow for fully laden ships greater than 1,500 TEUs.

Santos, with a draft of 13 meters allowing ships of up to 3,000 TEUs, has a high LLF value of 964,605 TEUs. Santos is the second most active port in South America. This current level of activity gives it an advantage, as ships are already calling in the port. Santos, however, has the notorious history of labor problems. Overall though, Santos has an above-average location and draft to develop into an even greater transshipment center.

Suape, which has a depth permitting ships of more than 7,000 TEUs, has an LLF of 70,403 TEUs, over half of which comes from its own activity. This rather low LLF value demonstrates that little container trade takes place near Suape. Therefore, if Suape is to become a transshipment center, it will act more like the global transshipment centers of the Caribbean and not become a concentration center for local trade (i.e., a feeder port). It is ideally located for the role of a transshipment center; the trade lanes both from the eastern side of South America and from the tip of Africa to Panama pass very near Suape. A modern container terminal has recently been completed and the port's infrastructure is now improved. However, Suape's opportunity to develop as a hub port will be severely hampered if large volumes of transshipment take place in the southern part of Brazil.

The Port of Sepetiba has some significant advantages in the competition for transshipment traffic. Sepetiba possesses a depth of 14.5 meters, making it capable of accommodating vessels large enough to carry 7,000 TEUs, more than twice the size of any ship currently traveling the route. Sepetiba has virtually no container traffic of its own. It is, however, well located to act as a concentration center for local container traffic as shown by its high LLF value of 583,676 TEUs. This ideal physical location is at the edge of some of the most economically powerful cities in South America, including Buenos Aires, Montevideo, Pôrto Alegre, São Paulo (and Santos), and Rio de Janeiro. Sepetiba also has a large hinterland, including São Paulo and Rio de Janeiro. The port has sufficient space for further development and has intermodal links with the Brazilian hinterland.[26] On the downside, Sepetiba will continue to have difficulty attracting container traffic as long as smaller ships serve the area. Rio de Janeiro and Santos can receive vessels capable of carrying up to 2,500 TEUs and 3,000 TEUs, respectively. Sepetiba's main advantage of depth will not be of primary importance until South American container traffic reaches a level requiring ships able to carry greater than 3,000 TEUs. This is many years, if not decades, away.[27]

Although Buenos Aires operates the busiest port on the continent (50 percent more TEU movements than the second largest, Santos), it appears that Santos will remain the primary center for transshipment in the region for some time to come. This dominance is because Santos possesses the depth to receive ships loaded with more than two times as many TEUs as ships currently calling in Buenos Aires. Therefore, Santos will likely be able to accommodate the largest ships traveling the South America East Coast route into the foreseeable future, leading to Santos' continued dominance over Suape and Sepetiba.

Conclusion

The chapter has identified criteria common to successful hub ports based on expert opinion and has considered some of these factors as variables in models describing current port activity and predicting future trends.

Although it is unlikely that a new hub port will be predicted, using the data contained in this chapter, the models and databases provide an accurate assessment of the state of affairs of transshipment in Latin America and the Caribbean, providing the tools for future research.

It is clear that there are varying opinions regarding the need for transshipment and the makeup of the ideal transshipment hub port. However, the methods used in the chapter suggest that Santos is in an ideal position to remain a leader in regional transshipment, even in the face of its neighbor Buenos Aires' larger volume of annual TEU movements. The global transshipment hub ports of the Caribbean are likely to retain their status within the region.

Notes

[1] Bruce Lambert, "Latin America's Relay Imperative," *Containerisation International* (November 1998), pp. 71-73.

[2] Ibid., p. 73.

[3] Ibid.

[4] Jan Hoffmann, "An Overview of Latin American and Caribbean Ports," Santiago, Chile, 1997, p. 31.

[5] Ibid.

[6] Lambert, "Latin America's Relay Imperative," p. 71.

[7] Ibid.

[8] Ibid.

[9] Ibid.

[10] Ibid.

[11] Ibid.

[12] Port Authority of Jamaica, *Annual Report 2000, Year Ending March 31, 2000* (Kingston, Jamaica, March 2000), p. 13.

[13] Lambert, "Latin America's Relay Imperative," p. 73.

[14] Gustaaf de Monie et al., Policy Research Corporation N.V., *Strategies for Global and Regional Ports— The Case of Caribbean Container and Cruise Ports* (Boston: Kluwer Academic Publishers, 1998), pp. 16-17.

[15] Jan Hoffmann, "Concentration in Liner Shipping: Its Causes and Impacts for Ports and Shipping Services in Developing Regions," *ECLAC Publications Online* (Santiago, Chile). Online. Available: http://www.eclac.org/publicaciones/transporte/7/lcg2027/hports.htm. Accessed: February 23, 2001.

[16] Jane Vickerman, "VZM/TransSystems Report on the Texas City Mega-Port Facility" in Lyndon B. Johnson School of Public Affairs, *Transportation in the Americas*, Policy Research Project Report Series, no. 135 (Austin, Tex., 2000), p. 47 (Table 2.1) (paper presented at a conference at the J. J. Pickle Research Campus, the University of Texas at Austin, November 9, 1998).

[17] Martin Stopford, "A New Revolution," *Containerisation International* (January 2001), pp. 46-48.

[18] Ibid.

[19] Ibid.

[20] Jose L. Tongzon, "Systematizing International Benchmarking for Ports," *Maritime Political Management,* vol. 22, no. 2 (1995), pp. 171-77.

[21] Telephone interview by David Wortman with Richard Couch, President, Osprey Line, La Porte, Texas, January 30, 2001.

[22] de Monie et al., *Strategies*, p. 67.

[23] Theo Notteboom, Chris Coeck, and Julien van den Broeck, "Measuring and Explaining the Relative Efficiency of Container Terminals by Means of Bayesian Stochastic Frontier Models," *International Journal of Maritime Economics*, vol. II, no. 2 (n.d.), p. 100.

[24] Lambert, "Latin America's Relay Imperative," p. 73.

[25] Ibid.

[26] Hoffmann, "Overview," p. 32.

[27] U.S. Department of Commerce, National Trade Data Bank, *International Market Insight: Sepetiba—A Hub Port?* by Etienne Kvassay (Rio de Janeiro, February 22, 2000). Online. Available: http://www.tradeport.org/ts/countries/brazil/mrr/mark0063.html. Accessed: April 3, 2001.

Chapter 5. The Mercosur Atlantic Corridor Consortium

Introduction

When the Summit of the Presidents of South America opened in Brasília on August 31, 2000, at the invitation of Brazilian President Fernando Henrique Cardoso, it marked the first time in history that all the heads of state in South America convened together at one place at one time. Realized in the context of the quincentenary of Brazil's discovery by Portuguese explorer Pedro Álvares Cabral in 1500, the summit discussed a wide range of issues affecting South America. Several themes emerged, namely, democratic consolidation, South American cooperation and trade facilitation, integration of infrastructure, narcotics trafficking, and information technology. In the area of trade and under the philosophy of "open regionalism," the heads of state resolved to begin negotiations for a free-trade area between the Southern Common Market (Mercado Comun del Sur, or MERCOSUR) and the Andean Community by January 2002 in addition to concluding agreements to bring Bolivia and Chile into MERCOSUR. The harmonization of South American trade regimes was designed to be consistent with World Trade Organization (WTO) regulations, with an eye toward consolidating and strengthening South America's bargaining position vis-à-vis the Free Trade Area of the Americas (FTAA) to be negotiated by 2005.[1]

On September 1, 2000, the Summit of the Presidents of South America released a communiqué emphasizing the importance of an integrated infrastructure (transportation, energy, and telecommunications). The communiqué directly addressed the continent's transportation infrastructure envisaging the optimum use of different modes (land, air, maritime, and inland waterway) in order to facilitate the border traffic of people, vehicles, and cargo. The presidents recalled efforts at infrastructure integration developed by the Working Group on Bioceanic Land Corridors. In sum, a significant emphasis of the first South American summit was placed on trade and development of transportation infrastructure along the region's prevailing corridors.[2]

In South America, the trade corridor has emerged as an important agent of economic development, with transportation its fundamental subsidiary component. Despite the tendency to restructure the state to become more normative and assume a regulatory posture, Latin American governments are still pressing forward to invest in transportation infrastructure. Though the Summit of the Presidents of South America addresses infrastructure needs, the investment capacity of South American countries is severely limited. Moreover, the monies being invested are heavily targeted toward highway construction and not toward more integrative and cost-reducing maritime, inland waterway, and intermodal transportation.

Facing a legacy of unintegrated and unstandardized highway, railway, river, and coastal transport networks, Latin America is developing a unique style of overcoming the obstacles to trade presented by its disparate transportation system. In the absence of a top-down comprehensive intermodal approach to transportation, public and private interests have coalesced in the nonprofit sector in the form of integration roundtables to make transportation more efficient, resolve disputes, attract more business, and stimulate more intermodal and waterborne transportation. The Mercosur Atlantic Corridor Consortium (and its predecessor, the Mideast Corridor Consortium) is an emanation of this style and subject of this chapter.

Originating in Vitória, the leading port and capital of the Brazilian state of Espírito Santo, the Mercosur Atlantic Corridor Consortium (hereafter Mercosur Consortium) brings together trade and transportation interests under the umbrella of central exporting ports and their hinterlands. The focus of the Mercosur Consortium is on generating regional economic development. To do so, it necessarily convenes a region's basic (exporting) industries, warehousing companies, transportation services, government, customs, labor, press, and shippers during integration roundtables in order to solve issues of congestion and inefficiency in addition to business development. The vehicles for the consortium are regularly scheduled integration roundtable meetings hosted in an exporting or port city. From small beginnings in the Secretariat of Economic Development of Espírito Santo in 1991, the Mercosur Consortium has grown from one integration roundtable in Vitória to more than 26 roundtables throughout South America. In so doing, the consortium has moved outside the competency of the government and into the nonprofit sector.[3]

These integration roundtables are centered on a regional port and indicate an evolving conception of integrated port networks in Latin America analogous to the port networks in ascendancy in Europe.[4] Through their regularly scheduled meetings, the Mercosur Consortium has promoted multimodal transportation, especially intermodal freight carriage favoring alternatives to the highway and truck. The Mercosur Consortium counts among its successes a rapid organizational expansion, the reduction of transport costs, increases in trade, the resolution of disputes, the promotion of a transportation logistics, and regional economic development. Through its model of integration roundtables, the Mercosur Consortium has emerged as a regionally endogenous form of problem solving now present in several South American countries. Moreover, this organizational model is easily exportable. As such, it represents a new way of thinking about transportation and trade corridors from a bottom-up approach.

Transportation and Trade Corridors as Units of Analysis

Trade and transportation corridors possess various attributes with the distinguishing characteristic that transportation corridors are features of a trade corridor. While trade necessarily takes place along transportation corridors, trade corridors cover a broad geographical area with a variety of services and linkages to labor, capital, and production. In contrast, not all transportation corridors are trade corridors. Transportation corridors where negligible trade occurs cannot be considered trade corridors, except in a latent sense. This section defines trade and transportation corridors and outlines their emergence in the United States and Latin America.

Various definitions exist that wrongly equate a trade corridor with a transportation corridor. A trade corridor can be defined as a geographical area over which significant amounts of trade flow. Such an area has a set of physical and operating characteristics that facilitate "the national and transnational movement of goods, services, people, and information."[5] They include

- a commercial infrastructure comprising distribution and warehousing facilities, foreign trade zones, a regulatory system for customs and inspection, and trade incentives;

- an integrated regional technological infrastructure with Electronic Data Interchange (EDI) and trade databases;

- business and professional know-how and expertise, including custom brokers, freight forwarders, accountants, attorneys, consultants, and academicians;

- well-developed social, political, and business linkages;

- a physical infrastructure of highways, rail, air, sea, and inland waterway;

- direct access to multiple markets;[6] and

- specific legislation and regulations.

Viewed as a system, the components of a trade corridor add value to a region's production in contrast to a transportation corridor.

A transportation corridor is a route along which trade travels. It is based on geography and traffic flows comprising the links, nodes, and transfer points, which serve outbound and inbound movements. It can be a right-of-way on the surface, air, or subsurface set apart to accommodate major multimodal transportation facilities. It includes arteries that connect truck, rail, sea, and inland waterways via highways, rail lines, air facilities, ports, and waterways. Table 5.1 gives a partial listing of components of a transportation corridor. In and of themselves, transportation corridors do not add value, but their interaction with the adoption of just-in-time (JIT) production and distribution make an efficient transportation corridor an asset and a principal component of a firm's logistics matrix. In this sense a firm's value can be affected by its location along efficiently functioning transport corridors.

Transportation corridors function more effectively for trade if they

- connect significant end points such as major urban centers, intermodal facilities like ports, and major commodity producing regions;

- cover wide areas spatially (hundreds of miles) through which freight is transported;

- do not rely on one mode such as road or rail and include a multimodal range with access to main highways, rivers, sea-lanes, trunk rail lines, and airways;

- carry regionally significant freight measured in cargo tonnage and truck volumes or twenty-foot equivalent units (TEUs) and forty-foot equivalent units (FEUs) for containers;

- serve intermodal facilities with container and trailer capabilities at airports, seaports, riverports, and inland intermodal terminals (dry ports); and

- serve important economic centers, such as cities or agriculture or mining regions.[7]

Table 5.1
Components of a Transportation Corridor

Land	Air	Sea
Motor carriers	Airports	Marine vessels
Railroads/rail yards	Aviation facilities	Barges
Warehouses	Airplanes	Rivers and seas
Trucks/truck terminals		Ports
Intermodal terminals		

Source: Leigh B. Boske and John C. Cuttino, "The Impacts of U.S.-Latin American Trade on the Southwest's Economy and Transportation System: An Assessment of Impact Methodologies (Special Project Report," Lyndon B. Johnson School of Public Affairs, The University of Texas at Austin, 2001), p. 5.

The concept of transportation corridors has been in use by planners for decades, originating in studies undertaken by the United Nations and World Bank to assess the transportation needs of Africa. In Latin America, the Brazilian Transportation Planning Company (GEIPOT), the transportation planning division of the country's Ministry of Transportation, adopted this concept.[8] GEIPOT understands transport corridors to be places or lanes that make trade possible; they are benefited by a complex array of social and economic services featuring the multimodal trunk systems of transport.[9]

In economic development parlance, there are three types of transport corridors: funnel corridors, dumb-bell corridors, and developmental corridors. Funnel corridors channel traffic flows through a specified port. Dumb-bell corridors join two productive regions often by bridge or tunnel. A developmental corridor takes advantage of economic concentration seeking to provide high-speed travel and transport within the cluster. In Latin America, the Rio de Janeiro-to-São Paulo corridor and the corridor connecting São Paulo-Rio de Janeiro-Curitiba-Florianopolis-Pôrto Alegre along major highways are examples. Efforts to promote corridors often involve investments that facilitate transport of base commodities. They are often international in scope with a host of institutional issues involved in corridor development and financing.[10]

In Latin America, the Organization of American States (OAS) has identified the trade corridor as a vital element for planning sustainable development. Stephen Bender, principal adviser on sustainable development, opines: "Trade corridors are a new class of region. They are not the products, by and large, of planning theory and practice . . .rather, they are increasingly the result of decentralized decision making, led by the private sector's understanding of changing, competitive markets, comparative advantages in raw materials, production capabilities and access to markets. The private sector is in a partnership with the public sector, which is divesting itself of those activities which it does poorly or inefficiently. . . . Trade corridors are generating their own set of emerging issues: new models of public administration."[11]

In Latin America, the coupling of democracy with globalization has presented an environment where corridor development can flourish. The shift away from central planning has stimulated regional mobilization around core strengths. Bender makes three very important observations on the development of corridors as regions. First, the pooling of public and private sectors come about in order to reduce the risks in decision making. Organization is not centrally planned. Second, development or lack thereof within a corridor is measured in financial terms easily understandable to business. Economic impact analysis aids in measurement. Third, those who do not participate will have less influence on the development of alternative transport modes. Moreover, they will quite possibly lose out on rapidly forming global trading relationships and capital, labor, and technology shifts. In sum, "Trade corridors are created, not to solve urban development problems, but to seek development opportunities."[12]

The Origins of the Mideast and the Mercosur Atlantic Corridor Consortia

In 1991, under the administration of Governor Albuíno Azeredo, the Secretariat of Economic Development of Espírito Santo elaborated a series of fundamental infrastructure investment projects, which as priorities of the government were not to be halted, terminated, or paralyzed. Such projects were also to be designed under the assumption of federal deregulation of transportation initiated during the term of President Fernando Collor de Melo (1990-92). The principal objective of this effort concentrated around the Port of Vitória and funneling imports and exports from Greater Vitória and the region's hinterland through Espírito Santo ports. As a funnel corridor, the span or hinterland of Vitória expanded to include many other states, including Minas Gerais, Mato Grosso do Sul, and Goiás. In developing the investment strategies for the new Espírito Santo government, a team from the Secretariat of Economic Development traversed the 1,800 kilometers of rail network to assess bottlenecks and congestion. During the survey, it was obvious that different owners of the rail system, Federal Railroad Company (Rede Ferroviária Federal S.A., or RFFSA) and Vale do Rio Doce Mining Company (Companhia Vale do Rio Doce, or CVRD) were not acting in harmony. In fact, the transportation corridor did not exist; it existed in parts.[13]

The Secretariat of Economic Development sought to funnel development through Vitória, using the vast railway network of RFFSA and CVRD. To do so, it convened CVRD,

RFFSA, the Valec Railway Consultancy, and the Port Authority for the State of Espírito Santo to find ways to leverage development of the region through transportation infrastructure. Since economic development did not serve only Espírito Santo, other states were enlisted to form an Interstate Council for the Mideast Transportation Corridor. In July 1991, ten governors met to formalize an agreement, and the protocol for establishing the Interstate Council for the Mideast Transportation Corridor (hereafter Interstate Council) was signed in October 1991. As the lead state for the Interstate Council, Espírito Santo formed an undersecretariat for Economic Development, which became the Office of Operations for the Interstate Council, which, through state government, worked on expanding growth. One of its first successes involved obtaining equipment (600 railcars and 12 locomotives) and trackage rights for export of grain along railways owned and operated by CVRD and RFFSA. Coming from as far as Goiás to the Port of Vitória by rail opened up new markets for grains and soybeans. Exports increased from 250,000 tons per year to 1.5 million tons per year. Whereas past grain shipments faced costs of $80-90 per ton and port costs at Santos and Paranaguá of $14 and $7, respectively, exporting through Vitória cost only $26 per ton with port costs of only $6-7 per ton.[14]

In 1994, the Office of Operations for the Interstate Council of the Espírito Santo Secretariat of Economic Development moved to the nonprofit sector. Faced with elections for governor and absent, yet, reelection in Brazil, the Secretariat of Economic Development feared that the new governor would not continue the Interstate Council projects, dismantling them as is often the case in Latin America. The corridor program faced the unique style of Latin American policymaking that economist Albert Hirschman in the 1960s dubbed "fracassomania," or the failure complex, which describes policy shifts of governments that do not continue a previous administration's policies.[15] Especially prevalent in "clientelistic" political networks, *fracassomania* is necessary for redistributing the government's resources to political allies. In such a situation, policies associated with a defeated candidate or lame-duck administration are terminated or discontinued, no matter how well conceived or implemented. In the area of public works, this abandonment results in the paralysis of many public projects at the expense of the Latin American taxpayer. In Brazil, unfinished public works (hydroelectric power plants, dams, highways, bridges, locks, nuclear power) have severely limited regional economic development. In the case of the Interstate Council, program managers anticipated some disassembly and shifted their efforts from the public sector to the private nonprofit arena, effectively avoiding the discontinuity and termination of public policy brought on by regime change through leadership elections.

When the Interstate Council was government run, the emphasis was on maximizing the potential for expanding export of the region's largest enterprise, the extractive and industrial complex associated with CVRD. Until 1997, CVRD was a state-owned enterprise running an elaborate vertically integrated operation linking mines in the state of Minas Gerais with the Port of Tubarão in the Vitória metropolitan region through the country's most advanced and modern rail and port complexes. In 1991, the Mideast Corridor Consortium (hereafter Mideast Consortium) was established as an instrument of economic development anchored at the Port of Vitória and serving a wide hinterland.

Among the problems the region had to address were the perceived underutilization of the ports near Vitória and the lack of regulation addressing them. Moreover, the railroads connecting manufacturing and agricultural regions near Belo Horizonte with Vitória, its closest outlet to international sea-lanes, were in dire need of investment.[16]

The Mideast Consortium gained political capital when nine state governors and the governor of the Federal District signed a protocol on October 22, 1991, creating an Interstate Council of Governors, throwing their support behind the Mideast Consortium. The nine states plus the Federal District included from west to east the states of Rondônia, Acré, Mato Grosso, Mato Grosso do Sul, Goiás, Tocantins, Minas Gerais, Bahia, and Espírito Santo. These nine states and the Federal District all fall within the Port of Vitória's zone of influence. The Office of Operations for the Mideast Consortium was constituted formally in March 1993. The political support supplemented by a congressional lobby of 150 representatives (of a total of 594 federal deputies and senators) added the political will to resolve disputes in an integrated manner.

Logistics

The principal objectives of the Mideast Consortium involved the articulation of the Mideast transportation corridor as an integrated logistics unit connecting the high plains of central Brazil to the Atlantic Coast. The logistics of freight movement cover a variety of actors and processes necessary to move raw materials, transport them through transformation into final goods when required, and deliver them through the distribution chain to the final consumer. In business, logistics entails "the managerial responsibility to design and administer a system to control the flow and strategic storage of materials, parts, and finished inventory to the maximum benefit of the enterprise."[17] This logistics framework is all encompassing and can include customer service, demand forecasting, documentation flow, handling returns, interplant movements, inventory management, parts/service support, materials handling, order processing, plant-warehouse site selection, production scheduling, protective packaging, purchasing, salvage scrap disposal, traffic management, and warehouse and distribution center management.[18]

Within a logistics system, traffic management is the most vital component to a clearer understanding of economic and transportation impacts of international trade. Traffic management focuses on "freight consolidation, carrier rates and charges, carrier selection, certain documentation, tracing and expediting, loss and damage claims, demurrage and detention, movement of hazardous materials, employee-moving services, and use of private carriage."[19] The broad scope of such a system extends beyond simple classification. A successful logistics network necessarily relies on transportation corridors that offer a broad variety of services as conduits for efficient trade. These transport corridors leading to and from economic markets are attractors for determining whether trade will take place. A transportation corridor can exist without carrying trade but a trade corridor cannot exist without its transport corridor.

Mideast Corridor Consortium

The Mideast Consortium, once outside the purview of government, moved to extend into the broader value-added services that constitute a trade corridor. Specifically, the development of integration roundtables assembled the key actors in the logistics network. A transportation corridor with a diverse set of logistics services facilitates international trade and can act as an attractor of international trade when it reaches a certain level of development. With much investment in transportation, knowing what these services and service levels are presents strategic information, vital for the efficient functioning of trade corridors. The Mideast Consortium holds such valuable expertise addressing the following items during their roundtables:

- Containerization

- EDI and telecommunications

- Documentation

- Industry consolidation (rail, port, trucking, liner shipping)

- Trends (intermodalism, consolidated shipments, vessel sharing agreements, hub-and-spoke feeder services, privatization)

- Inland dry ports

- Port costs, inland haul (rail/truck) costs, including surcharges

- Labor

- Damage and loss

- Security

- Robbery

- Actors (freight forwarders, consolidators, bankers, traders, consignees, carriers, shipper associations, inspectors, customs brokers)

- Congestion

- Infrastructure (ports, highways, railways, intermodal, air, inland waterway)

The Mideast Transportation Corridor

The Mideast transportation corridor comprises a multimodal trade corridor based primarily on the export of dry bulk goods and breakbulk, such as minerals, steel and steel products, coffee, soybeans, and grains. Its transport corridor consists of two main rail trunk lines of more than 1,800 kilometers, five ports, and major interstate highways. The jewel of the corridor's transportation infrastructure is the Vitória-Minas Railway (Estrada de Ferro Vitória-Minas). It links the mines of CVRD in Minas Gerais with its export complex at the Port of Tubarão. The other railway linked Vitória with the high plains and, in 1991, was operated by RFFSA. Figure 5.1 situates the Mideast Corridor. The port complex emanating from the Vitória metropolitan region includes the modern Port of Tubarão, operated by CVRD at a depth of 23 meters. Other ports include Vitória, Praia Mole, Ubu, Barra do Riacho, and Regência. In sum, the Mideast Corridor region accounts for 35 percent of the nation's gross domestic product (GDP).[20]

To facilitate economic development, expand trade, and reduce transportation costs and bottlenecks, the Mideast Consortium brought together for the first time in a coordinated manner rail, truck, and marine transporters, the state and municipal governments, the press, rail concessionaires, port concessionaires, business organizations (chambers of commerce and federations of industries), trade unions, port and terminal operators, warehousing and trading companies, airport representatives, steamship companies, customs officials, freight forwarders, and major exporting industries. The first major actor to give credibility to the Mideast Consortium was CVRD. The mining giant, and the nation's third-largest firm in 2000, was at first reluctant to buy into the program, but the Mideast Consortium quickly acted on bottlenecks obtaining new investment for the double tracking of the Vitória-Minas rail line in addition to the opening of a rail channel linking the high plains of central Brazil to the ports of Espírito Santo. At the Port of Tubarão, facilities were created to handle the export of bulk grains. As a result, these achievements had dramatic impacts on expanding the exports via Espírito Santo. Moreover, since CVRD was owner-operator of the Vitória-Minas Railway, any increase in export of a nonmining commodity reduced its marginal costs of shipping ore, as it gained from revenues charged to exporters of grains and soybeans. These first achievements demonstrated the large-scale development potential of an integrated multimodal approach evidenced in Table 5.2.

Figure 5.1 The Mideast Corridor Port and Highway Complex

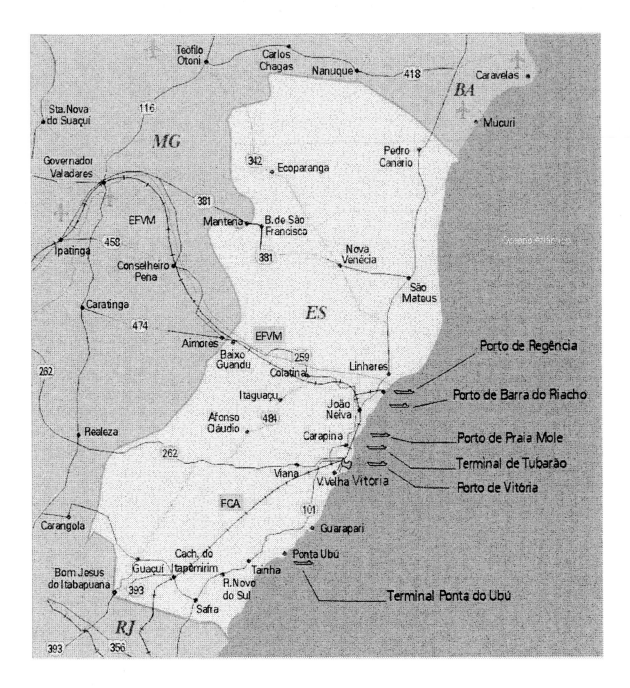

Source: Ministry of Transportation, Government of Brazil, Map of Espírito Santo. Online. Available: http://www.transportes.gov.br/bit/estados/iport/es.htm. Accessed: June 2, 2001.

Table 5.2
First Impacts of the Mideast Corridor Consortium

Problem	Action	Result
Transport and discharge of freight undertaken without continuity or planning	Organization of a mutual agreement, shared trackage rights, between CVRD and RFFSA	Private investment in warehousing and storage (225,000 tons)
Cargo volumes at 275,000 tons per year	Opening of the Port of Tubarão to dry bulk grains	Reduction of freight costs from $70 per ton to $27 per ton
Freight charges at exorbitant levels, approximately $70-80 per ton, plus the costs of port-related handling charges	Attraction of private investment	Explosive growth of grain shipments; within two years, grain cargo volumes increased from 300,000 tons per year to 1.5 million tons annually
Limited storage capacity at the port	Creation of door-to-door contracts	

Source: Information compiled from interview by John Cuttino with Pedrita Castiglioni, Economist, Mideast Corridor Consortium, Vitória, Espírito Santo, Brazil, August 21, 2000.

The Integration Roundtables

The vehicle for the Mideast Consortium to advance economic development and transport integration rests in the integration roundtables (sometimes referred to as roundtables). The roundtables are the sine qua non of the Mideast Consortium. They assemble the various actors involved in transportation and trade during regularly scheduled meetings. They hold their meetings in port cities counting among their membership the leading exporting and importing industries, public authorities, the press, labor unions, and transportation service providers. Members contribute financially to the operation and maintenance of the Mideast Consortium's organizational structure through dues, fees, and a commission on any business generated through the roundtables. Benefits accrue to participants in a variety of ways. First, the membership pursues integration by seeking reduced transport costs with the implementation of door-to-door contracts for freight movements along the transportation chain. Since Brazil passed its Multimodal Transport Legislation in 1998, finally implementing it in 2001, the Mideast Consortium is developing a database so that it can become a multimodal transport operator capable of offering door-to-door contracts through its participating members on one bill of lading. Second, new markets are being opened up as new transport solutions are applied via the roundtable deliberations. Third, regional economic development benefits from the attraction of new cargo to the region's ports, railways, airports, and highways. Finally, membership includes access to common pool resources of data readily processed into geographical information systems and logistics matrices.

For regional development, benefits are found in lower transport costs. The promotion of nonhighway transportation alternatives, such as inland waterway, rail, intermodal, or short-sea shipping, helps increase choice and reduce congestion and cost. The attraction of transportation interests via the roundtables contributes to clusters of value-added transportation services. The interaction augments regional capacity to trade by expanding a regional port's zone of influence. The focus on trade and transport aids in increasing trade and investment opportunities. Slowly, diverse interests work together on behalf of the region acknowledging that what is good for the regional economy is good for business. A regional identity begins to develop, which facilitates entrepreneurship and future growth.

At a more local level, the roundtables exemplify a new stage of economic development where a critical mass of mixed private and public social capital is mobilized. Here, the entrepreneurial sector is seen as a dynamic, creating synergies among business, government, and labor. In the past, Brazilian business waited for the state-owned enterprises or the federal, state, and municipal governments to move first as the motor of economic development. As the Brazilian state is becoming more normative, the entrepreneurial sector has used the roundtables to intervene directly into the matters that affect efficient functioning of trade corridors and transportation. The port cities have become the foci for logistics and integration.

Formal Operation of the Integration Roundtables

The roundtables are the focal point of activity of the Mideast Consortium. They provide forums for public and private interests to raise questions and problems affecting trade, economic development, and transportation. Meetings are scheduled monthly under the direction of the roundtable directors. If a member or nonmember of the consortium has an issue to be dealt with, it will be placed on the agenda and the staff will invite representatives from the relevant parties to convene at a roundtable. The meetings can often resolve at one meeting the problem just by assembling the necessary actors. In the case of a larger, more fundamental economic development issue, the roundtables can initiate the process of dialogue and, with staff resources, mediate and assist in resolving protracted problems. With the political support of regional executives, staff members are viewed as nonpartisan and objective actors. They are a respected common pool resource. Normally, there is one director of the roundtable who presides over each meeting, sets the agenda, and manages the interim tasks of acting on roundtable resolutions. The roundtable also serves a public relations or marketing function in disseminating information about the region and its potentialities.

A revised set of instructions for the Mideast Consortium outlines the following objectives:

1. Create an atmosphere favorable to the development of door-to-door contracts and intermodal logistics systems under the guiding concept of door-to-door service

2. Stimulate the exercise of positive-sum games, where all players win through their participation

3. Attract an increasing number of highway, rail, inland waterway, and coastal transportation providers in addition to ports, maritime companies, warehousing companies, unions, and shippers

4. Create winning door-to-door systems with regard to existing alternatives

5. Make explicit the problems to be resolved, bottlenecks to be removed, and solutions to be structured and forge partnerships to realize their implementation

6. Transform ports and the associated community into centers of logistic integration with their hinterland[21]

A high priority of the roundtable is in adding value through the development of information databases. In addition to dispute resolution, the roundtables offer strategic information capable of generating trade leads and business development. The databases become opportunities for investment and business between and among public and private organizations. Eventually, the roundtables seek to systematize trade and transport data, becoming a true repository for a corridor outlining transport costs and cross-referencing trade opportunities with transportation alternatives.

Mercosur Atlantic Corridor Consortium

The success of the Mideast Consortium, the economic stabilization since Brazil's implementation of the Real Plan in 1994, and the creation of MERCOSUR principally among Brazil, Argentina, Paraguay, and Uruguay contributed to the expansion of the Mideast Corridor into a full-fledged Mercosur Atlantic Corridor Consortium (hereafter Mercosur Consortium). Led by the efforts of Mideast Consortium Directors Sandra Stehling and Paulo Augusto Vivacqua, the Mideast Consortium exported the model of the integration roundtable to other port cities. The concept has met with fast success as roundtables have expanded to more than 26 in number. A listing follows in Table 5.3. Table 5.4 lists some of the key actors involved in the consortia.

A major advancement in the consortium concept emerged in the creation of cross-national roundtables established in Argentina, Peru, and Uruguay. A truly continental organizational economic development model is expanding based on assembly of key actors involved in the shipping process with the goal of reducing transportation bottlenecks and costs while increasing trade opportunities. In each new roundtable, a director is selected to run the local roundtables and manage the agendas. Since the Mercosur Consortium originated from the organizational structure of the Mideast Consortium, the Vitória office of the Mideast Consortium also functions as the marketing and public relations arm for the whole Mercosur Consortium.

Table 5.3
Mercosur Atlantic Corridor Integration Roundtables

Brazil	Argentina	Peru	Uruguay
Belo Horizonte	Bahia Blanca	Lima	Montevideo
Brasilia	Buenos Aires		
Campo Grande	Comodoro Rivadavia		
Fortaleza	Puerto Madryn		
Governador Valadares	Santa Cruz		
Ilheus	Zarate		
Imbituba			
Juiz de Fora			
Manaus			
Pôrto Alegre			
Recife			
Rio de Janeiro			
Salvador			
São Francisco do Sul			
São Luis			
São Paulo			
Vitoria			

Source: Data from Mercosur Atlantic Corridor Consortium, Consórcio do Corredor Atlântico do Mercosul, *Mesas de Integração Manual de Operações e Procedimentos de Implantação* (Vitoria, Espírito Santo, Brazil, 2000).

The Impacts of the Mercosur Integration Roundtables

The MERCOSUR integration roundtables have had numerous accomplishments. The reason for their rapid expansion across national boundaries stems from the success of the organizational model in giving participants value added for their participation. The rapid growth is also a possible weakness; as more and more roundtables develop, their range may exceed capacity unless Mercosur Consortium's organizational structure also adapts to accommodate the rapid growth. In addition to the previously mentioned achievement in grain exports in Espírito Santo, a summary of roundtable successes is listed in Table 5.5.

Table 5.4
Members of the Mideast Corridor Consortium

Name	Sector
Agep Construções e Empreendimentos	Civil construction
Aliança	Coastal maritime shipping
Andrade Gutierrez	Civil construction
CVRD	Mining, port, and rail operator
Development Bank of Minas Gerais	Banking and finance
Câmara Brasileira de Contêineres	Containers
Electrical Power Company of Minas Gerais-CEMIG	Power utility
Comigo-Cooperativa Mista dos Produtores Rurais do Sudoeste	Agricultural and livestock
Cominde Importadora e Exportadora	Trading company
Companhia de Armazéns Cerrado do Brasil	Warehousing
Silo and Warehouse Company of Minas Gerais	Warehousing
COIMEX Import/Export	Trading
Docenave	Coastal maritime shipping
Pereira de Almeida	Civil construction
Ribeiro Santos Advocacia	Law firm
Multiterminais	Intermodal transport terminals
RFFSA	Railways
Silocaf	Coffee export
Tora Transportes	Trucking
Viaçào Agua Branca	Bus and road transport
Samarco Mineração	Mining

Source: Information compiled from interview by John Cuttino with Pedrita Castiglioni, Economist, Mideast Corridor Consortium, Vitória, Espírito Santo, Brazil, August 21, 2000.

Table 5.5
Achievements of the Integration Roundtables

Problem	Action	Result
1. Wheat, corn, and malt * Wheat import restricted in Espírito Santo * Low storage capacity * High costs * Annual freight volumes of 150,000 tons per year	* Included wheat in the modeling of port activities * Attracted investment in new silos * Attracted trade lane Ghent-Vitória for the distribution of Braham malts to the southeast region	* Lowered costs * Increased storage to 60,000 tons * Increased grain throughput to 900,000 tons per year
2. Automobile imports * Absence of vehicle imports through Espírito Santo ports * Government legislation sanctioned auto imports only through São Paulo or Rio de Janeiro ports * Need a customs regime in a secondary area to serve the cargo movement of the primary area	* Previous government regulation eliminated * Obtained approval from Federal Revenue Department to establish three inland dry ports and one customs clearance terminal for the Vitória metropolitan region * Auction of three inland dry ports with customs clearance facilities	* Transformation of Vitória into Brazil's largest importer of vehicles by 1995 of 400,000 units
3. Energy * State of Espírito Santo imports 80% of its energy * Little potential for hydroelectric power * Large volume of ships arriving at ports in search of iron ore with the possibility of bringing coal for generation of power * Unused capacity of railway system * Need to reduce final transportation costs in Mideast Corridor	* Contracted study to identify viable alternatives to power generation * Conclusion on viability of creation of coal power plant in Minas Gerais * Attraction of Southern Electric International as investor * Association of Southern Electric International with CEMIG and Samarco Mining through intervention of Mideast Corridor	* Southern Electric International in association with another American company bought 33% of CEMIG valuing $1.3 billion

Problem	Action	Result
4. Energy II		
* Espírito Santos imports 80% of its energy * Petrobrás Oil Company is deactivating its research off the coast * Distribution of gas was the responsibility of the State	* Joint promotion with the Government of Espírito Santo for concession of gas distribution * Negotiation with Petrobrás of a contract with Espírito Santo for gas distribution	* Extension of pipeline serving region of Cariacica and Viana serving more than 10 businesses * Additional research on gas reserves resulting in the discovery of deposits of greater magnitude than those previously discovered * Linkage from Campos, Rio de Janeiro to Vitória * Two new plants under construction– Petrobrás in partnership with CVRD and Escelsa
5. Port of Ubú		
* Private terminal for mineral cargo of Samarco * 80 percent under capacity * Not taking advantage of port expansion at low cost * Only highway access to port	* Promotion of port as a business center * Feasibility study for linking the port to the Vitória-Rio de Janeiro rail trunk line * Stimulate the strategic planning to take advantage of unused capacity for attracting future cargo and port expansion	* New terminal expansion (4 new berths) * New cargo attracted, lumber and wood products, marmorite, granite, and coal * Formation of a consortium of private business for new investment in coastal railroad
6. Vitória/Zarate (Argentina) Association		
* Great dearth of knowledge of trade opportunities afforded by Mercosur on behalf of Corridor Consortia and MERCOSUR countries * Many opportunities if information passed along professionally	* Investment opportunity in port terminal at Buenos Aires * Inland dry ports for vehicle imports * Project driven Murchison-Cotia Trading between regions	* Association between Murchison Cotia Trading and inland dry ports * Investment in 2 berths and 100,000 m2 * Establishment of new weekly maritime service on Transroll-Vitória-Zarate
7. High costs of storage		
* Large volumes of cargo imported through inland dry ports of Espírito Santo * Storage cost surcharges doubling costs * Expansion of imports restricted by high final costs	* Benefit/cost analysis of single payment only at inland dry port	* Regulation permitting issuance of customs transit declaration * Warehousing is only paid in the inland dry ports, and cargo is liberated in four hours

Problem	Action	Result
8. Logistics of malt transportation		
* High costs of road haulage	* Create a new transport logistics	* Authorized CODESA to construct rail link
* Long distances	* Reduce freight costs	
* Freight costs affecting production costs directly	* CVRD proposed construction of rail link 100 meters from access to malt silos inside port	* Transfer of highway cargo to rail cargo
* Railroads without access to malt inside the port, prohibiting modal choice	* Meetings with Mideast Corridor roundtables brought together Brahma and Skol breweries, CVRD railway, and the Espírito Santo Port Authority (CODESA)	* First transport of malt via rail

Source: Information compiled from interview by John Cuttino with Pedrita Castiglioni, Economist, Mideast Corridor Consortium, Vitória, Espírito Santo, Brazil, August 24, 2000.

The Dorsal Fin Project and MERCOSUR Cabotage

Increasing cargo carried along coastal sea-lanes has been an objective of the Mercosur Consortium. In November 1996, the consortium convened a meeting of the region's ports, concentrating on using its integration roundtables to assemble the port actors. The consortium sought to build, through its MERCOSUR contract, a transport/trade database that would pool information from small- and medium-sized businesses. By pooling information, an increasing range of transport and trade options are made available as more cargo is available to freight carriers. Concomitant with more demand for freight, the consortium designed its MERCOSUR contract to be able to provide door-to-door multimodal logistics service, which is only feasible in scale if there is sufficient cargo to increase the offer of transport service. By targeting small- and medium-sized businesses, the consortium was seeking to stimulate new business development by pooling the market power of local businesses that had remained isolated from markets. Underlying the objective to promote economic and business development is also the promotion of nonhighway transportation. Here, the database would make intermodal transport more viable by providing transport providers with cargo that could be consolidated and/or transported by containers. The ambitious economic development goals of the Mercosur Consortium involved simultaneously developing trade and transportation alternatives.[22]

The idea of shifting cargo to nonhighway modes was evident in the early meetings. In 1998, at the roundtable of São Paulo, a manager of a trucking firm carrying freight from São Paulo to Fortaleza was seeking to remove a number of its trucks from the Fortaleza-São Paulo route.[23] A liner company suggested that it could serve the trucking company by moving freight from Fortaleza to São Paulo via cabotage. The consortium developed the idea into a larger framework for enhancing the region's cabotage with the stated objective to reduce the transport costs of the "Brazil Cost."[24] So was born the Projeto Espinha Dorsal, or Dorsal Fin Project. The Dorsal Fin Project is an ambitious project in the early stages of development, seeking to link trucking companies, port terminal operators, liner companies operating cabotage, and multimodal transportation operators in a logistics network. Similar to the MERCOSUR contract, the Dorsal Fin Project would create a backbone network, providing shippers with cheaper transport alternatives. Moreover, the multimodal aspect of the Dorsal Fin Project shifted cargo from traditional highway mode to intermodal, rail, inland waterway, and cabotage. On August 24, 2000, Brazil's Vice President Marco Maciel signed the Mercosur Corridor's Dorsal Fin Project Protocol of Intentions in a symbolic ceremony in Brasília. Figure 5.2 illustrates the proximity of cities hosting integration roundtables to the coastal and inland waterway navigation routes.

Notwithstanding the potential of pooling shipping databases for purposes of promoting cabotage and lower transport costs, the Dorsal Fin Project is in its nascent stage. For intermodal transportation to really grow, Brazil has some tax issues that must be resolved. Currently, the state value-added sales tax (Impostosobre Circulação de Mercadorías e Serviços, or ICMS) is levied more than once on cargo that travels across state lines and switches modes before arriving at its final destination. In other words, freight that uses multiple modes pays more taxes than cargo traveling solely by one mode. This tax burden is a disincentive for the Dorsal Fin Project or any multimodal movement seeking to shift cargo from highway to nonhighway modes. Any attempt to resolve the problem of double taxation will have to be addressed by the National Council for Finance Policy (Conselho Nacional de Política Fazendaria, or CONFAZ). CONFAZ assembles the state secretaries of finance and the minister of finance with the objective of debating and negotiating the fiscal policies of states. Because the states levy the value-added tax, any changes affecting its incidence on multimodal freight movements must be addressed by CONFAZ. However, CONFAZ must rule on issues by consensus, making dispute resolution almost impossible. Barring a change to majority decision in CONFAZ, the problem of double taxation on intermodal freight movements is likely to continue.[25]

The degree of transparency can also affect the future of the Dorsal Fin Project. Transparency can be measured in the willingness to share information developed as a result of the project. As stated in an agreement with a private logistics company, the Mercosur Consortium delegates the logistics services to be provided to one company, Danzas Logística.[26] The Dorsal Fin Project cannot be said to be neutral vis-à-vis logistics companies. Integration roundtables as generators of cargo movement would be funneling business to just one company. This result goes against the very intentions to provide a variety of transport alternatives. For the Dorsal Fin Project to gain momentum and increase cabotage, the consortium may have to expand into its own multimodal transport operator and become a door-to-door logistics nonprofit company, which would have the rights to any business generated by the roundtables. However, if this were to occur, it would risk alienating logistics companies that currently participate in the roundtables. It is worth noting that a conflict of interest forced the originator of the idea, Paulo Augusto Camello (representing Global Lines in 1998 when the idea arose, but now representing Aliança Navigation and Logistics) to withdraw from the Dorsal Fin Project. Camello views Danzas' participation as a nonneutral logistics service provider as an impediment to creation of the network.[27] While the idea to stimulate cabotage is engaging politically as observed by the attention of the Brazilian vice president, its implementation will determine its success.

Roundtable Dilemmas

Ports play an important role in the development of their cities and hinterland. The Mideast Consortium and Mercosur Consortium are active organizations that constitute one part of the logistics network along their respective trade corridors. By assembling the major actors on a regular basis, the roundtables of the consortia are able to articulate the needs of a logistics, transport, and trading system. They have created value as a promising and vital mechanism with which to address and resolve transportation issues outside the initiative of the state. In many ways, the corridor consortia are creating a new form of organization transcending political and geographical boundaries, so much so that the existence of a corridor roundtable aggregates value for a region. In addition to physical infrastructure, a defining characteristic of successful trade corridor in the future may be the existence of integration roundtables. The capacity to collect and disseminate information and resolve problems constitutes a tool that shippers and transportation providers may use to enhance their flexibility to react to market demands. The successes listed in Table 5.5 delineate early accomplishments of the roundtables.

Though clearly dominated by trade topics, the scope of the Mercosur Consortium has grown to include educational initiatives at the university and municipal levels, environmental programs, and alternative (wind) energy projects. The concept of corridor and the concept of sustainable development now overlap with much attention going toward addressing environmental and academic issues. The Mideast Consortium offices in Vitória are a training ground for addressing far-reaching issues of sustainability. One program being promoted seeks to educate disadvantaged children about the environment by showing, via satellite technology, how their communities are linked to other communities in the region. Taking place at the municipal level, the program seeks to be an exponential solution to the exponential problem of environmental degradation and population growth. By showing youth how their communities interact with others, the objective is to induce more environmentally friendly behavior in poorer communities.[28] To carry out these far-reaching initiatives, the Mideast Consortium created the Mideast Foundation (Fundação Centroleste). In so doing though, the Mideast Consortium is at risk of losing its transport identity as it ventures away from transportation. If it cannot follow through on the creative transport ideas that it is developing, such as the Dorsal Fin Project, then its credibility is at issue.

Figure 5.2
Mercosur Atlantic Corridor Integration Roundtables

Source: Adapted from Paulo Augusto Vivacqua and Sandra Maria Ferraz Stehling, "Mercosur's Atlantic Corridor: New Avenues for South America's Integration" (paper presented at Latin Ports and Shipping 2000, Miami, Fla. November 2000), p. 9.

The Mercosur Consortium is at a crossroads where it must either continue to grow and add capacity or pare down its portfolio to tasks to which it can adequately apply the necessary human resources. Future success of the Mercosur Consortium may not be a question of ideas or organizational structure but, instead, of human resources and commitment to those present and future initiatives. Another impediment to the Mercosur Consortium lies in the dominance of the Mideast Consortium. Justifiably so, as it provides the labor and resources used to organize a great part of the roundtables, the Mercosur Consortium is dominated by issues that involve the Port of Vitória and, hence, its Mideast Consortium. Rather than act as independent roundtables, integration roundtables can be viewed to some extent as satellites of Vitória, quasi embassies of the Mideast Consortium. Though these new integration roundtables owe their existence to the Mideast Consortium and, in particular, to its directors from Vitória, the success of the roundtables may depend on the degree to which they develop endogenously. In such a situation, following a schedule centralized in Vitória may be an obstacle to roundtable growth.

Conclusion

Coastal cabotage along the East Coast of South America depends a great deal on the network of shared information concerning shippers, service, markets, and transportation providers. The Mideast Consortium and, later, the Mercosur Consortium have emerged as new organizational units with which regions, led by port cities, articulate and resolve their problems. The legacies of uneven development in Brazil along the lines of an archipelago are ripe for expanding coastal cabotage and inland waterway transport by ship or barge. The consortia have sought to move South America toward integration through shifting freight from highway to nonhighway modes, in essence, connecting the archipelago or islands of port cities and their hinterlands by cabotage. The Dorsal Fin Project and MERCOSUR contract show how global trends for door-to-door transportation are addressed by an emerging transnational corridor unit of analysis. As they relate to maritime transportation in the Americas, the examples of the Mideast Consortium and Mercosur Consortium demonstrate the success and potential that a nonprofit organizational entity can have on economic development and problem solving. In the future, the development of a trade corridor may be conditioned on the existence and activity of integration roundtables based in exporting/importing cities. The integration roundtables are, thus, safety valves providing business and community leaders with the forum to address problems arising from complex and simultaneous processes of modernization, deregulation, privatization, and globalization. The success of the roundtables is also its weakness. The management of rapid growth will be the major challenge for the Mercosur Consortium. If it succeeds at disseminating information and generating business for cabotage, then it will be helping to build demand and capacity.

Notes

[1] Agência Brasil, *Comunicado de Brasília, na reunião de presidentes da América do Sul* (September 1, 2000), Radiobras Website. Online. Available: http://www.radiobras.gov.br/abr/integras/00/integra_0109_3.htm. Accessed: October 16, 2000.

[2] Ibid.

[3] Paulo Augusto Vivacqua and Sandra Maria Ferraz Stehling, "Mercosur's Atlantic Corridor: New Avenues for South America's Integration" (paper presented at Latin Ports and Shipping 2000, Miami, Fla. November 2000), p. 8.

[4] H. A. van Klink, "Creating Port Networks: The Case of Rotterdam and the Baltic Region," *International Journal of Transport Economics*, vol. 24, no. 3 (October 1997), pp. 393-408; Klaus-Jürgen Uhl, "The New Role of Ports as Railroad Operators and Builders of Hinterland Networks—The European Example" (paper presented at Latin Ports and Shipping Conference, Miami, Fla., November 10, 1999); and Robert Koenig, "Port 'Networks'—A Wave of the Future?" *Journal of Commerce* (July 19, 2000). Online. Available: http://www.joc.com/20000719/sections/edit/w50615.shtml. Accessed: July 20, 2000.

[5] Wilbur Smith Associates, *The CANAMEX Trade Corridor: Economic Opportunities Associated with Transportation Improvements* (Columbia, South Carolina, December 1998), p. 1-1.

[6] Ibid., p. 1-2.

[7] Western Trade Transportation Network, *Western Trade Transportation Network (WTTN) Final Report* (n.p., 1997), p. 3-2.

[8] Stephen O. Bender, "General Aspects of Trade Corridors" (Organization of American States: Washington, D.C., n.d.), p. 1.

[9] Empresa Brasileira de Planejamento de Transportes (GEIPOT), Ministério dos Transportes, *Corredores Estratégicos de Desenvolvimento*, coord. José Glauco Apoliano Andrade Dias (Brasília, February 1999), p. 4.

[10] Bender, "General Aspects of Trade Corridors", pp. 1-3.

[11] Stephen O. Bender, "Trade Corridors: The Emerging Regional Development Planning Unit in Latin America" (paper presented to the United Nations Centre for Regional Development, Regional Development Forum for Latin America and the Caribbean on "Regional Development Planning: Towards the 21st Century," Santafe de Bogota, Colombia, December 1-3, 1997), p. 3.

[12] Ibid., p. 5.

[13] Interview by John Cuttino with Sandra Stehling, Director, Mideast Corridor Consortium and Mercosur Atlantic Corridor Consortium, Vitória, Espírito Santo, Brazil, August 21, 2000.

[14] Ibid.

[15] Albert Hirschman, *Journeys Toward Progress: Studies of Economic Policy-Making in Latin America* (New York: Twentieth Century Fund, 1963), pp. 240-41.

[16] Stehling interview.

[17] Kenneth C. Williamson, Daniel M. Spitzer, Jr., and David J. Bloomberg, "Modern Logistics Systems: Theory and Practice," *Journal of Business Logistics*, vol. 11, no. 2 (1990), p. 67.

[18] Donald F. Wood et al., *International Logistics* (Boston: Kluwer Academic Press, 1995), p. 4.

[19] Ibid., p. 217.

[20] Stehling interview.

[21] Mideast Corridor Consortium, "Consórcio do Corredor Atlântico do Mercosur: Mesa de Integração—ES—Termo de Instituição e Posse (September 23, 1997)," in *Consórcio Operacional do Corredor de Transportes Centroleste* (Vitória, Espírito Santo, Brazil, n.d.), p. 12.

[22] Stehling interview.

[23] Interview by John Cuttino with Paulo Augusto Camello, Manager, Cabotage Operations Center, Aliança Navigation and Logistics, Rio de Janeiro, August 28, 2000.

[24] The so-called *Custo Brasil,* or Brazil Cost, includes high transport costs but also describes a variety of other factors that impede Brazil from importing or exporting, such as customs procedures, tariff and non-tariff trade barriers, inadequate infrastructure, taxes, theft, and corruption.

[25] Saïd Farhat, *Dicionário Parlamentar e Político-O processo político e legislativo no Brasil* (São Paulo: Editora Fundação Peirópolis, 1996), p. 176.

[26] Mercosur Atlantic Corridor Consortium, *Instrumento Particular de Constituição de Consórcio do Corredor Atlântico Mercosur e Danzas Logística e Armazéns Gerais Ltda.* (Vitória, Espírito Santo, Brazil, June 9, 2000).

[27] Camello interview, May 29, 2001.

[28] Interview by John Cuttino with Paulo Augusto Vivacqua, President, Mercosur Atlantic Corridor Consortium, Rio de Janeiro, May 30, 2001.

Chapter 6. Cabotage Law in the Americas

Introduction

Most maritime nations have a body of law that governs the marine transportation of passengers and cargo between domestic ports and restricts such trade to national flag vessels.[1] These laws are typically referred to as coastwise laws or cabotage laws.

The history of cabotage legislation in the Americas begins in the United States in 1789, when the First U.S. Congress enacted An Act Imposing Duties on Tonnage in response to the mercantilist Navigation Acts of England. The 1789 act favored the use of U.S. vessels over foreign-owned or foreign-built vessels through the levying of preferential tariffs and port fees.[2] The next significant piece of U.S. shipping legislation passed in 1817, when Congress enacted An Act Concerning the Navigation of the United States. It was this legislation that for the first time limited domestic trade to U.S.-flag vessels.[3] This law also placed additional tonnage taxes on U.S.-flag vessels that did not maintain a certain percentage of U.S. citizens among the crew.[4] The Merchant Marine Act of 1920 expanded the 1817 legislation by requiring that vessels participating in domestic shipping be U.S.-owned, U.S.-built, U.S.-crewed, and U.S.-flagged.[5] This law has since become known as the Jones Act after its sponsor, Senator Wesley Jones (Republican, Washington State).

In the 81 years since its passage, the Jones Act has become more than a simple piece of maritime legislation. Because of its multitude of restrictions on domestic shippers, in large part, the Jones Act has come to be known as the international standard by which other nations' cabotage legislation is judged.

What Cabotage Laws Exist in the Americas

As other countries throughout the Western Hemisphere became increasingly involved in maritime trade, many of them enacted cabotage laws resembling the Jones Act. Since the Jones Act's passage in 1920, it has become quite common for nations throughout the hemisphere to limit cabotage within their boarders to domestically flagged vessels. Crewing and ownership requirements are a phenomenon of the 20th century, likely precipitated by the passage of the Jones Act. Few nations in the Americas ever fully developed the shipyard capacity necessary to justify the enactment of domestic shipbuilding requirements.

Table 6.1 provides an overview of the exclusionary restrictions on cabotage shipping currently in place in many of the major maritime nations of the Americas.

Table 6.1
Domestic Shipping Laws

Country	Flagging Requirements	Crewing Requirements	Domestic Ownership Requirements	Domestic Construction Requirements	Fleet Subsidies
Argentina	X	X	X		3
Bahamas	X	X	X		X
Brazil	X	X	X	X	X
Canada	X	X	2		
Chile	X	X	X		3
Colombia	X	X	X		
Ecuador	X	X	X		3
Honduras	X	X	X		
Mexico	X	X	X		
Panama	1				
Peru	X	X	X	X	X
United States	X	X	X	X	
Uruguay	X	X			
Venezuela	X	X	X		X

Notes:

X–Country has restrictions of this type or offers fleet subsidies.

Blank–Country does not have restrictions of this type or does not offer fleet subsidies.

1–Country does not exclude foreign-flagged vessels but does have certain restrictions.

2–Country does not have formal ownership requirements but does have some minor restrictions.

3–Country provides benefits to its domestic fleet indirectly.

Source: Data from U.S. Department of Transportation Maritime Administration (MARAD), *A Survey of World Cabotage Laws: Summary of Responses from Countries* (Washington, D.C., March 1991), p. 61.

The table illustrates quite clearly the prevalence of restrictive legislation in countries throughout the Western Hemisphere. Not all the nations of North and South America are represented in this research but, rather, a sample of those nations most heavily engaged in maritime trade. The nations listed here cite similar reasons for the adoption of cabotage laws. The common justifications behind the existence of cabotage restrictions and individual circumstances that make cabotage in these nations unique will be presented below on a nation-by-nation basis.

Argentina

In Argentina, cabotage regulations exist "[t]o promote the development of the domestic shipping industry and related sectors in the industry and to promote economic growth."[6] The statutory authority for Argentina's registration, ownership, and crewing requirements dates back to legislation passed in 1944. Despite the longevity of cabotage legislation, cabotage trade in the country has been faced with many changes in recent years. The 1995 integration of Argentina, Brazil, Paraguay, and Uruguay into the Southern Common Market (Mercado Común del Sur, or MERCOSUR) brought with it the goal of eliminating nontariff barriers to trade.[7] Opening cabotage to the MERCOSUR group was discussed within MERCOSUR's marine transportation working group several years ago. Discussions have since been discontinued, and the marine transportation working group has since merged into another working group that considers both road and maritime issues.[8] Coastal shippers in Argentina have also recently been faced with increased competition from other transportation modes and a 1999 regional financial crisis.[9] According to industry officials, many small Argentine shipping companies were forced into bankruptcy by poor economic conditions.[10] In the past, the Argentine government supported its domestic shipbuilding industry with a tax on import and export trade. Given the economic troubles recently faced by Argentina, it remains to be seen whether this process will continue in the future.[11]

Bahamas

The focus of cabotage legislation is simply "to generate employment for Bahamian nationals."[12] This goal is hardly surprising given the number of island-hopping passenger vessels that visit the region each year. Through cabotage legislation, the Bahamian government ensures that any cruise ship desiring to make subsequent port calls within the country's boundaries must be registered in the country and must, to the extent possible, employ Bahamians among its crew. The Bahamian government subsidizes the operation of the nation's domestic mail boat service.[13]

Brazil

Accounting for two-thirds of all trade along the East Coast north-south market in Latin America, Brazil is the regional leader in trade in South America. The goals of cabotage legislation are "[t]o protect domestic shipping and shipbuilding."[14] It is one of only two countries in Latin America (see the section on Peru) that has enacted as many restrictions on domestic coastal shipping as the United States has in the Jones Act. The Shipping Law of 1967 represented Brazil's first attempt to bring the country's shipyards to full capacity by requiring ships engaged in Brazilian cabotage to be domestically built.[15] According to industry officials, at least one reason for the failure to develop a MERCOSUR-wide cabotage system stems from the fact that cabotage law in Brazil has been written into the Brazilian constitution and will not be revoked for trade negotiations.[16]

Even assuming that Brazilian cabotage law could be repealed for the purpose of fuller economic integration within MERCOSUR, the concept of MERCOSUR-wide cabotage does not sit well with many Brazilian shipping companies that believe that the country has nothing to gain from participating in Argentine cabotage.[17]

Canada

Part X, Section 592, of the Canadian Shipping Act states: "(1) No goods shall be transported by water or by land and water, from one place in Canada to another place in Canada, either directly or by way of a foreign port, or for any part of the transportation in any ship other than a British ship. (2) No ship other than a British ship shall transport passengers from one place in Canada to another place in Canada, either directly or by way of a foreign port."[18]

The government maintains that these statutes exist "[t]o protect Canadian seamen and support shipbuilding."[19] Though the Canadian Shipping Act does not explicitly state that ships engaged in Canadian cabotage must be owned by Canadians, it does require that ships wishing to register in Canada must be owned by a British subject or Commonwealth corporation.[20]

Chile

The goals of cabotage restrictions in Chile are "[t]o insure adequate shipping by providing Chilean vessels with a monopoly."[21] Decree Law No. 3059 states: "Coastal trade, ocean, river or lacustrian cargo and passenger trade between locations in the national territory, and between these and naval devices installed in territorial sea or in the exclusive economic area, is reserved to Chilean shipping companies, except when it deals with cargo volumes over 900 tons, and after a public bidding has been held."[22]

A shipping company is considered Chilean if more than 50 percent of the company is owned by Chileans.[23] "As a policy, Chile has no operational subsidies. However, there are subsidies for shipments to remote areas not served on a regular basis by any cabotage or passenger service."[24]

Colombia

Colombia also believes that its cabotage laws "protect the domestic maritime industry."[25] In addition to requiring that ships engaged in domestic trades be registered in the country, Colombian law requires that all officers aboard such vessel and at least 80 percent of the crew be Colombian citizens, and that national-flagged vessels operating in domestic service have a minimum of 60 percent Colombian ownership.[26]

Ecuador

Ecuadorian-flagged vessels must have greater than 50 percent domestic ownership, and, similar to Colombia, at least 80 percent of the crew of an Ecuadorian-flagged vessel engaged in domestic service must be of Ecuadorian citizenship including the captain and chief engineer.[27] Ecuador indirectly subsidizes the domestic operation of its nation's ships through the provision of low-cost fuel.[28] The country has recently entered into bilateral trade agreements with its neighbors to foster cooperation in trade and commerce. The 1998 Treaty of Commerce and Navigation with Peru has the effect of liberalizing

238

trade between the two signatories and also provides that "customary international practice will govern the navigation of cabotage and warships."[29]

Honduras

Since 1952, Honduras has participated in the Central American Economic Integration Program that attempts to liberalize trade between Honduras, Nicaragua, El Salvador, Guatemala, and Costa Rica.[30] This movement toward unfettered trade, however, has not infringed on the protection of domestic cabotage. Cabotage laws in Honduras exist "[t]o favor vessels that operate under the Honduran flag in order to increase government revenues from the registry of new vessels."[31] National-flag vessels operating in domestic service must be 100 percent Honduran owned and maintain a crew of at least 90 percent Honduran citizens if possible.[32]

Mexico

Cabotage traffic in Mexico goes back to the end of the 19th century when navigation became an important area for the development of Mexico.[33] Today, cabotage traffic accounts for 29 percent of the total cargo moved by Mexican ports or approximately 67.3 million tons.[34] The motivations behind the Law of Navigation of 1994 are

- to strengthen the domestic system of maritime transport,

- to drive the maritime transport of cabotage,

- to implement actions to make the Mexican shipping lines more competitive,

- to generate jobs for officials and subordinates of the domestic merchant marine, and

- to make the functions of the maritime authority more efficient.[35]

This 1994 legislation represents a substantial liberalization of cabotage policy from the General Law of Means of Communication that formerly governed the industry.[36] Before the Law of Navigation of 1994, vessels operating in Mexican cabotage were required to be 100 percent owned and crewed by Mexican citizens.[37] The Law of Navigation of 1994 clearly favors Mexican ships in cabotage operations, but, in certain cases, foreign ship owners or vessels may participate in Mexican cabotage if the country in which the vessel is owned or registered has negotiated reciprocity or equivalency with Mexico.[38]

Panama

The only activity restricted to national-flag vessels in Panama is fishing.[39]

Peru

Peru stands in stark contrast to Panama. Peru, Brazil, Indonesia, and the United States are the only countries in the world that have registration, crewing, ownership, and ship building requirements to participate in domestic maritime trade.[40] Peru requires that 100 percent of the crew be Peruvian but requires that ships engaged in cabotage trades only be 50 percent Peruvian owned.[41] The Peruvian government maintains that the enforcement of these restrictions protect and promote the development of national transport facilities.[42] Like Ecuador, Peru has traditionally subsidized firms engaged in cabotage trade through below-market fuel prices.[43]

United States

The rationale for the Jones Act is set out in the act's preamble, which states: "That it is necessary for the national defense and for the proper growth of its foreign and domestic commerce that the United States shall have a merchant marine of the best equipped and most suitable types of vessels sufficient to carry the greater portion of its commerce and serve as a naval or military auxiliary in time of war or national emergency, ultimately to be owned by private citizens of the United States; and it is hereby declared to be the policy of the United States to do whatever may be necessary to develop and encourage the maintenance of such a merchant marine."[44]

Uruguay

Coastal shipping in Uruguay is reserved for vessels that fly the Uruguayan flag, are commanded by a Uruguayan captain, and have at least one-third Uruguayan crew.[45] Uruguay declares that its "[c]abotage law is not intended to protect the small national industry, but to conform with practices of other regional countries."[46] In practice, however, there are very few nationally registered vessels engaged in cabotage, as these restrictions are not enforced.[47]

Venezuela

The Law for the Protection and Development of the National Merchant Marine exists to protect Venezuelan citizens by requiring that ships engaged in cabotage be at least 80 percent domestically owned and employ a crew of at least 80 percent Venezuelan citizens.[48] In June 1999, Venezuela passed the Law to Restructure the Merchant Marine, the goal of which is to lower ship registration costs in the country in order to make the Venezuelan registry more popular.[49] Carriers may also be enticed to re-flag in Venezuela by the country's policy of subsidizing fuel costs of its domestic operators.[50]

The Case against Cabotage

Despite its long legal history in nations throughout the Americas, cabotage laws in recent years have become an increasingly fertile subject for debate. Groups worldwide have argued against the continued use of cabotage and other restrictive shipping preferences. Much of the debate centers on the U.S. Jones Act as two camps have formed on both sides of the issue. Throughout the 1990s, the primary group leading calls to liberalize the Jones Act was known as the Jones Act Reform Coalition.[51] Formed in 1995, the coalition included many shippers of agricultural and mineral commodities who believed that the Jones Act led to higher shipping costs for their low-price, high-volume products.[52] In addition to lobbying Congress for reforms, the coalition was primarily known to maritime industry officials through its maintenance of a home page on the World Wide Web, which has recently discontinued operation.[53]

U.S. interests opposed to the Jones Act have found statistical support for their position from the U.S. International Trade Commission (USITC). Through a number of biannual reports, USITC has investigated the economic costs of import restraints, including the economic effects of proposed changes to the Jones Act. In 1995, the USITC conducted a general equilibrium analysis, which concluded that complete repeal of the Jones Act would result in an overall economic welfare gain of $2.8 billion.[54] The 1999 update to the USITC's earlier report includes economic analysis of a second scenario in which only the U.S.-build requirement is struck from the Jones Act. Under this option, U.S. domestic shipping would still be reserved in all other ways, except that cabotage operators would now be able to purchase less-expensive vessels from Korean or Japanese shipyards. In this event, the USITC maintains that shipyards might lose up to 15 percent of their production but that the price of cabotage services would be reduced between 5 and 12 percent, domestic revenues would increase between 2.5 and 6.8 percent, deepwater domestic-sector employment would increase between 8 and 22 percent, and cheaper cabotage services would result in a welfare gain of between $138 million and $380 million to consumers of those services.[55]

Though reform of the U.S. cabotage market has received the most attention, the United States is by no means the only place where reforms are being considered for economic reasons. Consultants recently reported to the Organization for Economic Cooperation and Development (OECD) that "cabotage policy is clearly market distorting [and] should be addressed by national administrations, and ideally removed or minimized."[56] As mentioned earlier, MERCOSUR has also considered the liberalization of cabotage laws among its own member nations.

The Case for Preserving Cabotage

In the United States, the Maritime Cabotage Task Force, a loose association of vessel owners and operators, labor organizations, shipbuilders, repair yards, equipment manufacturers, other transportation interests (air, rail, etc.), pro-defense groups, and trade associations, has formed to oppose the actions taken by the Jones Act Reform Coalition.[57] The Maritime Cabotage Task Force defends the continued existence of the Jones Act on the grounds that (1) the act provides direct employment for 124,000 Americans, (2) similar laws are found in more than 40 major maritime nations throughout the world, (3) the act is necessary to ensure that a qualified merchant marine is maintained in readiness in the event of war, and (4) the USITC study projecting large welfare gains as a result of revocation of the Jones Act is flawed because it assumes that repeal will necessarily result in a precipitous drop in waterborne freight rates.[58]

The staunchest opponents to change in cabotage laws are quite naturally the companies currently engaged in cabotage shipping. Brazilian industry officials maintain that coastal trade is not very profitable and that most of the companies engaged in such routes operate at a loss, rather than a profit in most years.[59] Others maintain that the difference in door-to-door transportation cost with or without cabotage restrictions is so minor that it is unlikely to make a substantial difference in the final price of consumer goods.[60]

Regional Cabotage in the European Union

Applications for Latin America

With the possibility that the Free Trade Area of the Americas (FTAA) will come into being around 2005, a system of regional cabotage could emerge in the hemisphere.

The Plan for the Free Trade Area of the Americas

The FTAA was born out of the Summit of the Americas in Miami in 1994, where the leaders of all countries in the hemisphere, minus Cuba, met and agreed to create a hemisphere-wide trade zone. At the summit, the goal was set to establish the FTAA by 2005, with substantial progress required by 2000. The following are the FTAA's statement of principles:

- to preserve and strengthen the community of democracies of the Americas,

- to promote prosperity through economic integration and free trade,

- to eradicate poverty and discrimination in our hemisphere, and

- to guarantee sustainable development and conserve our natural environment for future generations.[61]

After establishing these principles, 12 working groups were established to gather and compile information about the status of trade relations within the hemisphere. These working groups were later consolidated into nine "Negotiation Groups" to discover possible approaches to negotiations.

Although maritime policy has not been specifically discussed within the FTAA, some form of liberalized regional cabotage system will emerge from this agreement. The question then becomes, how will this regional cabotage system be implemented and what effects will it have on the maritime industries in the FTAA-member countries? Currently, the only model of an integrated cabotage system is found in the European Union.

The European Model of Cabotage

Within the European Union (EU), the process of liberalization of maritime transport is virtually complete, with operators having the right to provide service between two ports in a country other than the one in which the operator is currently established.[62] The only significant restriction is passenger service in the Greek Islands, which is presently closed to competition until 2004.

The primary directive governing European cabotage is Council Regulation 3577/92 of December 7, 1992, applying the principle of freedom to provide services to maritime transport within member states. Member states have adapted their cabotage restrictions to comply with this directive. Currently, cabotage in all northern European states (Sweden, Finland, Denmark, the United Kingdom, Ireland, Germany, the Netherlands, and Belgium) is open to all other EU-flag vessels. In regards to third-country flags, waivers are required for Denmark, Sweden, and Finland, while all the other countries mentioned have open-coast policies.[63]

The case is slightly different in the southern European countries (France, Spain, Portugal, Italy, and Greece). Cabotage services were slower to liberalize in these countries, mainly to protect island passenger services. Island passenger service can be a lucrative trade in the region, particularly in the summer time, generating a significant amount of employment. In 1997, 50,000 people were employed by south European member states' cabotage, all EU nationals. This issue is of little interest in the north, since there is little passenger service in the region; so opening it to competition would have little impact. This attitude differs significantly in the south. As a result, there is considerable fear by residents that further liberalization will cost jobs. There was a total decline of 1,000 jobs since 1995, explained mainly by rationalization in Italy and the decrease in fleet size of the conventional registry in Spain.[64]

Initial research by the EU has shown that liberalization of cabotage has not significantly affected employment, nor has there been a serious adverse impact on overall cargo trades in the region. Table 6.2 and Table 6.3 show the degree of flag involvement in liberalized trades and overall cabotage in Europe.

Table 6.2
Liberalized Cargo Trades by Market Segment and Country
(million tons)

Category	Bulk Cargo		General Cargo		Liquid Bulk		Total	
	1993	1995	1993	1995	1993	1995	1993	1995
France	1.1	1.1	-	-	0.5	0.5	1.6	1.6
Greece	1.9	2.8	0.2	0.1	-	0.5	2.1	3.4
Italy	5.1	4.9	2.1	3.6	0.6	0.6	7.8	9.1
Portugal	0.1	-	-	-	0.1	-	0.2	-
Spain	3.7	3.2	0.3	0.25	0.8	0.55	4.8	4.0
Total	11.9	12.0	2.6	3.95	2.0	2.15	16.5	18.1

Source: Data from Commission of the European Communities, *Report from the Commission: Third Report on the Implementation of Council Regulation 3577/92 Applying the Principle of Freedom to Provide Services to Maritime Cabotage (1997-1998)* (Brussels, February 24, 2000), p. 13.

Table 6.3
Flag Involvement in Southern European Cabotage, 1995
(million tons)

Country	Total Cabotage Trade	EU-Flag Involvement	Non-EU-Flag Involvement	Total Foreign Flag Involvement
France	7.9	0.25	0.3	0.55
Greece	21.9	0.05	0.05	0.1
Italy	60.3	0.1	0.2	0.3
Portugal	6.0	Nil	0.05	0.05
Spain	38.2	1.3	0.7	2.0
Total	134.3	1.7	1.3	3.0

Source: Data from Commission of the European Communities, *Report from the Commission: Third Report on the Implementation Of Council Regulation 3577/92 Applying the Principle of Freedom to Provide Services to Maritime Cabotage (1997-1998)*, (Brussels, February 24, 2000), p. 16.

It can be seen that foreign-flag vessels have not played a significant role in European cabotage. Nonnational vessels have accounted for 17 percent of liberalized trade (3.05 million tons out of 18 million total), which has grown in comparison with 1993 figures, where nonnational vessels accounted for 12 percent of cabotage. Looking at overall maritime cabotage, however, the market share of nonnational flags accounts for only 2.3 percent of overall trades (3.05 million tons out of 132.7 million). While no analysis has been conducted on the effects of liberalization on employment in this sector, it can be inferred from the aforementioned numbers that it has been minimally affected.

Overall, what is seen is that liberalization of the maritime industry has had little effect on overall trades in Europe. Prices overall have decreased, mainly because of increased competition and use of open-registry vehicles. Using this model, we can now look at the possible impact that a regional cabotage system may have on Latin America, particularly by examining who has the most to gain and lose through such a system.

Winners and Losers

If the FTAA comes to fruition as it stands, there are certain players who stand to benefit and others who stand to lose.

Mexico

The country that perhaps stands to lose the most if the FTAA comes to fruition is Mexico. With the implementation of the North American Free Trade Agreement (NAFTA), Mexico became the only Latin American nation with duty-free access to the largest market in the region, the United States. As a result, Mexico has gained leverage in negotiations with other countries in Latin America, leading to similar pacts with Bolivia, Chile, Costa Rica, Colombia, Nicaragua, and Venezuela. Negotiations are also underway with eight other Latin American nations, as well as with the EU, Japan, South Korea, China, and Israel.[65]

The majority of Mexico's exports go directly to the United States. This dependence is changing, however, with the new free-trade agreements. For example, between 1991 and 1998, Mexico's trade with Chile increased by 572 percent. Since 1994, trade with Costa Rica has increased by 202 percent, Venezuela by 80 percent, and Colombia by 41 percent. Mexico also has entered into negotiations with Guatemala, Honduras, El Salvador, Panama, Ecuador, Peru, Belize, and Trinidad and Tobago.

The question now arises whether or not Mexico will wholeheartedly enter into FTAA negotiations. It will be interesting to see to what extent Mexico will support the FTAA insofar as the country has more to lose than to gain by entering into an accord.

Puerto Rico

A potential beneficiary of the FTAA may be Puerto Rico, particularly in regards to maritime trade. Currently, the Commonwealth is attempting to use the FTAA to position itself as a regional trade hub. The Puerto Rican government is currently spending $3 billion in an effort to develop the island's infrastructure, primarily focusing on improvements to ports and airports. The government hopes this investment will help establish Puerto Rico as a trade bridge between North and South America and between the Americas and Europe.

Puerto Rico's initial goal is not to displace any current trade centers but, rather, to take advantage of the increased trade resulting from the FTAA. According to Carlos Vivoni, secretary of state for economic development and commerce: "Other locations such as Miami are operating at full capacity, and incremental business will have to find other locations . . . . The plan is not to displace other gateways, but to make use of an increase in trade between North America and South America. We have very good communications by sea and air to both North America and South America."[66]

Puerto Rico has certain advantages for conducting business in the region. Both English and Spanish are spoken on the island, facilitating communication with other nations. Additionally, Puerto Rico is not part of the U.S. tax structure, enabling businesses to keep costs at a lower level than at U.S. ports. In efforts to capitalize on these advantages, Puerto Rico has established offices in various Latin American countries, seeking to establish future business.

Panama

Panama is among the nations in Latin America most likely to see immediate benefits from the adoption of an EU-like model of regional cabotage in the Americas. Panama boasts one of the largest national fleets in the world because of its limited registration and monitoring costs. If cabotage privileges are extended to all countries in the FTAA, it can reasonably be expected that liners will abandon expensive U.S. and Brazilian registries and will begin re-flagging their vessels in Panama instead.

Brazil

Brazil poses an interesting case. Looking at Europe, it can be seen that liberalizing cabotage has had a minimal impact on the amount of foreign-flag involvement in cabotage trades. What distinguishes Brazil, however, is the sheer size of the country, in terms of both the internal market and in the size of its coastline, which provides operators with a far greater number of opportunities than most European nations. Operating under inexpensive flags and with lower-paid foreign nationals staffing the crew, liner shipping companies may look to the recently opened Brazilian cabotage market as a potential for high profits.

Issues for Further Study

Though observers can speculate about potential winners and losers in an FTAA-wide cabotage region, considerable research on the cost-effectiveness of such a system will have to be undertaken before the member nations of the FTAA will seriously consider such a system.

Cost-Benefit Analysis of the EU's Transition to Regional Cabotage

With the exception of the research already mentioned for the southern member nations of the EU, little is known about the effects of the transition to regional cabotage in the EU. This lack of empirical research has left reform advocates and opponents without economic evidence to support their assertions about the benefits or costs of cabotage. Though further research into the effects of the EU transition is unlikely to quiet those with interests in the outcomes of reform, increased empirical knowledge would provide policymakers within the FTAA with stronger evidence of how changes in cabotage law might affect their nations. One approach to such research might be to conduct an economic cost-benefit analysis of the EU transition to regional cabotage.

Possible Costs

Opponents of cabotage laws have long maintained that the liberalization of cabotage laws will result in a loss of employment in maritime trade. Though initial research seems to indicate that liberalization of cabotage in Europe was not accompanied by losses in employment, a comprehensive study of European employment in the maritime sector both before the regional transition and after the change might help to dispel this fear. Ideally, such a study would survey how many citizens of EU-member nations lost their jobs in the maritime sector as a result of the transition to regional cabotage and the amount of income they lost as a result. Any comprehensive employment survey should also attempt to explain where those jobs went after the transition. It is entirely possible that maritime jobs may have been transferred from EU nations with high labor costs to member nations with low labor costs.

246

In addition to transfers of maritime labor from nations with high labor costs to those with lower costs, it is also possible that ship owners might have responded to the opening of cabotage markets by re-flagging their cabotage vessels from EU nations with stringent registration requirements to member nations with less costly registers. It is important to make the distinction here that re-flagging within the EU has a very different economic effect than the flagging-out of vessels from EU-member nations to low-cost registries outside the EU. Both behaviors result in lower operating costs; however, ships re-flagged in other member nations would still be able to participate in cabotage anywhere in the region. Fees associated with the registration of vessels can represent a substantial source of revenue for a nation that could be lost to re-flagging of vessels in a regional cabotage system. In order to incorporate this measure into the overall cost-benefit analysis for regional cabotage, it will be necessary to survey the fees collected by each EU nation as well as the total numbers of vessels that re-flagged from one EU nation to another, both before and after the transition to regional cabotage.

Possible Benefits

Nearly all arguments for the reform of cabotage law stem from the belief that eliminating market barriers will lead to increased competition, lower shipping rates, and lower final product costs to consumers. Cost savings are the basis of the $2.8 billion welfare gain projected by the USITC for reform of the Jones Act in 1995.[67] Despite the size of this projected cost savings in the United States, no comprehensive attempt has been made to account for cost savings realized by EU-member nations as a result of cabotage liberalization in Europe. Research is necessary to test the validity of the theory that the reform of cabotage laws leads to cost savings.

In order to establish whether cabotage reform has led to cost savings in the EU, it is first necessary to examine whether opening the EU market led to increased competition in cabotage services. Both the number of competing firms engaged in cabotage shipping and the frequency of service will need to be sampled before and after the reforms to determine if more shipping services were made available to shippers as a result of the change. It would then be necessary to survey shippers to find out if shipping rates for comparable services declined with cabotage reform and, if so, by what amount.

It is not certain that lower shipping rates inevitably lead to appreciably lower final costs to consumers. If sufficient competition among shippers is not present, there will be no incentive for shippers to pass on the savings obtained through lower freight rates to producers. It will, therefore, also be necessary to conduct research on the number of shippers in the European market before and after cabotage liberalization. The monetary value of the goods being shipped also needs to be surveyed before any definitive statements can be made about the cost savings that will result from reforms to existing cabotage restrictions. For low-value bulk commodities, the cost of shipping represents a higher proportion of the overall final product price than it does for high-value refined or manufactured goods. It can be assumed that cost savings realized through cabotage liberalization will be more apparent in these products than in others, and it is, therefore, advisable that the costs of lower-value bulk goods be evaluated both before the opening of the EU cabotage market and afterwards to determine if the final market prices of these goods dropped as a result of cabotage reforms.

Applicability of the EU Model

One needs to address the appropriateness of applying a multinational trade model from one part of the world to another. Before categorically concluding that regional cabotage according to a EU model could or should be applied to the FTAA, several issues will need to be investigated more thoroughly. Following are a few of the issues that might justify further study before the FTAA considers adopting a regional cabotage system.

One of the more obvious differences between the EU and the FTAA is the relative length of coastline to be serviced. The longer distances between Western Hemispheric ports than between EU ports may discourage the development of a regional cabotage system and instead foster the development of subregions within an FTAA.

Differences in the population densities are another consideration. As opposed to the EU, much of South America in particular is very sparsely populated. These smaller markets may not offer enough profit potential to truly foster competition among shipping lines even after the liberalization of cabotage restrictions. Many of these areas may be better served by alternate modes of transportation that do not maintain such high fixed operating costs. The availability of alternate modes for the transportation of goods and passengers is also a considerable difference between the EU and the FTAA that may affect the applicability of the EU model in the Americas. Many areas within the FTAA are significantly behind the EU in the development of a modern transportation infrastructure. The practical result of this fact is that many FTAA nations are more heavily committed to maritime shipping than are EU nations. Where there is sufficient competition in the shipping market, this fact may actually increase the cost savings realized from cabotage reform in the FTAA above levels observed in the EU.

Last, regional re-flagging of cabotage vessels may generate additional concerns in the FTAA because of disparities that exist in environmental standards for vessels and working conditions for crews among the registries of the FTAA. While there are national differences in the registration requirements among EU-member nations, those differences are not as contrasting as potential differences between potential member nations of the FTAA. It is unlikely that the more safety-conscious nations in the Western Hemisphere will be willing to allow vessels with low environmental or labor safety standards to operate along their coastlines even if doing so resulted in lower-priced consumer goods.

Notes

[1] U.S. Department of Transportation Maritime Administration (MARAD), *A Survey on World Cabotage Laws: Summary of Responses from Countries* (Washington, D.C., March 1991), p. 1.

[2] Lyndon B. Johnson (LBJ) School of Public Affairs, *Port-Related State Programs and Federal Legislative Issues*, Policy Research Project Report Series, no. 117 (Austin, Tex., 1996), p. 50.

[3] Ibid., p. 51.

[4] Ibid.

[5] Ibid.

[6] MARAD, *A Survey on World Cabotage Laws*, p. 4.

[7] LBJ School of Public Affairs, *Transportation in the Americas: Its Role in International Trade, Economic Integration, and Sustainable Development*, Policy Research Project Report Series, no. 135 (Austin, Tex., 2000), p. 13.

[8] Interview by Cara Dougherty with Paulo Augusto Camello, Gerente, Centro de Operações de Cabotagem, Alliança Navegação E Logística Ltda., Rio de Janeiro, Brazil, January 23, 2001.

[9] Michael Fabey, "Cabotage Ups and Downs," *Traffic World* (December 4, 2000), p. 26.

[10] Camello interview, January 23, 2001.

[11] MARAD, *A Survey on World Cabotage Laws,* p. 31.

[12] Ibid., p. 4.

[13] Ibid., p. 31.

[14] MARAD, *A Survey on World Cabotage Laws,* p. 4.

[15] Interview by Michael Pratt and Matthew Gever with Paulo Augusto Camello, Gerente, Centro de Operações de Cabotagem, Aliança Navegação E Logística Ltda., Austin, Texas, October 11, 2000.

[16] Camello interview, January 23, 2001.

[17] Interview by Cara Dougherty with Caio Morel Corrêa, Director, Transroll Navegação S.A., Rio de Janeiro, Brazil, January 24, 2001.

[18] *Canadian Shipping Act*, part X, sec. 592(1)-592(2) (1984).

[19] MARAD, *A Survey on World Cabotage Laws*, p. 4.

[20] Ibid., p. 47.

[21] Ibid., p. 5.

[22] Asia Pacific Economic Cooperation (APEC), *Guide to the Investment Regimes of the APEC Member Economies*. Online. Available: http://www.apecsec.org.sg/GuideBook/. Accessed: November 15, 2000.

[23] MARAD, *A Survey on World Cabotage Laws*, p. 47.

[24] Ibid., p. 32.

[25] Ibid., p. 5.

[26] Ibid., pp. 40, 47.

[27] Ibid.

[28] Ibid., p. 33.

[29] American Society of International Law, *International Law in Brief, November 16-27, 1998*. Online. Available: http://www.asil.org/ilib/ilib0111.htm#02. Accessed: November 15, 2000.

[30] International Monetary Fund, *Secretariat for Central American Economic Integration*. Online. Available: http://www.imf.org/external/np/sec/dedco/sieca.htm. Accessed: March 12, 2001.

[31] MARAD, *A Survey on World Cabotage Laws*, p. 5.

[32] Ibid., p. 48.

[33] Inforport, *Cabotage Policy in Mexico*. Online. Available: http://www.inforport.com.mx/noticias/arts/art40w/htm. Accessed: November 21, 2000.

[34] Ibid.

[35] Ibid.

[36] MARAD, *A Survey on World Cabotage Laws*, p. 15.

[37] Ibid., pp. 43, 49.

[38] Inforport, *Cabotage Policy in Mexico* (online)

[39] MARAD, *A Survey on World Cabotage Laws*, p. 9.

[40] LBJ School of Public Affairs, *Port-Related State Programs and Federal Legislative Issues*, p. 52.

[41] MARAD, *A Survey on World Cabotage Laws*, pp. 43, 50.

[42] Ibid., p. 6.

[43] Ibid., p. 36.

[44] U.S. Congress, Senate, *Merchant Marine Act of 1920*, sec.1, 41 Stat. 988, chap. 250 (June 5, 1920).

[45] U.S. Department of Commerce (USDOC), International Trade Administration, *Uruguay—Overseas Business Report—OBR9209* (Washington, D.C., October 1992). Online. Available: http://www.umsl.edu/services/govdocs/obr/obr_0013.htm. Accessed: October 9, 2000.

[46] MARAD, *A Survey on World Cabotage Laws*, p. 6.

[47] USDOC, *Uruguay* (online).

[48] MARAD, *A Survey on World Cabotage Laws*, pp. 8, 44, 51.

[49] Organization of American States (OAS), *Inter-American Committee of Ports News*. Online. Available: http://www.oas.org/cipo/eng/news.htm. Accessed: March 18, 2001.

[50] MARAD, *A Survey on World Cabotage Laws*, p. 38.

[51] LBJ School of Public Affairs, *Port-Related State Programs and Federal Legislative Issues*, p. 53.

[52] Ibid., pp. 53-54.

[53] Ibid., p. 54.

[54] U.S. International Trade Commission (USITC), *The Economic Effects of Significant U.S. Import Restraints, Second Update 1999* (Washington, D.C., May 1999), p. 96.

[55] Ibid., pp. 102-03.

[56] Organization for Economic Cooperation and Development (OECD), *Discussion Document on Regulatory Reform in International Maritime Transport DSTI/DOT/MTC(99)8* (Paris, France, May 1999), p. 9.

[57] LBJ School of Public Affairs, *Port-Related State Programs and Federal Legislative Issues*, p. 55.

[58] Maritime Cabotage Task Force, *The Jones Act: Fact and Fiction*. Online. Available: http://www.mctf.com/jonesact.htm. Accessed: October 9, 2000.

[59] Interview by Cara Dougherty with Marcelo de Andrade Almeida, Wilport Operadores Portuarios S.A., Santos, Brazil, January 18, 2001.

[60] Camello interview, October 10, 2000.

[61] "FTAA—ALCA—ZLEA: Miami Declaration of Principles." Online. Available: http://www.ftaa-alca.org/ministerials/miami_e.asp Accessed: March 1, 2001.

[62] "Mt_1_en." Online. Available: http://www.europa.eu.int/comm/transport/themes/maritime/english/mt_1_en.html Accessed: November 29, 2000.

[63] Commission of the European Communities, *Report from the Commission: Third Report on the Implementation of Council Regulation 3577/92 Applying the Principle of Freedom To Provide Services to Maritime Cabotage (1997-1998)* (Brussels, February 24, 2000), p. 45.

[64] Ibid., p. 20.

[65] Esther Schrader, "Mexico Learns Lesson Well in Pursuit of Trade Accords; Exports: Pacts Similar to NAFTA May Hinder Clinton's Push to Form 34-Nation Free Trade Area of the Americas," *Los Angeles Times* (September 14, 1999), p. A-1.

[66] Editorial, "Survey—Puerto Rico," *Financial Times London* (March 11, 1999), p. 2.

[67] USITC, *The Economic Effects of Significant U.S. Import Restraints*, p. 96.

Appendix A. Port Principal Component Analysis

Appendix A contains the SAS Program used to calculate the values in the port principal component analysis model. Also included is the SAS output. Finally, an Excel spreadsheet is included with the original database and the standardized database. The standardized data were used with the PRIN1 and PRIN2 equations to calculate the PRIN values for the ports. These calculations are also shown.

SAS Program

```
*******************************************************************
*/      FILE NAME:CI2001-1                                      /*
*/      Port database as of 27-5-2001.                          /*

******************************************************************;
title;
data port;
infile 'C:\WINDOWS\Desktop\CI2001-1.prn';
input teu99 berth area storage cranes calls;
*****This line prints the database;
proc print data=port;
run;
*****This line runs the factor analysis and returns the correlation
matrix and the eigenvector matrix with the minimum eigenvalue set to
zero;
proc factor corr eigenvectors mineigen=0 data=port;
run;
```

SAS Output

Obs	teu99	berth	area	storage	cranes	calls
1	2084711	1505	288000	6200	6	41
2	1021973	4319	1240000	28595	15	100
3	878206	1340	370000	20000	10	69
4	871779	1600	505000	19500	10	116
5	771306	1220	110000	9150	5	54
6	689677	1901	766345	16050	10	56
7	590000	358	75000	560	1	39
8	543993	519	370000	10000	4	17
9	532472	510	420000	35000	4	47
10	496315	1250	10000	25570	0	77
11	415629	451	42000	2800	2	35
12	378000	555	235000	6750	1	48
13	376045	2000	56000	3700	0	65
14	374474	383	61000	1800	0	49
15	347023	1516	360000	12000	2	73
16	321893	250	135000	7000	2	54
17	252482	480	120000	3500	2	40
18	777821	3167	2630700	20000	14	109
19	771882	3661	628000	5100	10	29

The FACTOR Procedure

Correlations

	teu99	berth	area	storage	cranes	calls
teu99	1.00000	0.38193	0.23470	0.15036	0.50581	0.12850
berth	0.38193	1.00000	0.67248	0.34560	0.78040	0.50376
area	0.23470	0.67248	1.00000	0.42392	0.77866	0.56321
storage	0.15036	0.34560	0.42392	1.00000	0.49504	0.56274
cranes	0.50581	0.78040	0.77866	0.49504	1.00000	0.52249
calls	0.12850	0.50376	0.56321	0.56274	0.52249	1.00000

The FACTOR Procedure
Initial Factor Method: Principal Components

Prior Communality Estimates: ONE

Eigenvalues of the Correlation Matrix: Total = 6 Average = 1

	Eigenvalue	Difference	Proportion	Cumulative
1	3.45789442	2.43035651	0.5763	0.5763
2	1.02753790	0.35791358	0.1713	0.7476
3	0.66962432	0.26319486	0.1116	0.8592
4	0.40642946	0.10325269	0.0677	0.9269
5	0.30317677	0.16783965	0.0505	0.9774
6	0.13533712		0.0226	1.0000

6 factors will be retained by the NFACTOR criterion.

Eigenvectors

	1	2	3	4	5	6
teu99	0.25747	0.73574	0.51736	0.22065	0.17674	0.21168
berth	0.45169	0.17355	-0.35605	0.03301	-0.73987	0.30097
area	0.45552	-0.06869	-0.41394	-0.23239	0.62154	0.41967
storage	0.34799	-0.44726	0.64536	-0.45929	-0.15693	0.16372
cranes	0.49482	0.18451	-0.09303	-0.24071	0.05095	-0.80741
calls	0.39528	-0.43563	0.09521	0.79204	0.08845	-0.09882

Factor Pattern

	Factor1	Factor2	Factor3	Factor4	Factor5	Factor6
teu99	0.47878	0.74580	0.42336	0.14067	0.09732	0.07787
berth	0.83994	0.17592	-0.29136	0.02104	-0.40738	0.11072
area	0.84706	-0.06963	-0.33873	-0.14816	0.34223	0.15439
storage	0.64710	-0.45337	0.52810	-0.29281	-0.08641	0.06023
cranes	0.92014	0.18703	-0.07613	-0.15346	0.02806	-0.29703
calls	0.73503	-0.44159	0.07791	0.50494	0.04870	-0.03635

254

Port	99TEU	Berth Length	Terminal Area	TEU Storage	Gantry Cranes	Direct Calls	Standardized Matrix						PRIN1	PRIN2
							99TEU	Berth Length	Terminal Area	TEU Storage	Gantry Cranes	Direct Calls		
San Juan	2084711	1505	288000	6200	6	41	3.476	0.072	-0.254	-0.609	0.173	-0.668	0.42	3.18
Buenos Aires	1021973	4319	1240000	28595	15	100	0.887	2.462	1.302	1.634	2.022	1.541	4.11	-0.04
MIT (Panama)	878206	1340	370000	20000	10	69	0.537	-0.068	-0.120	0.773	0.995	0.380	0.96	0.06
Santos	871779	1600	505000	19500	10	116	0.522	0.153	0.101	0.723	0.995	2.141	1.84	-0.67
Coco Solo/Cristobal	771306	1220	110000	9150	5	54	0.277	-0.170	-0.545	-0.313	-0.032	-0.181	-0.45	0.42
Kingston	689677	1901	766345	16050	10	56	0.078	0.408	0.528	0.378	0.995	-0.106	1.03	0.15
Puerto Limon	590000	358	75000	560	1	39	-0.165	-0.902	-0.602	-1.174	-0.854	-0.743	-1.85	0.45
Freeport	543993	519	370000	10000	4	17	-0.277	-0.765	-0.120	-0.228	-0.238	-1.567	-1.29	0.41
Veracruz	532472	510	420000	35000	4	47	-0.305	-0.773	-0.038	2.276	-0.238	-0.443	0.05	-1.22
Puerto Cabello	496315	1250	10000	25570	0	77	-0.393	-0.145	-0.708	1.331	-1.060	0.680	-0.28	-1.35
Rio Haina	415629	451	42000	2800	2	35	-0.590	-0.823	-0.656	-0.949	-0.649	-0.893	-1.83	0.16
Guayaquil	378000	555	235000	6750	1	48	-0.681	-0.735	-0.340	-0.554	-0.854	-0.406	-1.44	-0.34
Callao	376045	2000	56000	3700	0	65	-0.686	0.492	-0.633	-0.859	-1.060	0.231	-0.97	-0.29
San Antonio	374474	383	61000	1800	0	49	-0.690	-0.881	-0.625	-1.049	-1.060	-0.369	-1.90	-0.18
Cartagena	347023	1516	360000	12000	2	73	-0.757	0.081	-0.136	-0.028	-0.649	0.530	-0.34	-0.87
Manzanillo	321893	250	135000	7000	2	54	-0.818	-0.994	-0.504	-0.529	-0.649	-0.181	-1.47	-0.54
Port of Spain	252482	480	120000	3500	2	40	-0.987	-0.799	-0.528	-0.879	-0.649	-0.706	-1.76	-0.25
Miami	777821	3167	2630700	20000	14	109	0.293	1.484	3.575	0.773	1.816	1.878	4.28	-0.60
Jacksonville	771882	3661	628000	5100	10	29	0.278	1.903	0.302	-0.719	0.995	-1.118	0.87	1.51
Mean	657667	1420	443266	12278	5.16	58.8	0.257	0.452	0.456	0.348	0.495	0.395	<PRIN1 equation	
Standard Deviation	410556	1177	611860	9984	4.87	26.7	0.736	0.174	-0.069	-0.447	0.185	-0.436	<PRIN2 equation	

255

Appendix B. Location Loading Factor

The location loading factor (LLF) is designed to relate the amount of TEU traffic that takes place in the area surrounding a port. The equation shown below defines the LLF. The second part of the right-hand side of the equation is an exponential decay function that gives an increasingly smaller value to TEU movements taking place at greater distances from a port.

$$\text{LLF}_{\text{Port A}} = \sum (\text{TEU}_{\text{Port xi}}) \cdot (e^{\wedge - (\text{distance from Port A to Port xi} / 150)})$$

The LLF's were calculated using the spreadsheet that follows. The distances were compiled from the Website http://www.distances.com. Some of the distances, especially the larger ones, were calculated by summing two other distances in the chart. Therefore, some distances may not be exactly correct. The effect will be negligible as the exponential nature of the equation quickly diminishes the contribution of TEU moves at large distances. For example, TEU moves at 600 miles are counted at only 1 percent of their value.

Local TEU Factor	ECLAC 98 & 99 Annual TEU Moves	CNTRY	PORT	Buenos Aires	Santos	Puerto Cabello	Cartagena	La Guaira	Montevideo	Port of Spain	Rio Grande	Rio de Janeiro	Paranaguá	São Francisco do Sul	Itajaí	Vitória	Willemstad	Salvador	Fortaleza	Suape	Manaus	Belém	Recife	Sepetiba
1,237,735	1107916	Argentina	Buenos Aires	0	973	4500	4960	4443	129	4119	411	1155	813	733	693	1387	4572	1767	2482	2160	3713	3069	2135	1105
964,605	787219	Brasil	Santos	973	0	3478	3940	3424	887	3147	598	197	161	241	281	419	3600	804	1525	1199	2756	2112	1174	125
728,829	491545	Venezuela	P. Cabello	4500	3528	0	452	65	4373	389	4087	3330	3631	3711	3751	3115	113	2675	2179	2340	1760	1567	2315	3380
374,688	336560	Colombia	Cartagena	4960	3940	452	0	517	4835	841	4549	3792	4093	4173	4213	3577	410	3137	2641	2802	2222	2029	2777	3842
642,885	270058	Venezuela	La Guaira	4443	3424	65	517	0	4318	324	4032	3312	3613	3693	3733	3097	151	2657	2161	2322	1742	1549	2297	3362
767,953	258060	Uruguay	Montevideo	129	887	4373	4835	4318	0	4042	301	1062	730	650	610	1294	4495	1689	2408	2083	3639	2995	2058	1012
332,487	254937	Trin y Tob	Port of Spain	4119	3147	389	841	324	4042	0	3756	2999	3300	3380	3420	2784	453	2344	1848	2009	1429	1236	1984	3049
428,065	243253	Brasil	Rio Grande	411	598	4087	4549	4032	301	3756	0	765	449	369	329	997	4209	1402	2124	1797	3355	2711	1772	715
481,639	201243	Brasil	R. Janeiro	1155	197	3330	3792	3312	1062	2999	765	0	354	274	234	232	3452	656	1377	1047	2608	1964	1022	50
647,760	178254	Brasil	Paranaguá	813	161	3631	4093	3613	730	3300	449	354	0	80	120	580	3753	958	1678	1353	2909	2265	1328	304
578,324	133909	Brasil	S. Francisco	733	241	3711	4173	3693	650	3380	369	274	80	0	40	500	3833	878	1598	1273	2989	2185	1248	224
534,468	132813	Brasil	Itajai	693	281	3751	4213	3733	610	3420	329	234	120	40	0	460	3873	838	1558	1233	3029	2145	1208	184
198,892	93516	Brasil	Vitória	1387	419	3115	3577	3097	1294	2784	997	232	580	500	460	0	3237	450	1162	830	2393	1749	805	282
434,340	74870	Curacao	Willemstad	4572	3600	113	410	151	4495	453	4209	3452	3753	3833	3873	3237	0	2797	2301	2462	1882	1689	2437	3502
82,343	65246	Brasil	Salvador	1767	804	2675	3137	2657	1689	2344	1402	656	958	878	838	450	2797	0	722	395	1953	1309	370	706
51,693	51676	Brasil	Fortaleza	2482	1525	2179	2641	2161	2408	1848	2124	1377	1678	1598	1558	1162	2301	722	0	337	1288	612	362	1427
70,403	44047	Brasil	Suape	2160	1199	2340	2802	2322	2083	2009	1797	1047	1353	1273	1233	830	2462	395	337	0	1568	924	25	1097
52,080	40529	Brasil	Manaus	3713	2756	1760	2222	1742	3639	1429	3355	2608	2909	2989	3029	2393	1882	1953	1288	1568	0	697	1593	2658
40,031	38563	Brasil	Belém	3069	2112	1567	2029	1549	2995	1236	2711	1964	2265	2185	2145	1749	1689	1309	612	924	697	0	949	2014
68,012	23101	Brasil	Recife	2135	1174	2315	2777	2297	2058	1984	1772	1022	1328	1248	1208	805	2437	370	362	25	1593	949	0	1072
583,676	0	Brasil	Sepetiba	1105	125	3380	3842	3362	1012	3049	715	50	304	224	184	282	3502	706	1427	1097	2658	2014	1072	0

$$ \text{LLF}_{\text{Port A}} = \sum \left(\text{TEU}_{\text{Port xi}} \right) \bullet \left(e^{\,\wedge\, -\,(\text{distance from Port A to Port xi}\,/\,150)} \right) $$

Example Calculation:

LLF (Buenos Aires) = B\$4*EXP(-E4/150) + B\$5*EXP(-F4/150) + B\$6*EXP(-G4/150) + B\$7*EXP(-H4/150) + B\$8*EXP(-I4/150) + B\$9*EXP(-I4/150) +
B\$10*EXP(-J4/150) + B\$11*EXP(-K4/150) + B\$12*EXP(-N4/150) + B\$13*EXP(-M4/150) + B\$14*EXP(-P4/150) +
B\$15*EXP(-O4/150) + B\$16*EXP(-Q4/150) + B\$17*EXP(-R4/150) + B\$18*EXP(-S4/150) + B\$19*EXP(-V4/150) +
B\$20*EXP(-T4/150)+B\$21*EXP(-U4/150)+B\$22*EXP(-W4/150)+B\$23*EXP(-X4/150)+B\$24*EXP(-Y4/150)